Blue Shadows Farm

A Novel

Jerry Apps

Terrace Books
A trade imprint of the University of Wisconsin Press

Terrace Books, a trade imprint of the University of Wisconsin Press,
takes its name from the Memorial Union Terrace, located at
the University of Wisconsin–Madison. Since its inception in 1907,
the Wisconsin Union has provided a venue for students, faculty, staff,
and alumni to debate art, music, politics, and the issues of the day.
It is a place where theater, music, drama, literature, dance, outdoor activities,
and major speakers are made available to the campus and the community.
To learn more about the Union, visit www.union.wisc.edu.

Terrace Books
A trade imprint of the University of Wisconsin Press
1930 Monroe Street, 3rd Floor
Madison, Wisconsin 53711-2059

www.wisc.edu/wisconsinpress/

3 Henrietta Street
London WC2E 8LU, England

1   3   5   4   2

Printed in the United States of America

Library of Congress Cataloging-in-Publication Data
Apps, Jerold W., 1934–
Blue Shadows Farm : a novel / Jerry Apps.
p.   cm.
ISBN 978-0-299-23250-4 (cloth: alk. paper)
ISBN 978-0-299-23253-5 (e-book)
1. Family farms—Wisconsin—Fiction.
2. Farm life—Wisconsin—Fiction.
I. Title.
PS3601.P67B58   2009
813'.6—dc22   2009007121

For
Sue, Kate, and Natasha

The invariable mark of wisdom is
to see the miraculous in the common.

–Ralph Waldo Emerson, *Nature*

Contents

Contents

Part 3

Part 4

Part 5

Contents

Part 6

Part 7

Part 8

Part 9

Blue Shadows Farm

Prologue

November 2000
Blue Shadows Farm
Link Lake, Wisconsin

I don't remember ever seeing the metal box. But here it is, dust covered, dented, and buried under some bigger storage containers. It is dull green, a couple feet long, a foot or so wide, and maybe a foot deep. I blow off the dust, slowly lift the hinged cover, and peer inside.

*S*ometimes the most logical decisions are the most difficult to make. At least that seems the case for me. Here I am, a seventy-four-year-old woman with arthritis in both knees, a perpetually sore back, and I'm still working as hard as ever. I own this farm called Blue Shadows. It has been in my family for three generations, but my friends tell me to sell the place and move to town. Truth be known, I am about tuckered out.

"Take it easy for once. You're working too hard, Emma Stark-weather," my friend Kate, the often cynical, sometimes arrogant, and always thorough editor of our weekly newspaper said. I've been putting off a decision. Part of me doesn't want to leave this place. I was born here, grew up here, and never left. I know the time is coming when I can't take care of it anymore. A farm needs taking care of—the buildings and the land and even the spirit of the place all need careful attention. I sure don't want the place to go to the dogs like some of the places around here.

I got a good offer for the farm from Modern Nature Educators, a company that says they want to do what I have been doing. Since 1986, I've operated Blue Shadows Farm mostly as a nature preserve and a place for kids to learn about the outdoors firsthand.

I think I've about made up my mind. I'll sell my place and buy one of those new condos right on the shores of Link Lake. Live high on the hog for a change. That's why this afternoon I'm up here in the loft of my farm's first log cabin. My grandfather Silas, who was a Civil War veteran, built this cabin when he homesteaded the place. Now I'm sorting through all these old boxes. Around these parts, when you move, you have an auction. And before you hold an auction you sort through all your junk and decide what's worth trying to sell, what should be tossed, and what you can't part with.

I haven't been in this loft for years. In fact, I can't remember the last time I climbed the ladder next to the old fieldstone fireplace and stuck my nose up here. This loft was once my grandmother's bedroom, when she worked for my grandfather as a housekeeper. Later she and my grandfather married. I didn't remember how small the place was. I can't even stand up straight without cracking my head on the cabin ceiling.

Now, here I sit with this old metal box. First thing I see when I lift the cover is a thin, greenish strip of metal a couple inches wide and maybe a foot long—a stencil of some sort—with the name "S. Starkweather" cut into it. Likely what my grandfather used to ink his name on his military gear. Underneath the stencil I find a tattered copy of Thoreau's *Walden*. Imagine, my grandfather read Thoreau. The old guy was tough as nails and filled with surprises.

4

Pressed inside the book I find a lupine flower, dry, brittle, and faded blue. Lots of them grow on Blue Shadows Farm these days; I didn't know they grew here when Grandpa first arrived.

In a corner of the metal box, I see a tiny yellow box. In it I find a Karner blue butterfly resting on a little piece of cotton. It has been carefully preserved with its tiny wings spread. Today, these little Karner blues are one of my favorite kinds of butterflies that flit around this farm. Digging further, I find yet one more little container in another corner of the metal box, this one crammed full of Indian arrowheads, some perfectly formed with sharp edges, others less perfect.

This box is a treasure trove of history. I keep digging. I find a battered old canteen, covered with faded blue wool, and a canvas haversack right next to it. Inside this, I find several notebooks, with page after page of meticulous handwriting. On the inside cover of each I read, "Property of Silas J. Starkweather." Each notebook has a number. I open the first one and begin reading.

Part 1

1

Ambush

March 1865
Somewhere in Mississippi

Private Silas Starkweather rode with his head drooping, fighting to keep awake as the hot Mississippi sun bore down on his heavy, woolen, blue Union uniform. The reins hung slack in his hands as his horse plodded along, each step turning up a little puff of reddish-brown dust. He rode just far enough behind the mule team and wagon to stay out of the dust the heavy wheels stirred up as the team pulled the high-wheeled vehicle with but one locked wooden chest as cargo. Silas had quit thinking about what was in the chest; it was none of his business. The corporal riding a couple hundred yards in front of the wagon told him as much when he first asked.

"Just keep your eyes and ears open and your weapon at the ready, Starkweather. That's all you need to worry about. What's in that chest is none of your business. All we gotta do is make sure it gets to New Orleans in one piece."

"Yes, sir," Silas had answered as he climbed on his horse and checked his rifle to make sure it was loaded.

Now, as both temperature and humidity rose, Silas wished he hadn't volunteered to accompany this mysterious shipment. At the time he held up his hand, he thought anything would be better than sitting in camp, doing nothing and wishing he was on the other end of the country, where the fighting was taking place. Or wishing he was back home in Watertown, New York, working in his father's harness shop. He'd be sewing leather now, hard work to be sure, but at least it was better than just sitting, which was what he'd been doing for almost a month. Until today.

At age twenty, Silas was tall and thin; gaunt might be a word to describe him. Since he joined the army he had grown a droopy brown mustache that curled down both sides of his mouth. His deep-set gray eyes stared from underneath the blue woolen cap that, with the rest of his uniform, was coated with reddish dust.

The road twisted through the pine woods like a big brown snake moving lazily along on a hot summer day. Most of the time Silas couldn't see the corporal, as he was always somewhere around the next corner. So Silas didn't see his leader fall from his horse when a minié ball tore off half his head, but the rifle's report caused both Silas and his horse to jump. He heard the muleskinner, Private Atkins, yell "Ha!" at the mules before he slumped over on the seat and fell to the ground, a minié ball passing clean through his chest. Almost simultaneously, Private Caldwell, who was riding shotgun on the wagon seat, fell to the ground, a hole in his head just above his right eye. His loaded weapon, without a shot fired, skidded into the weeds alongside the road.

The mules took off at a gallop, the wagon with its light load clattering behind. Silas looked around and saw nothing, no movement, no sign of where the shots had come from.

The last thing he remembered was a burning sensation in his head before he lost consciousness and tumbled off his horse into the dust. His horse stood near him, the reins touching the ground.

Four horsemen, wearing gray uniforms, emerged from the trees where they had waited since dawn. One rode after the mule team, stopping it a few hundred yards down the road. Another gathered up the corporal's and Silas's horses, but not before inspecting each of the Union soldiers to make sure he was dead.

"These Yankees ain't gonna do no more damage," the first soldier in gray said. He spat a stream of tobacco juice that splattered on the uniform of the dead corporal.

"Like shootin' fish in a barrel," the second soldier said.

"Wonder what they's carryin' in that chest?" the third soldier asked.

"What say we have ourselves a look?" the first soldier, the apparent leader of the ambush party, said.

The soldiers pried off the lock on the chest, which was about four feet square, and stuffed what they found in their saddlebags.

"Best we be on our way," the first soldier said. "Before somebody comes along."

"What about them mules and horses?" asked the second soldier.

"Shoot the mules. We'll take the horses with us," said the leader of the troop.

Two more shots echoed through the woods as the mules dropped in their tracks, their blood mixing with that of the Union soldiers.

Silas didn't know how long he had remained unconscious. He slowly lifted a hand to his head, which throbbed with more pain than any headache he could remember. He rubbed dried blood from his eyes and slowly sat up. It was eerily quiet as the sun slowly began sinking below the trees to the west.

At first Silas couldn't recall why he was sitting in the dust with dried blood all over his head. Then he saw the wagon sitting alongside the road, and what looked like bodies lying in the dirt. Slowly he got to his feet; the pain in his head was almost unbearable. He looked for his cap, which he found by the road. A bullet had gone through it from one side to the other. He felt his head and the little groove left after the minié ball had torn away a strip of hair and skin but had not done lethal damage.

As he approached the wagon, he found the bodies of Privates Atkins and Caldwell. Big black flies buzzed around them and crawled over their faces. Their eyes, still open, stared upward. Silas looked through their pockets for any personal effects that could be returned to their relatives. He reasoned that whoever came along the road, and someone was sure to come eventually, would strip the bodies clean.

Silas staggered further up the road, where he found the body of the corporal, lying face down in a puddle of dried blood. He looked through his pockets as well, with the same intention in mind. He found a brown envelope with the words "Commander, Camp New Orleans, New Orleans, Louisiana."

In the upper-left-hand corner was written "Link Lake, Wisconsin." Silas stuffed the envelope into his pocket and sat down, leaning against a pine tree that stood near the road. His head pounded, and blood continued trickling into his eyes. He soon lost consciousness again.

2

New Orleans Hospital

March 1865

Silas Starkweather dreamed of home, especially of his mother back in Watertown, where he was born. He dreamed of helping tap maple trees this time of year and making syrup. He dreamed of the sweet smell of the sap boiling on his mother's cookstove, and how pleasant it was. He dreamed of eating his mother's big meals, vegetables from her garden—fresh peas and sweet corn. Buttered beets and new potatoes. Fresh meat from a farmer the family knew.

He dreamed about the war and how for two years he was too young to enlist and join the other young men from the Watertown area who had marched off to join the great Union army. Lincoln's army, they called it.

He dreamed about how upset his mother had been when he told her that he had enlisted. He had talked to his pa about it, but had not mentioned it to his mother. He knew how unhappy she would be, how she would plead for him not to go. His mother had good reason for concern; already three boys from the community had been killed and would never return home. Silas was her only son.

Silas heard a rustling sound, and he didn't know if he was still dreaming or was awakening. And the smell, something sweetish he had never smelled before. Were these special flowers? He didn't see any flowers in his dream.

He heard a voice. It wasn't his mother's, but it was pleasant.

"Can you hear me, Private Starkweather? Can you hear me?" the soft, soothing voice repeated.

Silas slowly opened his eyes. A young woman dressed in white gradually came into focus.

"Can you hear me?" She touched Silas on the hand.

Silas looked around the long room. Everything was white: the walls, the ceiling, the bed coverings. Beds lined up one after the other, and each one occupied.

"Where am I?" Silas asked.

"In a Union military hospital," the young woman said.

Silas, now fully awake, heard moans coming from the bed next to him and the quiet snoring of a man sleeping in the bed on the other side of his. The smell permeated the crowded room, a clean one, but different. Not at all like the country scents that Silas knew so well.

"Why am I here?" Silas managed to say.

"You've been shot."

"Shot?" Silas was pushing his mind to recall the recent history. Slowly his memory began returning, like a haze that lifts from a country meadow on a warm summer day, revealing all previously obscured by the morning mist.

He recalled the secret mission he had volunteered for. How he and his fellow Union soldiers had been toting a wagon with a mysterious cargo along a hot dusty road. He remembered seeing everyone else shot and killed.

"You were shot in the head," the young woman said quietly. "You were very lucky."

Silas lifted his hand to his head, which was wrapped with a thick bandage. It still throbbed.

"Lucky?"

"The minié ball merely tore a little groove in the top of your head. Left most of your noggin in place." The young woman smiled. "Doctors don't think it did any serious damage, but we're waiting to see. Want to see if the inside of your head was affected. You're also lucky to have a head wound. They bleed a lot, and I'm sure you must have looked dead to those who shot you."

"How long will I be here?" Silas asked.

"A few more days. Maybe a week. We want the wound to heal— and we need to know if there was any more damage. How do you feel?"

"Got a headache. And I'm hungry."

"Good sign that you're hungry. We'll find something for you to eat."

A week later, still wearing a bandage, Silas Starkweather was discharged from the hospital and was cleared for limited duty.

The nurse brought him his clothes. He pulled on his trousers and shirt. They were dusty and dirty; it was obvious the hospital didn't have time to wash patients' clothes. He reached into his trouser pocket and there found a folded, brown, sweat-stained envelope. The memory returned. He had found it in the dead corporal's pocket and stuffed it in his pocket before he lost consciousness.

He carefully opened the envelope and unfolded the piece of paper inside. He couldn't believe what he was reading. The paper was a bill of lading. In detail it described the contents of the wooden chest the small group of volunteers was transporting.

He read the document again, this time more slowly. Then he smiled before carefully folding it and returning it to his pocket.

Limited Duty

April 1865

Silas, his head still wrapped in bandages, sat at a little desk in the headquarters building at the Union army's Camp New Orleans. His job was to file official-looking papers in brown folders and then carry them across the camp to another office. He did this each day, finishing by midafternoon. The rest of the day he spent in the barracks, where he rested, read newspapers, and kept track of the war.

A week after the hospital dismissed him, he returned for a checkup. A nurse told him that his wound was healing nicely. A doctor, wearing a white coat, asked him a series of questions:

"What is your name?"

"Silas Starkweather."

"What is your rank?"

"Private."

"What is your unit?"

"Company F, 35th Infantry."

Silas wondered why the doctor was asking all these questions. He caught a glimpse of the paper in front of the doctor. The answers he sought were on the paper.

"Stand up, please."

Silas did as he was asked. "Touch your right finger to your nose, then your left finger."

"Good," the doctor said. He wrote something on the pad in front of him.

"See that line on the floor?"

"Yes."

"Walk down it as straight as you are able."

"Good," the doctor said when Silas finished the task. He once more wrote something.

"Stand on your left foot," the doctor instructed.

Silas could never do that, not even when he was a child and kids played games where they stood on one foot.

"Try standing on your right foot."

Silas couldn't do that either. More notes on the pad. "Do you still have headaches?"

"Once in a while."

"I want to see you a week from today," the doctor said. "If your headaches get worse, come by sooner."

"I will," Silas said as he left the little white office and returned to his barracks.

A day after the doctor's examination, he received a note to appear at the camp commandant's office.

He was shown to a little windowless room where a man in civilian clothes sat behind a bare wooden desk. The gray-haired man, who wore a black patch over one eye, looked up when Silas entered.

"Sit down, please," the man said. His voice was firm and serious, without a southern accent.

"Your name is Silas Starkweather?"

"Yes."

"Your rank is private."

"If I could interrupt," Silas said. "What is it that you want?"

"Let me ask the questions," the man said. His voice was flat, without emotion.

"How were you wounded?"

"I think a rebel shot me in the head. But I really didn't see him."

"What were you doing when you were shot?"

Silas explained he was accompanying a mule-drawn wagon. He did not mention that it was a secret mission and that he had volunteered for it.

"What happened to the other men on the mission?"

"All killed."

"How did you survive?"

"I don't know. Lucky, I guess."

"Did you see who did the shooting?"

"No, I already told you that."

"How did you know they were rebels?"

"Guessed they were. Who else would shoot at us?"

"What did you do?"

"I didn't know what to do. I couldn't see which direction the shots were coming from. It happened mighty fast."

"You don't know for sure who shot you?"

"Never saw nobody. Musta passed out after I was shot."

"Did you ever regain consciousness?"

"Yeah."

"What did you see? What did you hear?"

"Didn't hear much. Quiet out there in the woods. Saw the dead soldiers layin' there in the dust with blood leaking out of them."

"See anything else?"

"Saw the dead mules. They'd been shot, too. Each one shot in the head."

"What about the wagon? Was the wagon still there?"

"It was," Silas said.

"What about the wooden chest on the wagon?"

How did this fellow know about the wooden chest? This was supposed to have been a top-secret mission.

"What wooden chest?" Silas asked. Now he wondered if he could trust this man with all the probing questions.

"I know all about the secret mission, Private Starkweather. Just answer my questions, please."

"The chest had been broken into. It was empty."

"What do you know about the mission?" the man probed.

"Nothing. Corporal said it was none of my business when I asked. So I didn't ask no more."

"What else can you tell me?"

Silas thought for a moment about the bill of lading that he'd found in the corporal's pocket. He quickly decided not to mention it.

"Told you all I know. Next thing I remembered, I was in the hospital here on base."

"Thank you, Private Starkweather," the man said coldly. "If you think of something else, please let me know."

"I will," Silas said as he walked out the door.

Back at the barracks, Silas dug out the bill of lading and read it once more: "Origin of Shipment, Link Lake, Wisconsin." Where was this place?

The recreational room at the camp had a modest library. There Silas found an atlas indicating the location of Link Lake, Wisconsin. The village was scarcely a blip on the map, located in Ames County, in the south-central part of the state. He also found a geography book for the Upper Midwest, one that described the effects of the several glaciers that had pushed through the region, especially their effects on the shape of the land in western Ames County.

All the soldiers received information about the recently passed Homestead legislation, which President Lincoln had signed in 1862. This new law made 160 acres of unoccupied, federally owned public land available without charge to former Union soldiers and others who were "twenty-one years of age, a citizen of the United States or who filed intention to become such, and who has never borne arms against the U.S. Government or given aid and comfort to enemies."

A week later, on April 12, 1865, he got the good news. General Lee had surrendered the Confederate forces to General Grant at Appomattox Court House in Virginia. The war was over.

Because of his wound and the need to recover, he stayed in the army through the summer and into the fall, when he was discharged. He spent the winter in New Orleans, picking up odd jobs and waiting for spring, when he traveled by steamboat to Dubuque, Iowa, and then hiked the rest of the way to Link Lake, Wisconsin, carrying his rifle, his pack on his back, his canteen at his side, and his haversack over his shoulder.

April 2, 1866

I decided I must write down some things so I don't forget. I am on a great adventure. I've been mustered out of the army. The war is over. Thank God for that. I don't know who will read these words, if anybody, but I must write them.

Some rebels shot me in the head about a year ago. I was lucky. They killed the others traveling with me. I lost only a little skin and some hair off the top of my head. Minié ball ruined my cap. Tore a hole in it from one side to the other. We were hauling a secret cargo to New Orleans when the bastards ambushed us.

I'm on a steamboat moving slowly up the Mississippi River on my way to Wisconsin. It's a long way from my home in New York.

I'm on my own secret mission and must not put anything in writing about it for fear others will find out. I will search out land in a county called Ames in the center of Wisconsin. Mr. Lincoln signed a law so I can have property free of charge if I do some work for it.

Part 2

4

Nature Hike

Emma
October 2000
Blue Shadows Farm

Not one of the hikers predicted the bolt of lightning. I know I didn't, and I had seen a good many lightning storms here at Blue Shadows Farm. Joe Crawford, Link Lake Middle School teacher, didn't see it coming. Not Mrs. Anderson either. Surely not Mrs. Ashley Anderson, who I noticed was wearing snow-white shoes and white designer pants on a nature hike. None of the twenty-five sixth graders from Link Lake Middle School saw it coming either.

"Ka-pow." The sound split the quiet, humid air. The bright light was beyond what anyone had ever seen before. The lightning bolt struck a tall white pine tree alongside the trail that led to the pond, a few hundred yards ahead of us. Right after the strike, it commenced raining like someone had opened a huge water tap right over us.

Immediately after it happened, Ashley Anderson screamed, "What was that?" and wrapped her arms around her daughter Jenny, who began sobbing uncontrollably. Ashley had come along on this annual fall nature field trip as a parent chaperone.

"Just a lightning strike," I yelled, trying to calm the group. In my many years living in the country, I'd seen a bunch of lightning strikes, but I must confess this one was spectacular, even though I didn't say that.

"Is everyone OK?" I heard Joe Crawford shout over the rain and children's voices. "Hold up your hand if you're OK."

Immediately all the students' hands shot into the air, except for Jenny Anderson's—she was still being consoled by her mother.

"Let's start back toward the bus," Joe said. Joe Crawford, tall, thin, and muscular with short brown hair and a tan complexion, an experienced teacher of twenty years, took the lead, hurrying back toward the bus parked near my barn. Joe's a good guy. I liked him from the first time I met him. Ashley Anderson and her daughter followed behind him, both of them now drenched, as was everyone else.

I heard Ashley say to Joe, "You'll hear more about this. There is no excuse for exposing children to this kind of danger. We could have all been killed!"

He didn't answer, pretending that he couldn't hear over the sound of pouring rain. But I knew he heard. He had been getting complaints about his nature field trips in recent years from parents like Ashley Anderson who were so protective of their children that a mosquito bite was a major catastrophe, and a skinned knee meant a trip to the emergency room. I just never could understand how someone could get so worked up over something so simple. Neither could Joe Crawford.

The children, except for Jenny Anderson, followed quickly in single file, laughing, giggling, and enjoying the surprise thunderstorm that had washed out the rest of their time in the country. The entire group was soaked. I walked at the back of the group with my crooked walking stick, rain dripping from my white hair.

I've been leading school groups on nature hikes on my farm for more than fifteen years. These have been the most fun years of my long life, and probably the most interesting, too. As far as these nature hikes go, the unexpected makes them the most fun. You just never know what will happen, what you'll see, what you'll hear, sometimes even what you'll smell. Nature is like that. Unpredictable.

This particular late September afternoon had started out warm and a bit cloudy, with no rain predicted. Earlier, I'd hiked the group to the back of the farm, where I stopped on a little hill and began explaining how the great glacier had formed this land fifteen thousand years ago. Later, when the group had stopped for a brief rest, I talked about my grandfather Silas Starkweather, who had homesteaded this land in 1866. I explained that Grandpa had been in the Civil War, and when the war was over he came here, built a log cabin, and started farming. I told them that Link Lake was just a one-horse town then, and one of the children asked me what that meant. I said it meant not many people lived there.

The group had just begun hiking again when the bolt of lightning and the drenching rain disrupted their afternoon in the outdoors. Regular gully washer it was.

Back in the bus, I heard Joe Crawford counting to make sure everyone was present and then asking, "What'd you think of this afternoon?"

"Cool," several kids said. The warm bus filled with the smells of wet clothing as the bedraggled group prepared to head back to the middle school.

I overheard Ashley Anderson say to Joe, "Expect to hear more about this dangerous field trip," as she stiffly stepped onto the bus, her new white walking shoes caked with mud, her designer jeans mud-splattered to the knees. She was having a conniption fit. Her daughter Jenny continued to sob, a trick she had apparently learned long ago in order to reap the full benefit of her mother's sympathy. But that's just the opinion of an old lady who never had children.

Once back in my house, I crumpled up some old newspapers, stuck a couple sticks of split oak wood in the kitchen stove, and touched a match to the papers. I took off my wet jacket, hung it on a nail, and pushed the coffeepot over what soon would be a warm place on the stove.

I couldn't get Ashley Anderson out of my craw. Just what is that woman's problem? I sat down by the stove and looked out the rain-streaked window. I think about all the problems Grandpa and Grandma faced surviving on this land, and the challenges my folks faced, and here we have a parent worried about her youngster being frightened by a clap of thunder and a lightning strike. We've had a few complainers over the years. Mosquito bites take first place. Hot, humid days and sunburn come in second. But mostly everyone has great fun tramping across my prairie, hiking through the woods, and spending some time checking on the creatures in and around the pond. I sure hope this Ashley Anderson thing isn't the beginning of a new trend. Maybe she'll change her tune when she has a little time to think about what happened.

5

Sophia

May 1866
Link Lake, Wisconsin

*W*hy are you sneaking around? I thought you were a bear. You scared the bejeebers out of me," Silas Starkweather said as he held up his broadax, prepared to defend himself. He'd been using the wide-bladed ax to square the sides of a pine log that he would use for his cabin. Silas had cut the logs in the pine woodlot on the west side of his newly acquired 160 acres. Having been government land before he homesteaded it, it had been set foot on by no white man, except for the surveyors who had plotted the township in the early 1850s. He didn't give this bit of history any thought as he focused on the job at hand.

The girl smiled and slipped easily off the side of the horse that she was riding bareback. She wore a thin cotton dress and no shoes. At age sixteen, she had clearly left behind her childhood appearance and was fast becoming an attractive young lady. Though it was only May, her face, arms, and legs were as tan as the horse's leather bridle.

"Who are you? Where'd you come from?" Silas said gruffly. He did not want to be interrupted from his work. The sooner he completed his cabin, the sooner he could begin plowing his new land. Having never been plowed before, he knew breaking the ground would be a challenge.

She put her hands on her hips and looked the young man square in the face.

"I am not a bear. I am Sophia," the girl said. She had long arms and legs and curly blonde hair.

"Sophia who?" Silas asked gruffly.

"I am Sophia Reinert," she said. Her blonde curls bounced when she talked. "I am daughter of Volfgang Reinert."

"Wolfgang's sure a funny name," Silas said. A hint of a smile snuck out from under his sagging brown mustache. He pulled off his faded felt hat and swabbed a handkerchief over his sweaty forehead. It was a warm, sunny, spring day, a promise of the summer to come. The big bluestem and the little bluestem grass had just begun to green up. The leaves emerging on the oak trees were about the size of a squirrel's ear, light green and crinkled.

"Volfgang is not funny. Volfgang is German. We German people are in this country five years already."

"German, huh? You speak English pretty good."

"Learn it at school. Five years already I go to school. Link Lake School. Good place to learn. Why you got a white streak of hair down the middle of your head?" Sophia asked, as she touched her hand to her head.

"Oh, that. Got that in the war."

"You fight in the war?"

"Yeah, I did. Got myself shot in the head, too. Stop asking questions. I've got work to do."

"I'll bet it hurt."

"Hurt like the blazes."

Sophia kept staring at Silas's head as he talked.

"How old are you, Sophia? Don't you have work to do at home?" Silas asked.

"I am sixteen years. How old are you?" Sophia smiled when she asked.

"I'm twenty-one," said Silas. "Lot older than you. That's all you need to know."

"Not so much older. You are age of my brother."

"What's his name?"

"Papa call him Fritz, I call him Fritzy."

"What does Fritz do?"

"He farms with Papa. I have another brother, Emil. He's seventeen. And little sister, Anna, too. She's only four."

"You have a big family. Are there lots of people around here? I came here to be alone."

"Not a big family. Other families are bigger. Some families have six, seven kids. Even more."

"Where'd you say you lived?" Silas asked. He put his hat back on his head and sat down on the pine log he was chopping, trying to think of a way of getting rid of this nosy girl. He didn't want a lot of people poking around his place.

"We live just over there. Over that hill. We are your neighbors." Sophia pointed toward the south. "Are you a farmer?"

"I plan on doing a little farming," Silas said. "But first I've got to build this cabin, and a shelter for my yoke of oxen."

"Our oxen do most of our work. They work hard for us. When your cabin be finished?"

"I don't know. Goes mighty slow, just me working alone. Why don't you go home now?"

"Can I help?"

"I don't need help. Besides you're kinda skinny and probably not very strong," Silas said, smiling.

"Skinny? Not too skinny, and I am strong," Sophia said, standing to her full five feet four inches and putting her hands on her hips.

"I'm sure you're stronger than you look."

"Ja, I am strong. Papa says I am strong for a girl."

"I'm sure you are," Silas said. "I've got to get back to work or I'll never get done with this cabin."

Sophia stood watching Silas work for a time, watched the chips fly as he swung his broadax against the side of the long straight white pine. Her horse stood nearby, grazing on the lush prairie grasses that had begun to grow since the weather had warmed.

"What's that tent for?" Sophia asked, pointing toward the old army tent that stood under a nearby oak tree.

"That's where I sleep," Silas said. "Until I get this cabin built."

"What is it like to sleep in a tent?"

"Not bad, not bad at all. Really nice in a gentle rain. Relaxing. But not good for winter. You sure talk a lot. Can't you see I'm working?"

"Tent be cold in the winter, huh?" Sophia said.

"It would be mighty cold, so leave me alone so I can finish my cabin."

"I'll go home now," Sophia said after a few minutes of watching without Silas so much as looking up from his work. She jumped on her horse with one motion, turned his head with the reins, and galloped off down the dusty trail. She waved her left hand as she raced off, her blonde hair flying in the wind.

Silas stopped chopping to watch Sophia and her horse disappear from view down the road; puffs of dust trailed behind. He thought about his new land and whether he would get along with his neighbors, especially people like the Reinerts, who had such a different background than he did. The Starkweathers, his people, had come from England shortly after the Revolutionary War and settled first in Massachusetts and then in New York, while Sophia's family had been in this country only a few years. Once more he picked up his broadax and began chopping.

Silas needed to finish this cabin so he could start doing what he had come here to do—and it wasn't building cabins and farming. He wasn't especially interested in getting to know his neighbors either— he preferred to remain by himself and not be bothered.

May 7, 1866

I'm building a log cabin on my new land. Not as easy as I thought it would be. Slow going, but I must have a roof over my head. This afternoon I met the neighbor girl. She belongs to a German family who has only been here five years. They live on the farm just south of me. A saucy young thing. Kind of cute, though. But she's nosy and talks too much. Wanted to know all about me. Rides a horse like a man. She wasn't even wearing shoes. Got to be careful talking with the neighbors. They could get in the way.

6

Accident

May 1866

Cabin-building proved far more difficult than Silas imagined it would be. Initially, he thought, What's so difficult about chopping down a few trees and stacking them up to make walls? Simple enough. Besides that, his new farm had nearly a hundred acres of trees, about half of them white pine, which made perfect logs for a cabin. Those were his thoughts when he once more shouldered his new chopping ax and headed for the woodlot on the west side of his property. Silas's father had taught him how to use an ax. But only for cutting firewood. Cutting logs for a cabin was new and, he soon discovered, far more difficult than merely cutting some deadwood to burn in a woodstove.

Silas had been cutting trees for nearly two weeks, and his cabin was only about one-fourth finished. It was taking much longer than he had planned. He also knew that the time he spent working on his cabin was time he should be breaking the land and putting in a crop—a requirement of the homestead law. He also desperately wanted to begin what he had come here to do.

Accident—May 1866

This May day dawned clear and cool, perfect for cutting several trees. Silas yoked his team of oxen, Dan and David, and headed toward the woodlot, the oxen walking slowly and deliberately, as is the nature of these beasts. Two weeks of dragging pine logs from the woodlot had formed a trail to the cabin site as the freshly cut logs dug into the soft, sandy soil prevalent in this part of Ames County.

Once at the woodlot, the oxen began grazing at the edge of the woods where Silas worked. His muscles, not accustomed to the hard work required in cutting trees, had slowly hardened as the days passed. The open air and hard work had been just the medicine he needed after his stay in the New Orleans army hospital where he had recovered from his wound and tried to put his life back together after his stint in the Union army.

Unfortunately, he had badly misjudged the amount of work it would take to get his new land up to the requirement of the homesteading contract he had signed with the government.

In the few weeks he had lived on his new place, he learned much. One important thing was how to predict which way a tree would fall once you begin chopping it. He learned to look for its natural lean and then notched the tree on that side to make sure the tree fell in that direction.

Silas was thinking about other things this morning, about the document he'd found the day he was shot, and he wasn't paying enough attention to his woodcutting. Too late, he discovered that the big white pine wouldn't fall in the direction he thought it should. With a mighty crack that echoed throughout the woodlot, it began falling, so fast that when Silas saw its direction it was too late. One of the tree's branches struck him on the side of the head, and he fell to the ground, unconscious. He regained consciousness once or twice, but each time he found he couldn't move because of the massive pine branch that had him pinned to the ground.

Minutes passed, perhaps even hours. He awakened to the sound of chopping and thought he was dreaming, thought it was an echo of his own work. Then someone was shaking him, and he heard a voice, "Ya hurt? Are ya hurt?"

Silas shook his head and focused his eyes; a bearded man was looking down at him as he lay on the soft pine needles.

"Ya hurt bad?" the man asked again.

"Don't know," Silas said as he tried to focus his eyes.

"First saw ya, I was afeard ya was daid. Than I heared ya moanin' a little. This here big branch that I chopped through and pulled off ya gave ya a glancin' blow. If the trunk of that big ole pine tree'd hit ya, you'd been a goner."

Silas sat up and looked around.

"Who are you?" Silas asked. Through bleary eyes he saw a heavy-set man with a red beard, wearing a rumpled felt hat.

"I'm your neighbor to the north, Meadows is the name, Justin Meadows. Heard yer ox bellerin' and wondered what was going on. So I came on over and found ya here. Ox probably saved yer life."

Meadows helped Silas to his feet.

"Ya got a nasty bump on yer head," Meadows said. "Gotta watch them big pines; never know which way they gonna fall. Anythin' broke 'sides a part of your head?"

"Don't think so," Silas said. "Much obliged you coming by and finding me."

"What's wrong with your hair? You look like a skunk—no offense."

"War wound," Silas muttered, not feeling up to providing more information.

Meadows helped Silas to his feet and supported him as the two men slowly walked down the sandy path. Dan and David ambled on behind, following the rutted trail, the logging chain dragging free behind and turning up little wisps of dust.

"Got a ways to go buildin' yer cabin," Meadows said when the log structure's foundation came into view."

"Taking a long time," Silas said. He was rubbing his head where a big lump had emerged.

"Ain't easy ta do. Nobody helpin' ya?"

"Nope, working all by myself."

"Can't do it alone, especially when the logs git up a little higher."

"Hadn't thought about that," Silas said.

"'Spect I could spare a little time and give ya a hand," Meadows said. "I'll ask Wolfgang Reinert and his big son, Fritz, ta help. I know Olaf Hanson will, too; that big ole Norwegian is a fair-to-middlin' carpenter as well. We'll git your cabin in shape in no time atall."

"Thank you," Silas said. He was feeling a bit woozy as he sat down on one of the logs he had pulled up to the partially completed cabin the previous day.

"Ya don't look too good," Meadows said. "Ya better rest for a spell."

Later that afternoon, Silas heard a rustling outside the flap of his tent. He crawled out to see Sophia Reinert slipping off her horse.

"Neighbor Meadows said a tree fell on you. Not good. Not good to have tree on your head. You better? Feel better?" the girl asked. She had a concerned look on her face.

"Much better," Silas said. He was actually glad to see her.

"I bring you supper," Sophia said as she opened up a bag she was carrying. "Bread and sausage that my ma make. She is good cook. Homemade cheese, too. Ma also make. You feel even more better after some supper." Sophia's wide smile lit up her entire face.

"I'm a good cook, too. But not as good as Ma. Ma is best cook. I am just good cook," Sophia said as she set the cloth bag on a stump.

"I'll bet you are," Silas said, smiling.

"I go now. You have good supper. I know you don't like company." Sophia climbed on her horse and turned the animal toward the rutted country road. With a free hand she waved as she turned back toward Silas and smiled.

May 15, 1866

Bad luck. A big tree fell on me today. Knocked me silly. I'd be a dead man if my old ox hadn't bellowed loud enough to catch the attention of my neighbor to the north. Justin Meadows is his name. Mighty nice fellow. Probably saved my bacon. If he hadn't come along, I'd still be under that tree. Way I feel tonight, I won't be doing any work for a couple days, maybe more. Got a helluva headache.

7

Cabin Building

May 1866

A couple mornings after his accident, Silas still felt stiff and sore and not up to his old self. The bump on his head had gone down, but it was still there—just to the side of where he had been shot. Someone in the New Orleans hospital had told him he had a hard head. He smiled when he thought of the comment and how it must be true.

Silas puttered around the foundation of the cabin that was slowly taking shape. He peeled bark from several of the logs in preparation for raising them into place. He was frustrated with his cabin building. He should be breaking some of his land so he could grow some crops, "prove up," and claim this place as his own, and he was still working on his shelter. He also had become impatient because he didn't have time to pursue his main reason for coming to Ames County.

Silas heard the squeaking wheels of an ox cart and looked up. Much to his surprise, visitors began arriving. Justin Meadows, driving his team of brindle oxen arrived first. He yelled, "Howdy, how ya feelin'?" Minutes later Wolfgang Reinert and Fritz, carrying axes and driving their ox team, drove into Silas's yard, followed by Olaf

Hanson, who was walking and carrying a big double-bitted ax over his shoulder. Others began arriving on horseback and by ox cart. They introduced themselves as they arrived. Emil Groskeep, Amos Blackwell, Joe and John Judd.

Silas was baffled. Where had all these men come from? How had they so quickly heard about his accident?

He asked these questions of a tall, thin young man who had arrived on horseback.

"I'm Adolph Lang; some of us are members of the Standalone Church in Link Lake," the man answered. "Our pastor, Increase Joseph Link, informed us of your predicament and said we should offer our assistance. Pastor Increase Joseph said you came from New York State. That was our home, too. Our congregation arrived here in 1851."

Silas and Adolph had a brief conversation about their common home state and discovered they had come from different parts of New York.

"We'll talk more later," Adolph said as he followed the parade of men, some driving ox teams and all carrying axes as they followed the winding trail to Silas's woodlot, up the hill beyond the building site. Soon the sound of axes biting into pine echoed through the woods and across the valley where the pond was located.

Pine logs began arriving at the cabin site, one after the other, pulled by teams of oxen. The snap of the ox drivers' whips cut the morning air. Silas stood in amazement as a crew of sturdy young men led by Fritz Reinert peeled the bark from the logs and began lifting them into place after first notching the corners so they fit properly together. Olaf Hanson supervised, showing the young men where to cut, how to notch properly, and where each log should be placed. The sound of axes cutting into wood and the sweet smell of pine filled the air.

Silas indicated where he wanted windows and where he wanted the door. When it was time to put in a window, Olaf made one without glass. He had brought along some white muslin, which he stretched over the window frame and then oiled to preserve it. Of course, Silas could not look out the window, but it did let in light.

At noon the men assembled in Silas's yard, in the shadow of the cabin that was two-thirds finished. Mrs. Reinert and Sophia, with Mrs. Meadows's and Mrs. Hanson's help, laid out a spread of food on blankets under a big oak tree not far from Silas's tent. They'd come riding horses and driving wagons around eleven.

Just before the men began to eat, a man dressed in black from head to foot and carrying a little red book arrived on horseback. He was tall and lanky and had long thin fingers and the most penetrating eyes Silas had ever seen.

"Are you Silas Starkweather?" the man in black asked.

"I am," Silas answered as he took the outstretched hand.

"I am the Reverend Increase Joseph Link," the man in black said. "Welcome to Link Lake."

"Thank you," Silas said. "I appreciate what your church members are doing for me."

"Your neighbor Meadows told me about your accident," Increase Joseph said. "Our church stands ready to help those in need, no matter who they are."

The hungry men, those who had spent the morning chopping trees, those who had pulled the logs down the sandy trail to the cabin site, and those who had been building the cabin, all lined up to eat. They were a dirty, dusty lot, but all were smiling, as they enjoyed working with each other and helping someone in need.

Increase Joseph climbed up on a white pine stump, removed his black hat, and with his other hand held his red book high in the air. In a loud, clear voice, he began, "Before we partake of this food, a few words of prayer."

The men all bowed their heads, as did Silas, who was not accustomed to praying. He hadn't seen the inside of a church since he left New York to join the army.

"Thank you Lord, for offering us the opportunity to help our brother in his time of need. Help us welcome him to our fine community, and let him know that he has friends and neighbors. And now let us join in this repast that has been set before us. Amen."

The men loaded their plates with thick slices of homemade dark bread, hunks of cold roast beef, piles of pungent-smelling sauerkraut, pieces of three kinds of sausage, and lefse plus Norwegian krumkake, for dessert—foods foreign to Silas. Sophia Reinert poured each man a cup of black coffee that Mrs. Reinert had made in a huge pot over Silas's campfire.

While the women packed away the food, the men began joking and telling stories, asking each other how spring planting was coming, and talking about the many changes that were taking place in Link Lake. They all wanted to talk about how things would be different now that the Great War that so divided the country had finally concluded.

With the meal finished, the men lit up pipes and sprawled in the shade of trees, for it was a sunny, warm, spring day without a cloud in the sky. Soon the men were back to work, and by day's end, the cabin was nearly complete. It was twelve by fourteen feet and had a woodsy and refreshing smell. The structure had one story, with one room and a sleeping loft overhead. All that remained to do was to finish the roof and build a stone fireplace, which would take up most of the space on one end of the cabin.

Justin Meadows and a couple of Welshmen who were stonemasons agreed to return in a few days to do the remaining work. Meadows said to Silas, "Drive yer ox team and cart over to my place. I've got a pile of stones I pulled off my fields that'll make a most suitable fireplace."

May 17, 1866

The best and the worst happened today. The best part: a huge crew of neighbors came and worked on my cabin. People came from

40

all around. A jovial bunch they were, laughing and telling jokes and working hard. Some could scarcely speak English, but that didn't seem to matter. They all worked together beyond anything I've ever seen before.

And the worst. Now everybody in God's creation knows about Silas Starkweather. How am I supposed to carry on when so many people have their eye on me? And all with good intentions, too, it seems. They all want to help out. Hard to believe so many people want to help me. If they ever found out what I'm doing here, they'd probably string me up from the oak tree in front of my new cabin.

8

Olaf Hanson

May 1866

*F*eeling better, Silas hauled stones all the next day, some as large as a big cooking pot, others smaller than a man's fist, and every size in between. Silas carefully inspected each rock before tossing it on the cart. Some were red, some multicolored, some black, some white with flecks of gray. They were the kinds of rocks he'd earlier read about when he studied the effects of the glacier that had come this way thousands of years ago.

By the end of the week, the cabin was completed, except for furniture. Silas had yet to build a lean-to for his oxen, but this could wait. He now must break some land for a garden and some field crops and finally find some time to do what brought him to central Wisconsin.

The next morning Silas got up early; the birdsong had awakened him. He had never heard so many birds before, and in the quiet hour of sunrise each competed with the other as to which could sing louder, or so it seemed to Silas. He sat on his porch with a cup of coffee and watched the sun creep over the tree line to the east, across the dirt road from his cabin.

Olaf Hanson—May 1866

He smelled the new pine lumber that comprised his new home, mixed with the scents of new growth—wild grasses that were growing everywhere, awakening from a long winter and a cold, wet spring. A brief thunder shower had rolled through the area during the night, the rain pounding on the cabin roof making sleep easy.

Silas thought about what had occurred in the few weeks since he arrived. And he considered how he had already failed in at least one major respect. He had not wanted to make much of a stir in the community. He wanted to keep to himself, but already he was indebted to a whole host of people who had come by to help him without even being asked. He surely appreciated what they had done; now he realized he could have never built the cabin by himself.

He heard the sound before he saw the ox cart pulled by a plodding team of roan oxen that appeared on the road and turned in toward his cabin. Another visitor. Olaf Hanson waved his arm as he approached the cabin. Silas quickly recognized him as his neighbor who had supervised the cabin building. Everything happened so quickly that day; Silas hadn't had time to talk with Olaf, who was tall, slim, broad-shouldered, clean-shaven, and had blond hair and deep blue eyes.

"Hallow. A gutt morning . . . to you, neighbor Silas," he said. His speech had a lilting quality to it, like a piece of slow-sung music.

"Good morning," Silas said, standing up.

"I come . . . for a visit," Hanson said. "To see . . . how you are?"

Silas listened carefully for he had little experience with a Norwegian accent.

"Would you like a cup of coffee?" Silas asked. He was actually glad to see a friendly face. He wasn't sure why.

"Ja, sure," Olaf said, smiling.

Soon Silas appeared back on the porch with a cup of coffee for Olaf and a refilled cup for himself.

"You . . . like your new cabin?" Olaf asked as he gazed at the building whose construction he had supervised.

"It's well made. Very well made. Couldn't have done it by myself."

"Tank you . . . I help build four, five cabins . . . in neighborhood. Couple log barns, too."

"You always a carpenter?" Silas asked.

"Ja . . . learned in the old country how to do . . . this work. In Norway. Working with my papa. . . . He was carpenter and farmer, too. Yust like me." Olaf took a big drink of his coffee and made a little face, but said nothing. He was accustomed to drinking much stronger coffee.

"Ja, I grow up . . . in Norway. Beautiful country. Big mountains. Lots of snow. Lots of water, too. Ocean close by. Smell the ocean most days. Miss all that here . . . no big water nearby . . . only small lakes. No mountains," Olaf said.

"So, why did you leave? Why'd you come here?"

Olaf's face turned serious. "I come from . . . family of four boys. I am third son. No land for me. To farm, I must leave . . . so I come to this country yust before your big war."

"And your wife?" Silas found himself interested in this man. Asking questions about Olaf's family was the least Silas could do as thanks for helping with his cabin.

"Ja, Ella. She a good woman. We married now . . . six years. Back in Norway we married. She from neighboring farm there."

"Must have been hard to leave."

"Ja, ja, very hard. Especially for Ella . . . she not want to leave her mudder and sisters. Many tears."

Olaf sat quietly for a bit, sipping on his coffee.

"Hard for me . . . too," the big man said. Silas saw tears in his eyes. "Will never see family again . . . a bad thing. Family important," Olaf said haltingly. He pulled out a big red handkerchief and blew his nose.

"How do you like it here in Link Lake?" Silas asked.

"So far . . . we like it . . . we both like it. Know why? Neighbors.

44

Good neighbors who help you . . . like family," Olaf said as he finished his cup of coffee.

With their coffee finished, both men filled their pipes with tobacco and lit up.

"What about you . . . Silas Starkweather? Where you from?"

"Oh, my family lives in New York State."

"They not from . . . old country?"

"Yes, but many years ago. They came from England, it was back in the late 1700s, a long time ago."

"You fight in War. Wolfgang told me. . . . He said . . . you were shot."

"Oh yeah, I was wounded in the war. Not much to it, except it left a streak of white hair down the middle of my head."

"So . . . how did you . . . Silas . . . decide on this place?"

"Always been looking for a place of my own," Silas lied. He had no intention of sharing with Olaf Hanson or anyone else, for that matter, his real reasons for homesteading this place.

"Ja . . . this make a good farm . . . need much work. . . . All farms need much work . . . at the beginning . . . and every day after that." Olaf chuckled. He had a deep laugh that lit up his entire face and made his blue eyes sparkle.

For a time the two men sat quietly, puffing on their pipes and enjoying the warmth of the sun as it climbed higher in the sky.

Finally, Olaf pulled out his pocket watch.

"Ja, I must . . . be going," he said as he stood up.

"Thanks for stopping by," Silas said.

"Oh . . . I am offering to build you furniture . . . chairs . . . table . . . dresser," Olaf said, smiling. "Reason I came . . . this morning. To tell you."

"But . . . but," Silas stammered. He didn't want to hurt his neighbor's feelings, yet he didn't want to be even more beholden to him.

"I will do it. . . . It's what neighbors do."

"But I planned to buy a couple chairs, a bed, and a table at the mercantile in Link Lake."

"No need. I . . . can build for you. . . . Will use your leftover lumber from the cabin. Help me load . . . on ox cart." Olaf walked over to his oxen, and they began moving toward the pile of logs and the few leftover roof boards, which Silas had sawed at the Link Lake Saw Mill.

Silas helped Olaf load the lumber and soon he was on his way. Silas stood on his porch watching Olaf Hanson and his slow-moving team go down the road. His neighbor smiled and waved his hand.

May 18, 1866

My neighbor Olaf Hanson stopped by this morning. He offered to build furniture for me. Can you imagine that? Said he'd do it for nothing. Stayed for a cup of coffee, and we chatted for an hour or more.

Hate to admit it, but I'm starting to feel a little guilty about lying to my neighbors. They all think I have my heart set on farming. Truth be known, I hate farming. I could never figure out why anybody wanted to make a living by grubbing in the dirt.

But I got to be careful. Only way I can get clear title to this place is to farm it. I must at least look like a farmer. I'm beginning to wonder if I made the right decision in coming here. I hope my stay is short.

9

Sophia's Garden

May 1866

The days became noticeably longer and warmer toward the end of May. One early morning, with dew hanging on everything and the sun creeping up over the trees to the east, Silas sat on the front porch of his new cabin with a cup of coffee. The smell of new pine wood mixed with the smells of the morning. He looked past the fenced barnyard that confined his sturdy team of oxen. He had just completed the wood-rail fence yesterday, so he no longer had to worry about his oxen wandering too far at night.

Silas looked across the plowed field, about five acres, just to the west of his cabin. His neighbors Wolfgang Reinert and Justin Meadows helped him with the plowing and had even lent him their oxen, because the breaking plow required several ox teams to pull it. They used Wolfgang's breaking plow, a sturdy implement with a heavy oak beam and a long steel moldboard that turned the heavily rooted soil and cut through the roots of the hazel brush and small scrub oaks that grew here and there in the otherwise grass-covered and hilly prairie. The pleasant, fresh smell of newly turned soil was new to Silas. With land plowed, Silas began to feel like a farmer, even though he knew his father back in New York wanted him in the family harness shop.

Silas had not written his father the real reason he had moved to central Wisconsin, to Ames County. He would in due time, but he wanted it to be a surprise, and besides, it was much too early to let him know. What he didn't need was someone, like a father, to dash his hopes and dreams in these early stages.

Meadows had lent Silas a small sack of corn kernels and showed him how to punch holes in the newly turned furrows, drop a kernel of corn in each small hole, and cover it with his foot. He had said, "When your crop comes in, you can give me back some seed corn."

Silas had agreed the deal was more than fair, but he was a little skeptical about whether he would get any crop at all. The sod was heavy with a fierce tangle of roots, not especially conducive to corn growing, Silas thought.

Silas lit up his pipe and leaned back in the chair that Olaf Hanson had made for him. He was waiting for Sophia Reinert to arrive. Wolfgang had volunteered her to help Silas plant his vegetable garden in a freshly plowed space behind his cabin. He heard the hoofbeats before he saw the horse and rider. Sophia, a big smile on her face, carried a small sack in one hand. She effortlessly slid off her horse.

"Got morning," she said. Her yellow hair shone in the sunlight. "You ready for garden planting?"

"Never planted a vegetable garden before," Silas said. "My mother always planted our garden at home and took care of it, too. I helped my pa with his work."

"Never too old to learn garden planting," Sophia said. She wore a loose-fitting gingham dress. Even with her loose clothing Silas could see that Sophia was developing into an attractive young woman.

Sophia showed Silas how to lay out rows in the garden, using a length of string she had brought with her to mark them. Together they planted carrots and radishes, turnips and potatoes, two rows of sweet corn, and several hills of squash and pumpkins.

As they worked, Sophia talked constantly. She was filled with questions.

"Silas, what from life do you want?"

"What?" Silas was a bit surprised by her question.

"Oh, I don't rightly know."

"You do not have a big plan?"

"I guess not," Silas said.

"You not want to be rich? Live in a big house? Have servants help you, like I read about in books?"

Silas laughed. "Maybe you're reading too much."

"No, no never read too much. Books how I find out. Learn about other places. Other people. Learn how other people live. What they want."

Silas decided to turn the tables. "What do you want when you grow up, Sophia?"

"Me?" Sophia smiled.

"I want to do something important. I want to be like famous men. George Washington, Thomas Jefferson."

"But you're a girl," Silas said matter-of-factly.

"Should not matter. Girl or boy. Man or woman. No matter if you wear dress or pants, you should be able to do big things. Be a famous person."

Silas laughed.

"You laugh at me. Don't you laugh! Papa laugh, too. I show Papa. I show you, Silas. I will be famous person."

"Why do you want to be a famous person?"

"Think it fun to have my picture in school books. See me in book. Sophia Reinert, famous person. Kids read about me. Look at my picture. Want to be like me. Even kids born and grow up on farms should have chance to be famous."

"You're probably right," Silas said as he scraped his foot across the hole where Sophia had just placed five squash seeds.

"I right for sure," Sophia said. "What this country is supposed to be about. Different from old country. Here anybody can be famous. Do big things. Get picture in school books."

With the garden finished, the two neighbors sat in the shade of the big oak in front of Silas's cabin.

"You got nice cabin," Sophia said. "New wood smells good."

"Thanks to your pa and the other neighbors."

"We glad to help. Pa say must always help neighbor. Can I ask another question?"

"Why not? You've been asking questions all morning."

"Why you spend so much time walking around in your plowed field? Corn crop not grow any faster whether you keep looking or not."

"Want to help the crop any way I can," Silas said.

"You strange man, Silas, with white streak across the top of your head," Sophia said. She paused for a moment. "Time for me to go. Ma has work for me this afternoon."

Sophia gathered the reins of her horse, slipped on its back, and headed down the road toward home. Silas sat back thinking of this young woman and her many questions. And her ideas of women becoming famous people. This was a new one for him. He watched as Sophia and her pony disappeared over the little hill that separated his farm from the Reinerts'. Her curly blonde hair bounced as she rode bareback, holding tight to the pony's reins. Silas looked over the little garden that they had planted together; he had to admit that Sophia had done most of the work, because he knew nothing about planting a garden. He wasn't especially interested in gardening but realized that it was one way for him to have fresh vegetables at no cost, except for a few hours of hoeing.

He looked over to the log lean-to that Olaf Hanson helped him build for his team of oxen, who stood by their manger munching dry hay that Justin Meadows, his neighbor to the north, had given him.

"This should hold ya until the grass grows a bit more," Meadows had said, smiling. He brought the wagonload of hay over on his high-wheeled wagon, pulled by his team of oxen, and pitched it into a pile near the barnyard fence that confined Silas's team.

Silas thought how unbelievably kind and generous his neighbors had been to him as he tried to establish himself on these 160 acres of free land. He, having grown up in a city, had not expected such. Indeed, he had hoped he could quietly go about his business, build his cabin, plow a few acres, and generally meet the government's requirements for homesteaded land with little notice. He had quickly discovered, especially when the tree had fallen on him, that he couldn't do it alone, that he depended on his neighbors more than he wanted to.

As he sat on his porch, whittling on a piece of pine, he thought about his father, John, back in Watertown, New York. John Starkweather, now in his early fifties, made harnesses, horse collars, bridles, halters, saddles, any equipment for horses. He was an excellent harness maker. Farmers and small-town and city people from miles around came to his little shop to have their leather equipment repaired or to have him make a new harness or some other leather item, according to their own specifications.

Silas had worked with his father in the harness shop since he was a lad, helping to clean up after a day's work, piling tanned hides, gathering up stray pieces of leather. As he grew older, his father taught him the harness-making skills he had learned from his father. How to sew leather with straight and uniform stitches, how to look at a tanned hide and decide which sections would work best for which part of the harness. Silas was a bright boy who learned quickly, and by the time he had finished his schooling was as good a harness maker as his father, perhaps even better.

Sophia's Garden—May 1866

John Starkweather had the hope of many fathers. He wanted his son, his only child, to follow in his path, taking over the family business when he could no longer do it. But Silas, although he enjoyed the smell of new leather and shared the pride of doing good work with his father, did not want to spend the rest of his life in a harness shop in Watertown, New York, where the snow was deep and the winters harsh. He wanted to travel, wanted to seek his fortune in other parts of the country, maybe even in other parts of the world. Wanted to make money more easily than toiling hour after hour in a harness shop.

When the Civil War began, he couldn't wait until he was old enough to enlist. His reasons for joining up were to get out of Watertown, different from most of the other young men, who enlisted because they were patriotic and favored the North's position on the war.

Now, as he sat here alone in the wilds of Wisconsin, he wondered if he had made the right decision to homestead this rather isolated sandy and hilly farm. It certainly wasn't the most productive land in the area, thus the reason some settler hadn't taken it over earlier. But for Silas, it should be just right. Exactly the right place to do what he wanted to do.

He often felt bad that he hadn't returned to Watertown and his father's harness shop, as both his parents had thought he would. Especially on days when his farmwork seemed never finished. He had written a letter to his parents while he was still in New Orleans and not yet released from the service. Their return letter was filled with disappointment, even a tinge of betrayal. Silas knew that his parents would never understand the reasons for his decision to homestead land in central Wisconsin, miles from any major city.

In the valley west of his cabin, Silas heard a sandhill crane. Its unusual call upset him, but he didn't know why. As the afternoon sun settled below the woods to the west, he walked into his cabin and started a fire in the fireplace. He lit his kerosene lamp and began reading from a new book he'd purchased at the Link Lake Mercantile. Later he wrote in his journal.

May 30, 1866

Finally, my crops are in. I'd never have got it done without my neighbors. They bend over backwards being nice to me. Tell you the truth; I'd rather they weren't so friendly. Planting crops is a tough job. Had to break the ground first. Not easy, especially with the prairie grass. That stuff is tough. You should see the roots. Takes a sturdy plow and three teams of oxen to turn the sod. Neighbor Meadows called the grass "turkey foot." He said in the fall the grass seeds come out on little branches that look like a wild turkey's foot. He said this turkey foot grass grows six feet tall. I've still got lots of it to plow.

Stopped by the mercantile in Link Lake. Owen Davies struck up a conversation. I can't get over how friendly everybody is. That goes for town people as well as the farmers. Davies knows I live alone. He asked me if I read much. I said I didn't. He said he had a book I'd like. I told him I didn't have much time for book reading. He said I might like to read this one because the guy who wrote it and I have things in common. "How was that?" I asked him. He said we both were from the east and both lived in small cabins. Said the guy's name was Thoreau, Henry David Thoreau. I paid Davies a quarter for the book, *Walden*.

After my chores were done, I opened the cover and thumbed through it. Not an easy book to read. Read a couple paragraphs here and there. Then I read them again. This guy Thoreau thinks a lot like I do. He wrote: "If a man does not keep pace with his companions, perhaps it is because he hears a different drummer. Let him step to the music which he hears, however measured or far away."

Sophia's Garden—May 1866

He's writing about me. I'm sure not like the rest of the folks around here. Most of them have noticed, too. They think I'm a little strange. But it's more than that. Maybe I do hear a different drummer that's telling me what to do.

10

Attack

October 1866

The summer days passed quickly as Silas worked hard to establish his farm. With the help of his neighbors, Silas broke ground for three more five-acre patches to be planted to winter wheat. Fall had arrived before Silas had even been aware of it. Great flocks of Canada geese winged overhead, on their way south, honking loudly. Some days the flocks stretched from horizon to horizon, hundreds of birds flying in formation, perhaps thousands of them, changing position as they flew, taking turns breaking a path through the cool fall air. Sometimes Silas heard them flying in the dark, creating a melodic chorus on a still, dark night, a haunting sound to someone not accustomed to it.

Silas saw the robins, gathering in huge flocks, preparing for their trip south, away from the harshness of a midwestern winter, and the blackbirds, too, and the sandhill cranes gathering in his fields, preparing to leave, calling to each other, a mixture of sounds, sounds of fall.

On dark fall nights, with no moon and clouds obscuring the starlight, he often heard an owl calling, and then another returning the call. "Who cooks for you? Who cooks for you?" he thought they asked. At first the sound troubled him, even frightened him a little, but then he came to enjoy it, for it broke the quiet of the night.

Much to the surprise of everyone in the Link Lake community, all summer Silas had dug holes, set fence posts, and fashioned wooden fences around each of his fields. It astonished everyone that he would do this. All the other wheat farmers in Ames County made their fields as large as possible. None was smaller than ten acres, and many were as large as forty acres or more. But not Silas Starkweather's.

As neighbors will do, they began talking about him and his strange ways. It was one thing to arrange your farm in five-acre plots, but it was quite another to surround each little plot with many fence posts and a wooden pole fence.

No one had the nerve, not even his closest neighbors, Justin Meadows and Wolfgang Reinert, to inquire about this considerably unusual way of farming. Perhaps it was how they farmed back in New York, some thought.

Someone asked Preacher Increase Joseph what he thought about Silas's farming strategies.

"He perhaps knows more than the rest of us," Increase Joseph said. "The soil will remain in place when it is in small plots. It will not blow away in huge clouds of dust, as we have sometimes seen when a windstorm visits us."

The preacher's answer made sense to some people. Others, who knew about Silas's war wounds, wondered if the injury to his head might be affecting his behavior, if he might be mentally off a bit.

Silas also spent hours prowling his fields, walking up and down the fence rows, and hiking the newly plowed areas that he had planted to winter wheat, which was just coming up. How much inspection did a wheat crop need anyway? some of the more curious neighbors wondered.

One cool but sunny afternoon, Wolfgang Reinert stopped at Silas's cabin on his way home from trading in Link Lake.

"Hello," Wolfgang cried out when he arrived in Silas's yard. Silas came around the corner of the cabin when he heard the greeting. He had been working in his garden, digging the remains of his potatoes, carrots, and onions. Pulling the ripe squash and pumpkins from their vines. Snapping the ears from the field corn. All of these crops would be welcomed when the winter winds swept around his cabin and piled snow high against its walls.

"Howdy," Silas said when he saw his neighbor and now friend.

"Ve butcher pig, tomorrow," Wolfgang said. "You have time to help? Ve give you meat for help."

Silas was pleased to assist; he felt a considerable obligation to Wolfgang and his family for all they had done to help him become established during his first season in Link Lake. He had thought of offering to repair Wolfgang's horse and oxen harnesses but considered that if he did the leatherwork for Wolfgang, then others would want their harnesses repaired as well. He did not come to Link Lake to fix harnesses, after all.

After the butchering, Silas stayed on to help with the meat cutting. Wolfgang showed him how to cut the meat into pork chops, how to cut pork roasts, how to save the ribs and their meat for cooking, how to carve out the hams, which would be smoked. Silas even assisted with the grinding of the smaller and often less desirable pieces of meat that would go into sausage. He watched Mrs. Reinert cut the pig fat into small chunks, which she tossed in a kettle that stood on their cookstove.

She put pork chops and other pieces of choice pork in a pottery crock and poured the melted fat over them. When it cooled, the lard would keep the meat from spoiling.

At the end of the day, Silas started home, along a little path through the corner of the woods that separated his farm from the Reinerts'. Wolfgang had given him a hunk of pork, enough for several meals. He carried the meat under his arm, wrapped in brown paper that Mrs. Reinert had gotten from the mercantile in Link Lake.

As he walked, Silas smelled fall everywhere, and it was pleasant. He shuffled through newly fallen leaves of oak and maple, of aspen and birch. Much fall color remained and the sun, low in the western sky, created hillsides of many shades and hues—the purplish stems of the big bluestem grass not yet plowed, the yellow of the aspens in the distance, and the red maple trees growing near the pond.

As he walked he thought about what he had accomplished in the few short months since he had arrived at Link Lake. But he was frustrated. Although he had done much, he also had accomplished nothing toward his real goal. Perhaps next year will be better, he thought, now that he'd gotten a start with his farming and had made good progress toward owning this land.

He was shaken from his thoughts by a sound in the shadows behind him. A squirrel, perhaps, or maybe a rabbit. But this one was different, louder than either of these two creatures could make. It was a sniffing sound and a low growl. Something he had not heard before and couldn't identify.

It then occurred to him. Justin Meadows had told him that a few bears roamed these parts and could be a menace if you tried to raise pigs. A bear would come in the night, grab a little pig, kill it with one bite of its mighty jaws, and then run off with its prize.

Silas could sense the animal trailing him was coming closer, no doubt smelling the fresh pork he clutched tightly under his arm. He began to walk faster; his cabin was now only a quarter of a mile or so away. He felt the hair on the back of his neck tingle, and, though the late afternoon was cool, he began to sweat.

He glanced back along the trail, and deep in the shadows he saw the beast, a gigantic black bear, sniffing the air and making low growling sounds. Silas began to run, not knowing if he could outrun a bear or not. One thing he had failed to ask Meadows was how fast a bear could run; he surprised himself by how fast he was moving, even with a large hunk of fresh pork under his arm. It occurred to him as he ran that if all else failed and he sensed the bear gaining on him he would drop the meat. He hoped it would appeal to the beast more than a badly frightened and skinny man.

He ran on, the rustling behind him becoming ever louder. He burst into the cabin, slammed and latched the door, and sat down, out of breath. He was wringing wet; his hands shook so badly he could hardly put the meat on his table. After a moment or so, he gathered up some courage and lifted his rifle from the pegs above the fireplace.

Carefully he opened the cabin door and peered out into the twilight of early evening. He stepped off his porch and glanced down the trail. Nothing. Cautiously he walked around the cabin, toward the barnyard where Dan and David were confined. He heard Dan bellowing, something the big beast seldom did.

The oxen, normally grazing or resting, were clearly agitated. They were flicking their tails and moving their massive heads up and down.

Silas glimpsed the big bear at the barnyard fence, clawing at the rails and snapping its massive jaws. The bear saw him about the same time he saw it. The huge animal stood on its back legs and let out a mighty growl that sent a shiver through Silas.

He tried to take careful aim, but the barrel of his gun was jumping up and down as his arms shook. The bear growled again, and Silas pulled the trigger. The blast echoed through the valley by the pond. The big bear, a massive hole in its chest, fell to the ground, pulling down one of the fence rails as it did. It lay on the ground, blood pumping from its wound and seeping from its mouth. The bear's legs flailed in the air, as if looking for traction they couldn't find. And then the beast lay still.

Silas let out his breath and for the first time realized that he was shaking. Arms shaking. Legs shaking. He returned to the cabin, placed the rifle on its pegs, and sat on a chair by the fire for a long time, staring into the flames, waiting for the shaking to stop.

The next day, Silas asked Justin Meadows to help skin the beast and carve its meat into manageable hunks. Silas gave an ample amount of it to Meadows and gave even more to the Reinerts, who thanked him profusely. Hope Meadows said she would render the fat and give Silas the bear grease to help preserve anything made of leather.

A fellow in Link Lake tanned the massive hide, leaving on the hair. Silas put it on the floor in front of his fireplace, a reminder of the day he had first met a bear and shot it dead. News of what Silas had done flew around the neighborhood and beyond. Of course, with each telling the bear got larger and Silas's exploit more heroic. Someone had even started the story that the bear had attacked Silas and he had killed it with an ordinary butcher knife, while he lay on his back in his garden, the bear on top of him. Silas had been wise enough in his telling not to mention the sweating and the shaking, that he had been scared out of his wits, or that he took must of the night to calm down.

For years after the event, whenever anyone mentioned Silas Stark-weather, they remembered him as the man who killed a big black bear single-handedly. He did nothing to quell the stories. Better to be remembered for killing a bear than for what he was really doing on these hilly acres.

October 19, 1866

Shot a bear yesterday. Can't believe I did it. The animal scared me badly; nothing has ever frightened me this much. Never killed anything so big before. Not even in the army. All it took was one shot. And a lucky shot it was. Really lucky. I was shaking so badly when I fired the rifle, I could as easily have killed one of my oxen.

Animal followed me home from Reinerts' farm. I figured he wanted to steal a hunk of fresh pork Wolfgang gave me after I helped them butcher.

I'm still shaking a little.

October 25, 1866

I stopped at the Link Lake Mercantile today. Everyone had heard my bear story, including Owen Davies, who owns the place. He said to me, after he inquired about the bear, "You need to get yourself a dog, any kind of dog. Bear won't bother you if you have a dog."

I said I didn't know where to buy a dog. Davies offered me one of his dogs, a young animal that he said was "a bit short on looks, but appears to be smart. He goes by Rex."

So now I've got me a dog, a short-legged brown mongrel, but very friendly. I think we'll get along just fine.

People are beginning to wonder about all the fences I'm building. Let them wonder. I surely don't want them to figure out the real reason. Besides, the small fields do prevent the wind from blowing the soil away. Happened to a couple of my neighbors this spring. They have forty-acre fields. The wind blew for three days, turning the sky yellow with blowing sand.

I once more turned to reading *Walden*. It's the only reading material I have in the cabin. Someday I should buy a Bible I suppose. But so far I haven't felt the need.

I know some folks think I must be lonely living here all by myself. Thoreau wrote about that. He said, "I am no more lonely than a Mill Brook, or a weather cock, or the North Star, or the south wind, or an April shower, or a January thaw, or the first spider in a new house."

That about covers it, I'd say. I guess a person is only as lonely as he wants to be. I've been too busy to think much about it.

11

Gardening

Emma
October 2000
Blue Shadows Farm

*H*ello," I said, answering the phone that hung on the wall across the kitchen from my wood-burning cookstove. I'd traded in my dial phone a couple years ago for one of those fancy push-button phones. But I insisted the installers hang it on the wall. The phone has always hung on the wall, from the day when we had party-line telephones in our neighborhood, starting back in the early 1900s. I'd never find it if it were anyplace else. I'm not against change, except when it comes too fast and goes too far.

"It's Kate, at the newspaper."

"Mornin', Kate. Aren't you up early for a Saturday morning?"

"Got work to do. Facts to check."

I've known Kate Dugan since she was a little girl helping her dad in the newspaper office. She was a spunky little thing as a child; she still is. Kate doesn't take guff from anybody. She's one of those young women who can cut the mustard, no doubt about it. I had been good friends with her father, Ira, and her mother, Eleanor. I liked them both. Ira was a good newspaperman. Wrote what he thought. Made a few people angry over the years. Kate's a chip off the old block. She and I go out for coffee once a week or so. I have her over for dinner on occasion, especially since her husband was killed in a car accident a few years ago.

"What can I do for you, Kate?" I asked. I wondered what she wanted so early on a Saturday morning.

"Heard you had a little excitement at your farm yesterday," Kate said.

"Do you mean the lightning strike?"

"Yup. Ashley Anderson came storming into the office yesterday afternoon. Boy, is she a piece of work. She was soaked to the skin and having a hissy fit. Madder than anything."

"You don't say," I said. I knew she was upset—I could see that when she climbed on the bus with the kids—but I thought she'd get over it once she got home and dried off her daughter.

"She said her kid had been traumatized. Said all the kids had been in severe danger when lightning struck a tree. Said I should write a story about it and put it on the front page of the newspaper." Kate paused. "Emma, were the kids in real danger?"

"No, they were not. The students were nowhere near the tree when the lightning hit."

"I just needed to hear your side of the story," Kate said without expression.

"Kate, in all the years classes have been coming here, there hasn't been one child hurt—except for some sunburn, once a little poison ivy, and lots of mosquito bites."

"I had to ask, Emma. In my business, it's what we do. I go for the facts."

"Well, you heard my take on the situation," I said. "Did you talk to Joe? He'll give you the facts."

"Hey, Emma, calm down. I figured as much. Just doing my job.

Oh, you need to know, Ms. Almighty Anderson," Kate especially emphasized the *Ms. Almighty,* "is starting a crusade against nature hikes."

"You don't say," Emma said rather sarcastically. "You running Ashley's story?"

"No, I'm not," Kate said.

"Nature has a way of offering surprises," I said.

"How's the garden project?" Kate asked, changing the subject.

"Going well. Bunch of folks coming out today."

"Glad to hear it. Those community gardens are a great example for Link Lake."

"Thanks," I said. We talked for a few more minutes before hanging up. I had long appreciated Kate's support of my various projects at Blue Shadows Farm. I remember a couple years ago when the paper received an AP story saying vegetable gardening was old-fashioned and mostly a hobby. The article concluded with the statement, "A few large farms can grow all the vegetables the country needs. With modern transportation and refrigeration systems, vegetables and fruits can be shipped throughout the country in a matter of hours."

After the paper ran the story, Kate asked me if I'd like to write a letter to the editor with a response. I wrote, using the most high-falutin' language I knew:

Dear Editor:

I read with interest the recent story proclaiming the end to vegetable gardens. I totally disagree. With a garden, families can grow most of their vegetables right at home and save a lot of money in food costs. Also, if kids have a chance to work in a vegetable garden with their parents—plant some seeds, care for the growing crops, and help with the harvest—they're more likely to respect the land.

For me, gardening is a religious experience. A gardener has faith in the soil and the weather. Gardening is the path to a better future in this country.

Signed,
Emma Starkweather
R.R. I, Link Lake, Wisconsin

Ever the optimist, I expected some positive reaction to my letter. But the folks around Link Lake talk a lot in private but don't say very much publicly.

Only one letter appeared in the paper the following week. One that surprised me a bit. It was short and to the point. I pasted it in my scrapbook right next to the copy of the letter I had written.

Dear Editor:

I must take issue with the recent comments made by Emma Starkweather in this newspaper. As a man of the cloth, I resent her implication that in some remote way religion can be associated with gardening. As all believers know, religion is about saving souls and finding a way to the Promised Land. Growing a few radishes is not the way to do it.

Sincerely,
The Reverend Ridley Ralston
The Church of the Holy Redeemed

Never one to back away from a good argument, especially with a preacher, I fired back this response, using my everyday approach to writing.

Dear Editor:

I read what the Reverend Ridley Ralston said in your paper last week. All I have to say is, "What's the good of sending a soul to heaven and at the same time allowing the land to go to hell?"

Sincerely,
Emma Starkweather
R.R. I, Link Lake, Wisconsin

Well, I tell you, those few words about heaven and hell got people talking. Nothing else appeared in the newspaper, but I heard the talk in town and throughout the county, for that matter, was rich. And the pious folks, already wondering about my non-church affiliation, now knew for sure I was headed down the road to a fiery end.

But that was a couple years ago. This morning, I saw several of the garden families arriving for the fall harvest of their gardens.

Back in 1986, I laid out the community garden plots in one of the fenced fields near the road and not far from the farmhouse. At the beginning I had but two rules: (1) Keep your garden reasonably free of weeds and (2) Respect your neighbor—don't allow your little ones to traipse around in someone else's garden. The system has worked well. Only two families have been asked to leave in fourteen years. And I didn't do the asking. The twenty families gardening here organized the Blue Shadows Garden Association in the late 1980s. The association makes sure that everyone follows the rules.

For my payment, each year at Christmastime the gardeners take me out for dinner, give me a big box of Link Lake Creamery cheese and a fifty-dollar gift certificate to the Bookworms Bookstore in Willow River.

This morning, families began arriving at their gardens at eight o'clock. They dug white and red potatoes and bright orange carrots, pulled yellow-purple rutabagas and deep red beets, picked the last of the green beans, cut the spiky broccoli that had begun growing well since the cool weather returned, sliced off big green cabbage heads, and picked the last of the not-completely-ripe tomatoes. The rich, pungent smell of freshly turned soil hung in the air, a smell no one has been able to duplicate in a laboratory as hard as they might try.

The gardeners would return in a week or so for the gourds: little orange ones; some yellowish green and grotesquely shaped; some striped yellow and green; some large enough to dry, hollow out, and make birdhouses. And the squash: acorn and old-fashioned Hubbard, butternut, and buttercup and big orange Halloween pumpkins with sturdy green handles, pumpkins so big that a five-year-old could scarcely carry one, but carry them they do for they will be "their" Halloween pumpkins after they and their parents carve the faces and set the candles.

After the first killing frost, they will pick the ornamental corn, each ear a surprise when the husks are stripped back, some deep red, some ears a mix of red, yellow, and brown kernels, each one different. And they will cut the cornstalks, tie them into bundles, and stand them beside their front doors—a decoration for autumn in town, a reminder of their garden in the country.

I had the fire going in the cookstove as I had promised to help those with extra tomatoes make homemade soup. Soon, my big kitchen was filled with tomatoes and people. Three families were making tomato soup. They sliced the juicy, red tomatoes and then tossed them into a huge kettle on top of the stove. They added some slices of celery and garden-grown onions to the mixture. The kettle's contents were soon bubbling, sending wonderful smells throughout the house, historic smells that I remembered from my childhood when Ma made soup just like this, on this same stove, with the same ingredients. I can't explain why, but the smells of cooking on a woodstove always appealed to me; they still do. I wondered if making homemade soup had the same affect on the people working in my crowded kitchen on this Saturday morning.

As the families worked, Marilyn Johnson, one of the mothers, said to me, "Kids saw quite a storm on the field trip the other day."

"That they did," I said. "One of those unexpected things that happens."

"Good for kids to be surprised once in a while. So much of life is planned these days," another mother replied.

"You hear what Ashley Anderson plans to do?" a third mother asked.

"She's filing a formal complaint with the school board and asking that they stop all outdoor field trips. Claims they're just too dangerous. She says kids can learn about nature in much safer ways; they don't need to go on scary field trips to do it," the third mother reported.

"Expect the school board will listen?" asked Emma.

"They might. They're always looking for ways to cut the school budget. This would be another excuse to save a few dollars," one of the fathers piped up. "Expect there might be a liability question, too. Insurance problems."

I continued stirring the big kettle of soup. "It'd be a mistake," I said. "Students need these field trips." I wondered what the board would do with the complaint.

My steamy kitchen was filled with activity. A couple mothers washed dishes. Children were playing outside and then storming into the kitchen, tracking in mud from yesterday's storm. I didn't say anything but was enjoying it all.

Cooking tomatoes brought back memories of the days when I stood with my mother, at this same stove, making tomato soup and talking. How natural and pleasant it was to work with Ma, to help her with an important task. I knew the children would remember this day when they become adults.

Part 3

12

School Board Meeting

Emma
October 2000
Link Lake High School

Ashley Anderson, true to her promise, filed a complaint with the Link Lake School District about what had happened on the field trip to my farm. She also wrote a letter to the newspaper, which I read with great interest.

Dear Editor:

Field trips into nature, such as the one my daughter Jenny experienced recently, are dangerous, unpredictable, and should be permanently suspended. My daughter still wakes up in the middle of the night screaming about the terror she experienced when lightning struck a huge tree and it literally exploded in front of her. I have two younger daughters, and I do not want to subject them to the trauma Jenny experienced in the name of environmental education. My husband and I have asked the Link Lake School District to eliminate these perilous and ill-planned trips.

Either the school district makes the appropriate decision or my
husband and I will be forced to take legal action.

Signed,
Ashley Anderson

"What a crock," I said out loud when I finished reading the letter
in the paper.

When I arrived at the high school that dreary October evening, I
saw Ashley and her husband, Jacob, sitting in the front row of chairs
in the multimedia center—I still call it the library. I suspect everyone in the area knows the Andersons. Jacob owns Ames County Real
Estate and has clients throughout the county and beyond. I heard
that Ashley quit her job as a realtor there when their first daughter
was born. That's when she became a professional volunteer; it's what
I call her anyway. Let's see, she serves on the Link Lake Library
board, volunteers with the Link Lake Historical Society, and is president of the Link Lake Women's Club. I may have missed some. Oh,
and of course she volunteers at the middle school.

I remember when the Andersons moved here from Milwaukee
twelve years ago. They were treated as newcomers, of course, and
still are. That's the way people are around here. Unless you are born
here, you're a newcomer—forever. I'll give it to the Andersons.
They've worked hard to fit in and contribute to the community,
even though Ashley's head seems screwed on cockeyed some days.

I counted about thirty folding chairs in the room. Fifteen people
turned out for the meeting; I suspect some of them were there because they'd read Ashley's letter in the paper. Joe Crawford, looking
uncomfortable in a sports jacket and tie (I'd never seen him in a tie),
came in after I did and sat down beside me.

"What do you make of all this?" he whispered to me.

"Don't know," I whispered back.

"Can't believe this is happening," he said.

Kate Dugan, with her notepad at the ready, slid in beside Joe.

"How you doin' Joe?" I overheard her say. I noticed she touched him on the arm. I thought something might be going on between these two. They make a nice-looking couple.

I spotted some parents whose kids had been on the hike and who had gardens at my place—they were strong supporters of nature hikes. I knew most of the other people, some not well.

After dealing with several routine board items, Ruth Prescott, school board president, glanced down at the papers in front of her and began speaking. Prescott, a tall, thin, intense woman, on the dark side of forty, ran a gift shop in downtown Link Lake. A strand of loose hair, which she unconsciously pushed back from time to time, hung down the side of her face.

"Next, we need to discuss a complaint we've received from one of our parents. As you know it concerns a recent nature hike at Emma Starkweather's farm. Emma is here this evening. First, I want to thank her for the many years she has allowed children to visit her farm. Her generosity has made a great contribution to the Link Lake community. Emma, do you have any comment before we go on?"

"Thank you," I said as I stood up. I glanced at some notes I'd earlier made, guessing I might be asked to say something. "I believe strongly that the only way children can begin to understand nature is to have an opportunity to see it firsthand. I am pleased to make this important contribution to our children's education, and I plan to continue doing it as long as I am able. Thank you." After I'd heard myself talk, I realized I didn't really talk that way. What I wanted to say was, "What a bunch of malarkey. On the one hand, you thank me, and on the other, you question what I'm doing with my nature hikes." What I wanted to say to Ashley Anderson was, "We plowed that ground before." Of course when you are in your 70s, you sometimes, not always, have the wisdom to hold your tongue—or speak in code, which is probably what I had done. I sat down and was surprised to hear many people clapping. I glanced to where the Andersons were sitting. They were not clapping.

When it was quiet again, Ruth Prescott said, "Each board member has a copy of the Anderson complaint letter." Board members nodded.

"The Andersons are here," Prescott said, glancing toward the grim-faced couple sitting in the front row. In her usual monotone, she read the newspaper letter from beginning to end. With one hand she pushed back the strand of hair that fell over her eye.

"Do the Andersons have anything further to say?"

Ashley stood up. She wore a fashionable brown skirt with a tan blazer. She began reading from her notes in a strong, confident voice. "I believe we all are in agreement that our children and their needs should come first. I think we also can agree that the safety of our children must always be foremost in our minds. My husband and I see a basic contradiction between what we say we all agree with and some of the practices here at Link Lake Middle School. Of course, I'm referring to the old-fashioned and dangerous idea of taking children on field trips into the wild. At one time it may have been necessary to do this, but with new modern curricula enhanced by computer technology, these field trips are no longer necessary or appropriate. They should be abandoned immediately."

Upon hearing this, I turned toward Joe Crawford. He rolled his eyes but didn't say anything.

"Thank you, Mrs. Anderson. Does any board member have a question for either Mr. or Mrs. Anderson?"

"Yes, I have one," Fred Jones, a farmer from north of Link Lake and longtime board member, said. "First, let me commend you, Mrs. Anderson, for volunteering your time to accompany your child on field trips. We all appreciate your interest in the education of your child and her schoolmates. Was you or your daughter or any other youngster or adult injured on this field trip?"

"Not physically, Mr. Jones, but psychologically. Even now, many days afterward, any loud noise traumatizes our little Jenny. She is a sensitive and highly intelligent child. That shocking event has seriously disturbed her, and we hope and pray it hasn't permanently damaged her."

Walter Johnson, one of those who gardened at Emma's farm, stood up. "Mr. Johnson," Ruth Prescott said. "Do you have a comment?"

"Yes, a question for Mrs. Anderson." He spoke the "Mrs." louder than the "Anderson."

"Your child wasn't hurt, right? Isn't that what you just said?"

"I said she wasn't hurt physically. She was psychologically injured."

"Were any other children on the trip psychologically injured?" He emphasized the words "psychologically injured."

"I don't know."

"Did you bother to ask?"

"No, I didn't. And it doesn't matter. One child injured is too many."

"Did it matter to you that several of the children enjoyed the trip and learned from the lightning strike?"

"I'm not concerned about other children," Ashley said curtly.

"Earlier you sounded like you were concerned about all children," Walter Johnson said with a strong, almost too loud voice.

"Now, now," Prescott said. "We are here to discuss the facts of the matter."

There was a brief pause, the only sounds from some chairs squeaking and some feet shuffling.

A short, thin woman wearing dark-rimmed glasses stood up.

"Yes, Linda, do you have a question?"

"More of a statement, madam president." She had a high-pitched, annoying voice—at least it struck me that way.

"Yes, go on."

"Those of you who know me are aware that I work with computers, the Internet, and virtual imagery. For those who may not know what virtual imagery is, it's a way of capturing reality digitally. Putting what's out there in the real world into a format where it can be manipulated with a few strokes on a computer keyboard."

What is she talking about? I wondered. I glanced around the room and saw other faces with the same look: *What is this woman saying?*

Linda went on in her squeaky voice, "We now have the technology to capture the outdoors and bring it inside—to use the illustration of the discussion at hand."

Dead silence in the room. Linda and her fancy computer words seemed to float over the crowd and not find a place to light. I wanted to ask her a question, but I didn't know enough about what she was saying to open my mouth, so I didn't. I suspect other people felt the same way.

"Thank you Linda," Ruth Prescott said. "Let's go on. I've asked Joseph Crawford, who teaches sixth grade science, to attend our meeting. Mr. Crawford was the teacher in charge of the field trip. Would you share a little more about what happened that day?"

Joe Crawford walked slowly to the front of the room.

"Thank you for an opportunity to speak," Joe said in a quiet, measured voice. "First, I, too, want to thank Mrs. Anderson for volunteering to chaperone our recent field trip to Emma Starkweather's farm." He nodded toward Ashley Anderson. "We at the school all appreciate Mrs. Anderson's interest and support. I am sorry for the little surprise we experienced that day in the woods. I checked the weather forecast before we left, and it said there was a 30 percent chance of scattered showers. The sun was shining brightly when we left the school and did for the first hour of our field trip. Then the little storm came up.

"Let me point out that no one was hurt or even close to being hurt. The tree struck by lightning was more than three hundred yards away from us. True, we all got to see it, and what a sight it was. In all my years working in the outdoors, I've never seen lightning strike a tree—it is a sight to behold.

"I sincerely hope that this one event, this surprise thunderstorm, will not sway you toward dropping our nature-study field trips to Emma Starkweather's farm. As a longtime science teacher, I am convinced that the only way to learn about nature is to be out in it. No matter how sophisticated a technology might be, nothing replaces the real thing. I agree that the many new learning technologies can assist and supplement nature study. But to truly learn about nature, you have to experience it directly. Field trips are one excellent way of doing that. We carefully plan these trips. We design them to meet educational goals and specific science objectives. We have carefully integrated our field trips into the science curriculum at Link Lake Middle School. Thank you."

"Thank you Mr. Crawford. Does anyone have a question for Mr. Crawford?" the board president asked. She almost immediately followed with, "Hearing none, I'd like to hear what Superintendent Gullickson has to offer on this matter."

Duncan Gullickson, Ph.D., stood about five foot five. He was mostly bald, and he shaved the little hair he had. I'd heard that some of the kids at Link Lake High School called him B. B. Gullickson, the "B. B." for "Bowling Ball." I agreed. His head did look ever so much like a big pink bowling ball; eyes and mouth were where the holes should be. Gullickson was probably thirty pounds overweight and always wore a suit and tie, even to the grocery store.

"Mr. and Mrs. Anderson. Ms. Starkweather. Members of the school board, friends," Gullickson began. "We have an extremely important issue before us—our children's safety. We must not drop the ball on this one. No sir, as I always say, there is no 'I' in team, and as a team we will work together to make sure we split the uprights."

I couldn't stand to listen to the man. He's the kind of guy that gets my dander up. He could hardly spit out a sentence without including a sports metaphor.

"I have tossed the ball to a special committee of teachers I appointed just to look at this problem," he continued. "How can we best teach our children about the natural world and at the same time score a touchdown with our science curriculum? The committee has already huddled twice. I can assure you all, especially the Andersons, that Link Lake Public Schools responds to input from its parents. We are thinking outside the box on this one."

I saw Gullickson turn toward Ruth Prescott. "Ms. Prescott, I will have the special committee's recommendation to you before the next meeting of the board. You can be assured I am keeping my eye on the ball."

Then he looked toward the Andersons and said, "I have personally attended the first meeting of the special committee, and I think you will be pleased with the recommendation forthcoming."

"Thank you, Dr. Gullickson," Ruth Prescott said. "Is there any further business to come before the board?"

A woman in the back of the room stood up.

"Yes," Prescott said, recognizing the person.

"My name is Nancy Alcott, and my daughter was on the field trip you've been talking about."

"And what was your daughter's experience?" Prescott asked.

"One of the most interesting field trips she's ever been on. She still talks about it. Especially about the lightning striking the tree. The first thing she said that night when she got home from school was, 'I saw the coolest thing today.' Then she told about the lightning hitting a big tree and making a sound louder than even Fourth of July fireworks. I'm sure you're not planning to cancel field trips because of one little complaint."

With the words "little complaint," I saw Ashley leap to her feet, her face beet red.

"I've not met you, Ms. Alcott, but I am deeply offended by your comment."

I noticed Jacob was tugging on his wife's sleeve for her to sit down, but she brushed his hand away.

I knew Nancy Alcott. She worked as a cook at the Link Lake Retirement Center and Nursing Home and had a reputation for standing up for what she believed and backing down to no one.

"I've not met you either," Nancy Alcott said, quietly. "But I know lots about you. You've done some good things for our community, and we appreciate it. But when you start criticizing something you don't know much about, well maybe that's not a good idea."

"So you think I don't know much about nature hikes. My good woman, I was there. I saw lightning strike that tree."

"Molly Brown was there when the *Titanic* hit an iceberg and sank. They didn't quit building ships after that, did they?"

"Ladies, ladies, it's time I interrupt," Ruth Prescott said. She was now vigorously wringing her hands. "I think we understand each of your positions. The hour is late, and it's time we wrap up this meeting. Hearing no other comment, this meeting is adjourned."

"Well, that was something," I said to Kate Dugan as we walked out of the meeting together.

"Indeed it was," Kate said, smiling. "Kind of an interesting meeting for once. Not so boring. I've got it all down, too, word for word. Even the quip about the *Titanic*. See you later, Emma. I want to catch up with Joe."

I watched Joe and Kate walk out of the school together and climb into Joe's old Ford pickup. They headed out of town, the taillights of Joe's truck disappearing into the night.

Memories

Emma
October 2000
Blue Shadows Farm

A week after the school board meeting, I sat by my old cookstove. I could see the dishtowels drying on the same rack that my mother used. I heard the snap and pop of burning wood, and smelled the occasional whiff of oak smoke that snuck out from the stove lids. I loved that smell, even though the smoke did tend to darken the ceiling. It was a drizzly, cool, fall morning, and I was wrapped up in my thoughts. The warm cup of coffee I held with both hands provided a comforting feeling, one of the little things I'd come to appreciate, especially on damp mornings when my arthritis kicked in. The smell of freshly brewed coffee on a woodstove was right up there with oak smoke, newly plowed soil, and fresh-cut alfalfa hay.

As my daily routine, I wove my long white hair into a single braid that hung down my back nearly to my waist. I wore my favorite old, loose-fitting, cotton flannel shirt. It had once been a rather bright green but with many washings had faded to a dull, nondescript color. It had also become a bit thin at the elbows. My gray cotton work pants and heavy, scuffed shoes completed my usual attire. Not especially ladylike, but who wants to dress like a lady when you're my age? Far better to be comfortable.

I stared out the rain-streaked kitchen window of my weathered old farmhouse as I did every morning. I was born in this house on May 15, 1926, a surprise to my folks, who thought they couldn't have children. I'd like to believe I've been surprising people ever since.

I let my mind wander. I thought about hiking my nature trails all seasons of the year. I thought about the garden families, some of them second generation, who planted gardens each year on my farm and had a grand time doing it. And, I thought about Ashley Anderson. I had trouble understanding the Ashley Andersons of the world. They volunteered to help at this thing and another and took a great interest in every aspect of their children's lives, but, oh, they could be such a pain in the behind. I just can't understand how some people overprotect their kids and deny them a little adventure and an opportunity to gain something beyond what's in a textbook or even what their teacher had in mind for the kids to learn.

What I know about nature I've learned on this old farm—walking its trails, listening to its sounds, watching the seasons change. I love this place. It's been in my family since 1866. One hundred and sixty sandy, hilly acres. A treasure.

I've developed a reputation for speaking out for the environment, for going out on a limb and saying what I think. I write letters to the editor, especially to the *Link Lake Gazette*—and I usually get in trouble for it. The Reverend Ridley Ralston from the Church of the Holy Redeemed goes out of his way to remind his flock of "that old woman's transgressions," as he calls my reminder that taking care of the land is as important as watching after people's souls.

"The land needs a voice," I say. "Needs someone to take its side when it is misused."

People sometimes laugh at my words and often argue with me. But I stand up for what I believe. When you've got something to say, stand up and say it. That's what I believe. Just because you're walking a little short doesn't mean you can't speak out. Surprise people. Surprise them that you know what's going on in the world and that you listen to what people have to say, especially those who disagree with you. Surprise people that you read widely and have an opinion on a variety of issues. Surprise them that you're willing to express yourself, take a position, and argue for it. When you catch them barking up the wrong tree, call them on it. These thoughts flashed through my head when I thought about the Ashley Anderson situation.

"Most stubborn old woman in Ames County," Jon Jessup, our mayor, once said of me. "Everyone think like her and we'd never see a new condo, never see another housing development or new recreational park, or see any new industry come to our area."

My thoughts returned to the hundreds of children who have hiked Blue Shadows' trails, dipped their hands into the pond, examined snapping-turtle nests, listened to birdcalls, and learned the difference between a red pine and a white pine. I wanted to believe that these children would grow up having a deeper appreciation for the land than those who watched only TV, did Internet searches, and read about nature in a book. In my mind, nothing takes the place of being outside. Joe over at the school agrees with me. You don't learn how to swim by reading about it or watching a film, he says. You get in the water. That's how you learn to swim. Same thing with nature. You have to feel it, smell it, taste it, see it, and hear it yourself. You've got to be a part of it before you can learn it.

I sighed and sat back in my chair. I thought, "What will happen to this good earth if nobody wants to take care of it anymore?" I feel every one of my seventy-four years as I peer through the morning mist at the farm's outbuildings. I see a small barn that once housed twenty milk cows; a larger, more modern barn; a pump house; a chicken house where I still keep a dozen layers—enough for fresh eggs every day and sometimes a few eggs to spare for baking. Near the chicken coop I glimpse the small two-story granary and next to that a corncrib, maybe twenty feet long, wider at the top than the bottom, with spaced wooden boards on its sides. The granary and crib have been empty since I quit farming in 1986. All of the buildings could use a good coat of paint, but outside of that, they're generally in good shape.

I can't forget the log cabin, the one my grandfather built with the help of his neighbors. Grandpa Silas Jefferson Starkweather, Civil War veteran, farmer, and builder of fences.

People say my Grandpa Silas was a strange man with unusual habits and mysterious desires. Both the written and unwritten histories of Link Lake contain many stories about Grandpa. There were some who said he didn't know if he was afoot or on horseback. Beyond the buildings, I see the fences, miles of fences that Grandpa built. Fences around every five-acre patch of ground he farmed. He built no fences through the woods but surrounded the whole plot of trees with a fence, which was unusual.

The fences run this way and that, up hills and down, through the valleys, and next to the five-acre pond in a valley a quarter of a mile or so west of the farm buildings. Travel lanes connect the five-acre farm fields, just wide enough so a farm wagon pulled by a team of horses can pass between the posts and wire. These aren't ordinary fences either, for Grandpa Silas's fences had twice as many wooden fence posts as any other fence I've ever seen. The posts are spaced sometimes as close as four feet apart and never more than ten feet.

Blue Shadows Farm looks like a giant porcupine with all the fence posts, each one exactly the same height, with four strands of barbed wire nailed to it, each strand of wire exactly the same distance apart. I've given up thinking about the reason for the fences, why Grandpa spent hours building them, replacing posts, digging new postholes. He was forever digging new holes.

I've heard stories from my neighbors, stories passed on through the generations about the Starkweather fences. Some said Grandpa

Silas simply liked fences, that he felt more comfortable around them and more protected inside them. I've heard that old Increase Joseph Link, the Standalone preacher in Link Lake, often applauded Grandpa for his small, fence-surrounded fields, which suffered less soil erosion than larger ones, which allowed the dry winds to get at them more easily.

People still remind me that they'd heard Grandpa Silas suffered from his war wound and that his mind sometimes wasn't just right. Even today, people know the story of Grandpa Silas walking his acres with no apparent purpose, with his head down, humming some strange little tune.

One person in Link Lake, I forgot who it was, said she thought my grandfather must have been an artist and building fences was his way of demonstrating his artistic talent. I conceded the beauty of the fences as they march across my farm, crossing and crisscrossing the rolling land.

I often wondered why my dad, Abe Starkweather, hadn't pulled up the posts, rolled up the wire, and plowed larger fields. Once horses replaced oxen, and the farm equipment became larger, bigger fields would have made for easier farming. I once asked my dad about that. He had said, rather curtly, "I promised Pa that no matter what, I would keep up his fences." And so he did. I remembered the many hours I spent as a little girl, helping Pa fix fences. It seemed a run of barbed wire always needed repair, a fence post had toppled over, or a tree had fallen on the fence and broken off several posts and snapped the wire. Like my dad, I, too, keep up the fences. I still spend hours each summer repairing them, twisting broken wire together, digging holes and replacing rotting posts. The only reason I do it is that Pa did it, and Grandpa did it before him. Building fences has become a Blue Shadows Farm tradition. I wish I'd had a chance to meet my grandparents Silas and Sophia Starkweather. I'd have asked Grandpa about the fences.

I noticed as I stared through the gloomy haze a few flakes of snow mixed with the cold, drizzly rain. Though it was still October, another winter would soon arrive.

14

Snowstorm

December 1866

Snow began falling shortly after noon, a few scattered flakes at first but as the storm grew in intensity, the wind picked up, swirling the snow around. Fall had turned quickly to winter. After the first hard frosts, Silas busied himself taking care of his team of oxen, puttering around the cabin, making another chair and bench (he'd learned how from Olaf Hanson), and reading. Earlier in the fall, Silas had struck an agreement with Wolfgang Reinert that Sophia would stop by his cabin on her way home from school each afternoon. She would straighten up, make his evening meal, and prepare food for the next day's breakfast and lunch.

Silas paid Wolfgang a few dollars a month for Sophia's work, which Silas very much appreciated. With winter coming on, he saw less and less of his neighbors. He only got to Link Lake for provisions about every two weeks, so he welcomed Sophia's company for the hour or so she spent at the cabin each day. He didn't know why he enjoyed her brief visits; perhaps it was because she was filled with curiosity and questions and readily shared what she was learning in school. Maybe it was just her bubbly personality, which always brightened up a gloomy day.

Silas kept up with the local news by reading each week's edition of the *Link Lake Gazette,* which Sophia brought him. In addition to his continued reading of *Walden,* he devoured the books Sophia brought him from her school library: Mary Mapes Dodge's *Hans Brinker and the Silver Skates,* Harriet Beecher Stowe's *Uncle Tom's Cabin,* and Ralph Waldo Emerson's *Nature.* Though it had many pages, he especially enjoyed *Uncle Tom's Cabin.* It helped him understand a bit more about the Civil War and what the fighting between the North and the South was for and about slavery and how the institution had so profoundly affected millions of black people.

The arrangement with Sophia worked well, until the big December storm blew in. It had snowed in early November, an inch or two, which melted. Snow fell again in late November, this time six inches or so, and much of it stayed on the ground, turning the landscape into a world of gray and white, punctuated with the green of white pines. The snowflakes flew on the northwest wind. Silas had become accustomed to the sound of this wind that often blew during these days of late fall, tearing the remaining leaves from the trees and shaking the naked limbs of the maples and aspen, making a mournful sound. And in his snug cabin at night, he heard the wind rattle the windows and whistle as it gusted around the corners of the sturdy log building.

The December storm began with a few scattered flakes of dry snow that flew on a stiff wind. Almost sleetlike, the snow felt like tiny knives slicing into Silas's face as he tossed hay to his oxen from the stack he had made in the fall. With his scythe, Silas had cut an acre or so of native grass from an area of land that he had not yet broken. Some of the dry grass was taller than his head and so thick the scythe blade resisted when Silas attempted to slice it off. Once cut, Silas raked the dried grass with a homemade wooden rake— Justin Meadows had made it for him—loaded it on his ox cart, and then piled it by the lean-to where his oxen could get out of the wind on stormy days. Now, as he forked the sweet-smelling hay, he was reminded of the summer days when he cut it, the hot sun baking his back and the sweat running down his face and soaking his shirt.

The oxen, with their backs to the wind, stood waiting for Silas and the hay they readily consumed. Snow had already accumulated on their broad backs, now covered with long hair that had come in thick as the weather turned colder.

Silas's little brown dog, Rex, the one he had gotten after the bear incident, ran through the accumulating snow, jumping and turning, and making little yips as he tried to catch snowflakes in his mouth. Rex was Silas's constant companion, a homely dog but a faithful one. On cold, lonely, dark nights when the wind tore around the corners of the cabin, Silas talked to Rex. The animal listened, too. Cocked his head to one side and looked Silas straight in the eye when he spoke.

Earlier in the fall, Silas replaced the muslin windows with panes of glass; the muslin let in light, but he couldn't see out. Now, back in his cabin with Rex resting on the bearskin rug, his stubby nose on his paws, Silas watched out the window as the storm grew in intensity. The snow fell horizontally, sometimes so thick he couldn't see the barnyard and the oxen only a few hundred yards away. The sound of the wind ripping around the tight cabin sent a shiver through him. He was glad those who had helped build it had taken their time and carefully chinked the logs so the cold wind could not sneak in.

Silas grew concerned as he checked his pocket watch. Sophia should have arrived at his cabin by now. Snow was accumulating on the porch and piling up against the side of the cabin. Silas had heard stories of people losing their bearings in storms like this, becoming lost and dying in the cold.

He checked his watch again. She was a half-hour late. Once more Silas glanced out the window and saw nothing but a wall of snow flying on the northwest wind and burying everything in its path. He decided to walk toward the school, meet Sophia part way, and guide her to the cabin in case she was having trouble finding her way in the storm. He pulled on his heavy woolen coat, the one he had in the army, a cap with earflaps, and woolen mittens that Mrs. Reinert had knitted for him. ("You need varm mittens," she had said.)

"Come, Rex," Silas said as he pushed open the cabin door and stepped into the storm. Visibility was near zero, similar to walking on a foggy day, except it was wet, driving snow. Silas constantly rubbed his mittened hand across his face to clear the moisture from his eyes. The wind nearly took his breath away.

The road by his farm—which continued on to the school on the outskirts of Link Lake but a mile away—had all but disappeared with the accumulating snow. Walking was difficult; each step soon became an effort. Silas tried to look ahead for Sophia, but he all saw was snow. It was like facing a white cliff that moved as you walked into it.

Rex bounded along behind him, jumping in and out of his tracks, but occasionally making giant leaps in the snow as he struck out ahead of Silas. Silas became even more concerned about Sophia as he and his dog slowly made their way through the storm.

"Sophia!" he yelled. "Sophia!" The words flew back in his face. He yelled again, "Sophia!" and heard nothing but the wind, the relentless wind howling through the tops of the bare-branched trees and driving the moving wall of snow.

Silas lost sight of Rex, who had run ahead, enjoying the snow and wind. Then he heard Rex's bark, off to his right, away from where he thought the road ran.

"Rex!" Silas yelled when he heard the barking, now less distinct than before.

"Rex!" he yelled again. This time he heard the dog but barely. The roar of the wind nearly drowned out all sound.

Silas stumbled on. Walking through the snowdrifts that buried the road had become all but impossible. He followed the dim, fading sound of barking. At times the barking became stronger and then so faint it sounded miles away. Now he was concerned that he was lost as he no longer had a sense of direction.

He continued listening for his dog, and as he walked the barking gradually became louder. And then, directly in front of him, he saw Rex, the dog's brown coat entirely covered with snow. The animal was white from the tip of its nose to the end of its tail.

He patted his dog on the head and spoke to him. Silas glimpsed Sophia sitting next to Rex, near a huge snowdrift that provided some respite from the wind.

"I'm cold. I lost my way," Sophia said as she made out the man in front of her. She was shivering so violently she could hardly speak.

"Can you stand?" Silas yelled. The wind almost tore his words away.

"I can stand. Trying to be out of the wind. Waiting for storm to stop," Sophia said. "Your dog, Rex, good dog. He found me."

With Rex leading, Silas and a shivering Sophia made their way through the storm. Within a few minutes, the dog led them to the cabin. Silas had been disoriented, and though he probably walked a mile, Rex had found Sophia nearly in front of Silas's cabin.

Once inside, Silas tossed a log on the fire as Sophia warmed herself. She sat with Rex, patting the dog on the head.

"I must go home, now," Sophia said. "Papa and Mama will worry."

"You are not going out in this storm, Sophia," Silas said. "You will spend the night here. You can sleep in the loft. You'll be warm there."

December 3, 1866

I've never seen such a snowstorm. Everything is buried. Sophia got lost on her way from school. Rex found her. I think she would have frozen to death had he not. Everybody who lives in the country needs a dog. No question about it.

The storm is still raging as I write this. I hate this place. Why would anyone want to live here? Why am I here? I question the decision I made when I got out of the army. Too hasty? Maybe.

15

Wolfgang and Amelia

December 1866

The snowstorm blew itself out during the night. In the first light of morning, Silas crawled out of his snug bed to a cabin that was frigid cold as the outside temperature had plummeted during the night. Rex rested in front of the fireplace, on the bearskin rug. A few coals still glowed in the remaining ashes. Silas tossed in some kindling and soon a trickle of flame appeared. He added a couple larger hunks of wood from the box he had filled the previous night. He and Rex then headed outside to feed the oxen. He pushed hard on the cabin door to move the snowdrift aside, and a blast of cold air engulfed him as he stepped into an expanse of white.

Once outside, Rex made a giant leap off the cabin porch and disappeared into a huge snowdrift. Soon the snow-covered dog's head appeared as he leaped into the air and jumped into another drift. Obviously enjoying the deep snow, he barked with each jump he made.

Silas wallowed through the near waist-deep snow, holding his mittened hand to his face to deflect the frigid northwest wind that lifted little swirls of fresh snow and sent them skittering along the tops of the drifts.

Upon arriving at the log lean-to, he found his team of oxen munching on hay he had put in their manger the previous night. He pushed through the snow to the nearby haystack and carried a big forkful of the grass hay to refill the manger. The animals had withstood the storm with no apparent problems.

Returning to the warmth of the cabin, he saw that Sophia was up and busy cooking a big pot of oatmeal.

"Good morning," she said. A big, sleepy smile spread across her face.

"Did you stay warm last night?"

"Good and warm," Sophia answered. "Wind blowing. Scary sounds. But it was nice upstairs. Didn't sleep well. Mama and Papa worry about me. I must hurry home."

"Thank you for starting breakfast," Silas said as he hung his heavy coat on the wooden peg near the cabin door. Rex was standing near the fireplace; Sophia patted the dog's head as she stirred the oatmeal with her other hand.

"Good dog, Rex," she said. "You find me in storm. Good dog."

Rex wagged his tail and moved closer to the girl.

"Let's get you on home," Silas said when they had finished breakfast. "No school today."

"Ja," Sophia said. "Mama and Papa worry much for sure."

The wind had picked up some, but was mostly at their backs as they headed south along the drifted road to the Reinerts' farm. Rex was out front, leaping through the deep snow. Next came Silas, and following behind was Sophia, wrapped in a blanket. She tried to step in Silas's tracks. Snow blowing on the northwest wind sifted across the road in front of them, swirling and twisting and making interesting patterns. The sun was up but scarcely visible through the blowing snow.

They hadn't gone but a quarter of a mile or so when they glimpsed a figure coming toward them, trudging through the deep snow. It was Sophia's father. They hurried to meet him. He wrapped his big arms around Sophia.

"You are safe," he said. "You are safe. I was looking for you last night but couldn't see, almost got lost in the storm. Your mama worried sick. We were up most of the night, hoping you would come."

After stopping several times to rest, the threesome glimpsed the Reinerts' house, a thread of smoke coming from its chimney.

Upon reaching the house, Sophia burst inside, followed by Wolfgang, Rex, and Silas. Sophia's mother, Amelia, was working at the kitchen stove; the rest of the family was seated around the kitchen table.

"Oh, Sophia . . . Sophia," her mother said as she took her daughter in her arms. "Ve vorry about you so much in big storm. Wolfgang go out looking for you last night. Not find you. Could see nothing."

"I know. Silas and Rex found me in the storm. I stayed at Silas's cabin," Sophia said. "He got good place to sleep in loft."

"Need to thank my dog, Rex, here. I couldn't find Sophia in the storm either. Rex did though," Silas said.

"Good dog," Wolfgang said as he looked in Rex's direction. Rex and the Reinerts' dog, Max, were eyeing each other, looking each other over and smelling. Max was a big, black, nondescript dog with long hair and a short nose.

"Max," Wolfgang said along with some words in German. Max quit sniffing, but the dogs kept staring at each other.

The Reinert children, busily eating breakfast, looked up when Sophia arrived, but didn't say anything, except for little Anna. She jumped down from her chair and ran and put her little arms around Sophia and hugged her. "Sophia," the girl said.

"You eat breakfast?" Amelia inquired.

"Oh, yes. We ate at home," Silas said. "Sophia fixed it."

"Good," Amelia said. "You have cup of hot coffee?"

"Sure, hot coffee would be good. Cold day. Miserable wind blowing out of the northwest; snow blowing all over the place."

Sophia hung up her coat and sat in the empty chair next to her little sister, Sophia's regular place at the table. Silas sat on a chair that Fritz had gotten for him from the dining room.

With breakfast over, the Reinert children went off to do their various chores. Fritz had the heavier tasks to do, such as carrying hay for their team of oxen, their horses, and their couple of milk cows and splitting wood. Emil fed the chickens and hogs and carried in wood for the Reinert woodstoves, one in the kitchen and one in the dining room. Sophia left for the chicken house, where it was her job to scatter some corn and pick the eggs. There was something for everyone to do, except for Anna, who was petting Rex and Max, one dog with each hand.

The Reinert kitchen was quiet but for the snapping and crackling of the wood burning in the woodstove, and the rustling of dishes as Amelia Reinert cleared the table. Both Wolfgang and Silas lit their pipes and pipe smoke curled up toward the ceiling.

"Be a long vinter," Wolfgang said as he took his pipe from his mouth. "Blizzard in December not good."

"Long winters in New York, where I come from," Silas said. "Thought it might be better here, shorter winters."

"No, every vinter cold. Snowy. Last vinter like that. Year before, too. Ja, ve have heavy vinters here," Wolfgang offered.

"I've been thinking about Sophia," Silas began.

"Ja, Sophia good girl. Good vorker. Good cook, too," Wolfgang said. "Has one fault."

"What's that?"

"She read too much. Nose in book all the time. Every chance she get. Reading books—German books, English books."

"Reading's a good thing," Silas offered.

"Not ven work to be done. Vork first. Then reading."

"What would you think," Silas began and then hesitated. "With this tough winter weather and all. What would you think if Sophia stayed at my house during the week, at least through the winter? I could pay you a little more for her work," Silas said as an afterthought.

"Hmm," Wolfgang said, puffing on his pipe.

Amelia, who had been listening to the conversation, looked at Wolfgang and said, "Nein." And that's all she said as she turned back to the breakfast dishes.

A thick silence filled the room.

"I must discuss with wife," Wolfgang said quietly. "Ve will talk, wife and I."

"Nein," Amelia said shaking her head. "Sophia needed here. Ve have work for her. People will talk. Daughter living with bachelor in cabin. People will talk."

"Well, I guess I must be starting back home," Silas said as he pulled on his coat that he had draped over his chair. "Come on, Rex."

"Thank you once more for taking good care of Sophia in big storm," Wolfgang said as he shook Silas's hand. "Amelia and I talk about our Sophia," Wolfgang said quietly as he held the door for Silas.

A blast of frigid air struck Silas full in the face as he and Rex headed off for home. Silas hoped he hadn't caused a family problem with his offer. What he hadn't considered was tongues wagging about a sixteen-year-old girl living with a twenty-one-year-old bachelor. He had never considered Sophia as more than a hired girl, someone to help prepare his meals and clean up around his cabin.

December 4, 1866

Winter is here. No question about it. Asked the Reinerts if Sophia could spend the winter in my cabin. I think he's for it. Mrs. Reinert is dead against it. I didn't think about how it would look. I am just trying to help out, a little payment for all the Reinerts have done for me.

I pulled out my Thoreau book and read some more. Good night for reading. Temperature below zero. Northwest wind shaking the cabin windows. Warm by the fireplace. Kerosene lamp casts plenty of light. I wonder about this Thoreau fellow. He doesn't sound like much of a farmer. I wonder why he built a cabin way off in the woods. He wrote, "I went to the woods deliberately, to front only the essential facts of life, and see if I could not learn what it had to teach, and not, when I came to die, discover that I had not lived."

Now that's a mouthful. I suspect he's getting at the facts of life. But that's not why I'm here. Here's where this guy Thoreau and I differ. He had his reasons for moving to the country. I have mine.

16

Housekeeper

December 1866

The weather had warmed some the following day and the wind had gone down. After a light noon meal of bread and sausage, Silas sat in a chair by his fireplace, reading *Walden*. He heard a knock on the cabin door.

"Come in, come in," he said. He put down his book and stood up.

Wolfgang and Amelia Reinert came into the cabin. They both wore long, black, heavy coats, and he a black fur cap on his head and she a gray, woolen scarf tied around hers.

"Varmer day," Wolfgang said. Through the still-open cabin door Silas saw that Wolfgang had tied his blanketed team to the barnyard fence. The team was hitched to a bobsled.

"Yes, much more pleasant," Silas said, closing the door. "How are you Mrs. Reinert?"

"Ja, I good. Feel pretty good, even in cold."

"Well come over here by the fire, warm up," Silas said. He seldom had visitors and didn't quite know what to do. "Let me take your coats." Silas hung the long winter coats on the pegs near the door while the Reinerts stood in front of the fireplace rubbing their hands together.

"You got nice place here," Amelia Reinert said. "Varm and cozy."

"It's a tight cabin. It's built well, thanks to Wolfgang, your son Fritz, and the other neighbors."

They both stood quietly by the crackling fire, neither saying anything. Silas knew they had come to say something about Sophia, but he also knew it might take them a while to get around to saying it. This characteristic of country folks still bothered Silas. Coming from a city, he was accustomed to having people say what they had to say without dancing around the topic.

"Vhat is up there?" Amelia asked, pointing to the wooden ladder that led to the cabin loft.

"Oh, that's the loft. That is where Sophia slept. A nice warm place to sleep."

"Could I see?" Mrs. Reinert asked.

"Sure. Have a look."

Mrs. Reinert made her way up the ladder; the wooden rungs creaked under her weight. She pushed her head through the opening.

"Not big," she said, slowly stepping down the ladder.

"Nope, but about right for a sleeping room."

"Ja," Mrs. Reinert said, shaking her head up and down. She returned to the fireplace, where she resumed rubbing her hands together. Again silence.

"Vare you cook?" Amelia inquired.

"Right here, by the fireplace. Plan to buy a stove as soon as I have money saved."

"Ja, stove good. Make cooking easier. Specially baking. Baking hard with fireplace. I like stove," Amelia said, waving her hands as she talked.

All this while, normally talkative Wolfgang stood by the fire-place, rubbing his hands together vigorously. Silas thought his hands surely must have warmed by now, but he kept rubbing them anyway.

"I've got some warm coffee. Would you like some?" Silas asked. He realized he should have offered coffee sooner.

"Ja, I like coffee," Wolfgang said.

"Ja, I, too," said Amelia.

Wolfgang and Amelia took chairs at the little homemade table that sat by one of the cabin windows as Silas found cups on the shelf above the table and put them in front of the Reinerts. He lifted the handle of the big gray coffeepot from the hook near the fireplace, then took a handkerchief from his pocket and grabbed its side handle.

He poured the steaming coffee, first in Amelia's cup, then Wolfgang's, and then his.

"Ja, coffee smell good on cold day," Amelia said as she put both hands around the big white cup. She lifted the steaming coffee cup to her lips.

"Sorry I don't have any cookies to go with the coffee," Silas said.

"No expect cookies from bachelor. Most bachelors can't cook," Amelia said, smiling.

"I try," Silas said. "Sophia has helped me. She's cooked good evening meals, wonderful meals in fact. She is a good cook."

"Ja, Sophia good cook. Learn from her mudder," Ameila said, smiling again. This was the first time Silas had ever seen Amelia smile. Usually it was Wolfgang who was smiling and laughing. Today he said almost nothing. He sipped his coffee and gazed out the window at the snowbanks that extended as far as he could see.

"Ve came to talk about Sophia," Wolfgang began, haltingly. "Amelia and I, ve talk yesterday after you leave. Ve talk again last night. Ve talk this morning."

"My offer still stands," Silas said. But after he said it, he wondered if his words had been appropriate. Obviously, having young Sophia working as his housekeeper had become a sensitive issue with the Reinerts.

"Ve make up our minds," Wolfgang said.

"Ja," said Amelia.

"We decide Sophia can work as your housekeeper, live here with you, for payment you say," said Wolfgang.

"Ja," said Amelia. She took another drink of coffee. "But Sophia must sleep upstairs, in that room." She pointed to the loft.

"Well, sure. That's where she would sleep. There's no more room down here," Silas said, pointing to his bed on the opposite wall from the table where they were sitting.

"Also," Wolfgang said, "she must have time to help out at home on Saturdays and Sundays when she not in school."

"Sure, that would be fine," said Silas.

"Then ve have deal," Wolfgang said, standing up and thrusting out his hand to shake Silas's.

Silas noticed that Amelia was no longer smiling but staring at her coffee.

"I get her things," Wolfgang said, putting on his long coat and cap and heading out the cabin door. Soon he returned with a bag containing some clothes and a few books.

"Sophia good girl," Wolfgang said. "But lots of spirit. She give you trouble, you let me know."

December 5, 1866

Learned something important today. Learned to be patient and keep my mouth shut. Wolfgang Reinert and his wife came by. Sat for a long time. Drank some of my bad coffee. Looked around the cabin. Did they come to tell me that Sophia couldn't stay here? Almost asked a couple times if they'd decided. But I didn't. Kept

my tongue. Just before they left they said Sophia could live here
through the winter. I was surprised. Figured Mrs. Reinert held the
upper hand in the family. Maybe not.

Kitchen Stove

January 1867

The arrangement worked well. Sophia continued going to school each day, spent the weekday evenings working and sleeping at the Starkweather cabin, and walked home to help her mother on Saturdays and Sundays. She returned each Sunday afternoon to the little log cabin that she had come to like.

Silas wasn't always in agreement with Sophia's ideas, but he seldom argued with her. She made curtains for the cabin windows; with her mother's help she made a beautiful quilt for his bed and turned the cabin loft into a pleasant sleeping area for herself. It wasn't long before she said, "When will you buy cookstove, Silas? I bake bread, pies, cakes, cookies for you if you have stove."

Without telling Sophia, Silas had stopped by the mercantile on his last trip to Link Lake and had ordered a new cookstove. Mercantile owner Owen Davies said he expected a shipment of new stoves any day. In mid-January it arrived. When Sophia entered the cabin one afternoon, she opened the door and immediately saw the new appliance standing off to the side of the fireplace, with its black stovepipe stuck into the fireplace chimney.

"You got new stove," Sophia said, her blue eyes wide with excitement. "Pretty stove, so shiny." She walked up and began inspecting it.

"Be careful, it's hot," Silas said.

"I am careful. I know stoves. Ours at home is like this, but not so shiny. This stove is so shiny."

She pulled open the doors on the warming oven above the stove's cooking surface. She lifted the door of the hot-water reservoir on the right side of the stove. It was filled with steaming water. She pulled open the oven door and looked inside. A blast of warm air struck her in the face.

"Is good," she said. "Is very good. I now do better cooking for you, Silas." She ran up, wrapped her arms around him and kissed him on the cheek." He immediately turned a bright red.

"You blush," Sophia said, smiling. She turned, hung up her coat on the wooden peg that had become hers, and began preparing supper. She sang a little song in German; Silas didn't know the words.

"Thank you for the new stove. My work easier now."

Soon the smells of supper cooking filled the little cabin. When they had finished eating their evening meal, Sophia cleared and washed the dishes, using the warm water from the new stove's reservoir.

"Now I bake bread for you, Silas," Sophia said. "I make good bread. Mama say my bread nearly as good as hers."

That night when Sophia climbed the cabin stairs to her room in the loft, three freshly baked loaves of bread stood on the cabin table, cooling. The smell of fresh bread filled the room. Silas's head was filled with thoughts of Sophia. How she had changed in just the few months he had known her. She was becoming a beautiful young woman. Every day she seemed more attractive. And always smiling and laughing. He couldn't remember ever seeing her sad, and if she was, she hid it well. He was pleased with his decision to hire her as his housekeeper. He knew that her help would be even more appreciated when he could return to working in his fields and doing what he had come to Link Lake to do. So what if some of the neighbors talked. It was none of their business.

January 8, 1867

I have fresh-baked bread cooling in front of me. Bought a new cookstove. Sophia baked bread tonight. She's a good cook. I didn't know she could bake bread.

Wonder what Thoreau would have thought about this. Having someone do your cooking for you. Seemed like he was against that sort of thing. Bet he didn't have a blonde German girl sleeping in his cabin's loft. He never even mentioned having a loft in his cabin.

Silas fell asleep that night and dreamed of eating fresh bread his mother had just pulled from the oven. And then his mother left and a beautiful young woman came into the room. She had curly blonde hair and striking blue eyes, and she offered him a slice of homemade bread, covered with butter and strawberry jam. But he couldn't see her face; for some reason it was blurry. She stood by a shiny cookstove, a dishtowel in her hand.

18

Opportunity

Emma
October 2000
Link Lake, Wisconsin

*H*old your horses," I said out loud as I wiped my hands on a dish-towel and walked to the phone that had already rung four times. I picked it up and said, "Hello."

"It's Kate."

"How are you, Kate?" I asked.

"Doing OK, Emma, but I need to talk to you."

"About what?"

"You plan on coming to town today?"

"Hadn't thought that far ahead."

"A visitor stopped by this morning," Kate said.

"Visitor?"

"Guy from out of town. You comin' to town, Emma?" Kate repeated. "Like to talk to you about this fellow and what he had to say."

"Can, I guess. Running out of groceries."

"Stop at the paper, and I'll buy you a cup of coffee and fill you in."

"Free cup of coffee, huh. Never one to pass up something free," I said, laughing. I wondered who she was talking about and whether the fellow had anything to do with the school board meeting and the incident on the nature hike. I still have Ashley Anderson's reaction stuck in my head. Is she an example of the new parent, I wondered? If so, God help us all, especially our kids.

I grabbed my old denim jacket and felt hat that hung back of the woodstove, fired up my old Ford pickup, and headed to Link Lake in the fog and drizzle of the early morning. Soon I was parked in front of the *Link Lake Gazette* office on Main Street, one of the oldest buildings in town. It looked it, too. Sometime I need to tell Kate she should hire one of the town boys to slop a little paint on the building, spruce it up a little. Give it a little zing. But I know Kate is too much like me. If something works, leave it alone; don't fiddle with it. The building seemed to serve Kate and the paper just fine; that's what she'd say if I mentioned painting the place.

I heard the ding of the little bell above the door as I entered the rather dark and somewhat dreary newspaper office. Kate came walking up to the counter from someplace in back, where the printing presses had once been located. (Now she shipped the paper off to Willow River, where the printing was done each week.)

"You didn't waste any time getting to town," Kate said by way of greeting. She pushed back the wire-rimmed glasses that forever slid down on her nose.

"Not every day I get a free cup of coffee and a chance to chat with a friend," I said, smiling.

We walked a few yards down Main Street to the Eat Well Café, the local coffee shop named by John Jackson, a Chicago man who'd bought the place a few years ago. J.J., as he liked to be called, was working behind the counter.

"Hello Kate, Emma. What can I put in front of you two?"

"Couple of black coffees, J.J.," Kate said. "Do you have any big caramel rolls?"

"Yeah, I do. Fresh, too."

"Give us a couple of those."

"Comin' right up."

"You heard any more from Ashley Anderson? She's sure fired up," I commented once we had settled into the booth. I had been curious what Kate might have heard since the school board meeting. And I was even more curious if her visitor was somehow involved with the story.

"No, I haven't," Kate said matter-of-factly.

"Guess we'll have to see what happens," I said.

"Can't imagine it'll amount to much. Hope not anyway. But that's not what I want to talk about."

J.J. put two enormous caramel sweet rolls, two cups of coffee, and a coffeepot in front of Kate and me.

"Darndest thing happened first thing this morning," Kate said.

"I'm listening," I said. I had just taken a big bite of the sweet roll. I wondered if this was going to be another of Kate's long, convoluted stories that ran here and there and back and forth and around and around and didn't seem to go anywhere until the very end, when everything came together and made sense. She wrote newspaper stories the same way, requiring a certain amount of patience from her readers, who needed to read an entire article before deciding what she was trying to say. But most people liked her writing because she was a storyteller and usually had a powerful message. She also did her homework. She had a reputation for digging out facts many others overlooked, sometimes to the annoyance of her readers who'd just as soon some facts were forgotten.

"I was sitting at my desk when I heard the door open," Kate began. "I got this week's paper off to the post office last night, so I was the only one around this morning. As you know, it was kind of a sleepy morning, with the drizzly rain and all."

"Yup, a dreary morning," I agreed.

Kate went on, "I remember glancing at the clock on the wall. It was nine o'clock. I no more than heard the bell ringing on the door when I heard the sharp 'ding' of the bell on the counter.

"'I'm looking for Mr. Dugan,' the man at the counter said. He didn't say 'hello,' 'hi,' 'good morning,' or anything. One of those serious business types. He wore a long, tan raincoat, one of those fancy expensive ones that you don't see much around here. So I said, 'Good morning, kinda wet and chilly out there.'

"'Is Mr. Dugan in?' the man asked again. He pushed his hat back on his head. He had blond hair.

"'Nope, he isn't in,' I said. 'The reason is that he died four years ago.' I kind of smiled when I said it, not meaning to be rude but just wanting to share the truth.

"'Oh,' the fellow said, somewhat taken aback. 'Then, is the editor of this newspaper in? I'd like to talk with him.'

"'Editor isn't a him, it's a her,' I said.

"'Well, then, is she in?' the man said curtly. I noticed he wasn't wearing a wedding ring."

"You sure enjoy giving them outsiders the business, don't you, Kate?" I interrupted. Kate had a reputation for her humor, sometimes at the expense of others, especially if they were from out of town. Kate smiled and continued her story.

"'She's in,' I told the guy. I glanced out the rain-streaked window and saw a shiny red car with Minnesota license plates.

"'Well . . .' the fellow dragged on, 'can I please talk to her?'

"I said, 'You certainly can.' I stared straight at him and noticed he had green eyes. He stared back at me.

"'So, what can I do for you?' I said, smiling, because I had really fooled him. 'I'm Kate Dugan, editor of the *Link Lake Gazette* as well as reporter, office manager, advertising director, sometime janitor, and part-time photographer.' I held out my hand to shake his.

"'Oh,' said the man. He had a rather slight build, and I thought he must be in his late forties.

"'Well, why didn't you say so?' he said. He had a 'you're wasting my valuable time' tone to his voice.

"'You didn't ask,' I said politely. 'So how can I help? Would you like a cup of coffee? Got a little extra back there somewhere,' I said.

"'No, no thank you. My name is William Steele and I want to place an ad in your paper, a big ad.' He seemed a bit flustered that I was a woman.

"I said I'd look for my notepad, and I began rummaging around back of the counter. I asked him what he wanted the ad to say.

"'I have it for you,' he said curtly and opened his thin leather briefcase and handed me a computer disk."

As I listened to her tale, Kate began fishing around in her purse. Finally, she found the printout for the ad and handed it to me. I put down my coffee and read:

Wanted: Land. A national destination tourist attraction, regional educational center, and associated manufacturing plant is seeking to locate one of its complexes in the Link Lake area. Will pay top dollar. The development requires about 160 acres, preferably with access to a lake or river. Send letters of interest in care of this newspaper, Link Lake, Wisconsin.

"He whipped a checkbook out of his briefcase, wrote a check for the amount I told him, and handed it over.

"I said, 'thank you,' and before I could say anything more, Mr. William Steele wheeled around and walked out the door without saying another word. Glancing at the check, I saw it was from Modern Nature Educators, Inc., with a Los Angeles address."

"Why you telling me all this?" I asked. "Sounds like one of Mayor Jessup's cockeyed ideas."

"Indeed it does," Kate said. "Since Jessup got elected he's had one mission—cut taxes and develop new business."

"You got that right," I said. "The school budget is busted, the roads need fixing, and they've cut the police force from two guys to one."

"But taxes are less than they were a year ago," Kate said, smiling. She had a cynical look on her face.

"Kate, paying taxes is what we've got to do to have a decent community."

"I know, I know," Kate said, holding up her hand. "But there's a growing number of people who think the lower the taxes, the better the community."

"Kate, that's a bunch of bull and you know, it," I said, perhaps a little too loudly. A couple of locals drinking coffee at the counter turned and looked in our direction.

"Jessup's got one thing right," Kate said.

"And that would be?" I asked sarcastically.

"Increase the tax base, and you collect more taxes without raising taxes."

"Sounds good—on paper," I said.

"I'm not one of Jessup's fans, but I think he's on the right track with this idea. I suspect it was his idea to invite Modern Nature Educators to town."

"Maybe so," I said. "But doesn't he want more people moving here so he can sell houses? Seems his real estate company does a good enough business already."

"Jessup's got to make a living. Being mayor doesn't pay anything," Kate said.

"Jeez, whose side you on anyway?" Emma said.

"The community's side," Kate said, touching me on the hand.

"So back to this William Steele guy. What's all this got to do with me?"

"Well," Kate began, "I thought of you and Blue Shadows Farm when I read his ad. Why don't you sell your farm to Modern Nature Educators, Inc. and move to town? Retire and take it easy. Bet you can get a good price for your land from them."

I couldn't think of a thing to say.

"Well, you think about it, sounds like an opportunity for all concerned," Kate said.

Back at home, I sat at the kitchen table reading the copy of the ad Kate gave me. Perhaps this was the time to sell the place and move to town. I didn't mention it to Kate, but with another winter coming on, I had been thinking about moving. I've been pretty tuckered out lately. Maybe this Nature Educators thing is a sign. Maybe I should answer the ad and see if they have any interest in Blue Shadows Farm. "Nothing ventured, nothing gained," my ma always said.

Part 4

19

William Steele

Emma
October 2000
Blue Shadows Farm

A few days after my visit with Kate Dugan, I was working in my garden, gathering up the trash left over from the growing season— dead tomato vines, tangles of squash and pumpkin vines, rutabaga and beet tops—that sort of thing. I was using a six-tine barn fork. Once I've removed the clutter from the garden patch, I'll climb on my old Farmall A tractor, hitch it to my rusty disk harrow, and work up the ground. I like driving the tractor and often tell people when they ask about its age: "I'm older than the tractor, but we're both going strong." Some days, especially those when my arthritis flares up, the tractor may have the edge, but I don't tell anyone that.

Once I've stirred up the ground, I'll plant it to winter rye. If it rains and we have some warm weather, this will grow several inches before freeze-up—providing feed for the deer, turkeys, and rabbits— and keep the soil from blowing if the snow cover is slight or nonexistent. In the spring I plow down the rye, providing organic material to the soil. I've followed this same routine for thirty years, and it works. I'm not one to brag, but my garden spot is one of the best in the area, although the competition has gotten slight in recent years as fewer people grow vegetable gardens. The exception, of course, is the families from town who garden here at Blue Shadows Farm. It's been fun watching them keep an eye on my garden during the growing season—a kind of unspoken competition as to whether they could outgrow me. They often do, with certain crops, anyway.

I heard a car approaching and looked up to see Mayor Jon Jessup's new-model Buick pulling into my yard. He had someone with him I didn't recognize. I stopped working, pushed the gardening fork into the ground, and leaned on the handle.

"Hi there, Emma," Jessup said as he walked toward the garden. The man with him had blond hair and wore khaki pants and a green jacket. And he was skinny. He was so skinny I didn't think he'd cast a shadow.

"Nice day for working outside," Jessup said, all friendly and pleasant-like.

"Sure is. Not many of these days left this fall," I said, wondering about the man standing alongside the mayor.

"I'd like you to meet someone," Jessup said. The fellow, as if on command, stepped forward a couple steps.

"This is William Steele. He represents Modern Nature Educators, Inc. You've surely heard of them," Jessup said, almost gushing.

"Yes, I have," I said. "I'm pleased to meet you, Mr. Steele. I heard that you were in town."

What I didn't say was that I had decided to answer the ad in the *Link Lake Gazette,* the one asking for people interested in selling land to his company. I had the letter all ready to mail. What a coincidence. Here was the company contacting me.

"Oh, call me William," the man said, smiling broadly.

"Well, William, what can I do for you?" I said. I continued leaning on the fork handle.

"I've heard so much about you, Emma. All the good work you've done for the schools in the area, and the Scouts and 4-H Clubs and just about everybody who has an interest in nature. All the learning that's taken place here at Blue Shadows Farm."

"Thank you," I said. Long ago I learned to suspect people who tried to butter me up with praise. I had little time for bootlickers. If this guy had some interest in buying my farm, why didn't he just come out and say so?

"Mr. Steele's company is looking for land in this area," Jessup said. "I immediately thought of your place, thought it would be a perfect fit for what Modern Nature Educators has in mind."

"I . . ." I hesitated for a moment. "I haven't decided if I want to sell the place," I said.

Jessup winked. "A little bird told me that you might be thinking of moving to town, retiring, and taking it easy for a change," he said, smiling at Steele.

I wondered who that little bird had been. Had Kate put him up to this?

"Well as long as you're out here, would you like a look around?" I asked.

"No, that won't be necessary. I've got a good aerial map of the place—shows me about all I need to know," Steele said.

"I could show you the pond and the nature trails, you could see the oak woodlot and the prairie restoration I've been doing?"

"Not necessary. Got all I need right here." Steele was holding the black and gray aerial map in front of him.

"What about the buildings? Don't you want to have a look at the barns and the log cabin over there? My grandfather built it, you know."

"Not necessary. Mainly wanted to meet you. Get to know you a little. Always interested in talking with someone who loves nature."

"Okay," I said, a bit taken aback by his seeming lack of interest in any of the details of my place.

"By the way," Steele began. "Exactly what are you doing here in this field?"

I laughed. "Putting my garden to bed for the winter."

"Garden, huh. Didn't know people gardened anymore."

"Some of us still do," I said, trying to smile when I really felt like giving Mr. Steele a lecture on why gardening was important, even beyond the fresh vegetables harvested. It hadn't taken me long, but I'd already soured on this guy.

"Well, Jon, guess we'd better be on our way. Don't want to take any more of Ms. Starkweather's time," Steele said. "Oh, and be sure to see our presentation at the high school next week. You'll learn all about us." He took my hand and shook it. Later I noticed he was rubbing his hands together as he and Jessup walked to the Buick. I guessed that William Steele hadn't had dirt on his soft hands for some time.

20

Blue Shadows

February 1867

*F*rom doing farmwork, Silas Starkweather's hands became tough and calloused, his muscles hard. He was surprised how all the hard work had agreed with him. The time had passed quickly since he arrived in Link Lake last spring. He'd planted ten acres of wheat in five-acre plots, each surrounded by a fence he had built with his own hands, black locust trees for posts and pine for the connecting pieces. His neighbors quit asking him why he built so many fences. The way they saw it, the only ones he really needed were the ones encircling the pasture where his loyal oxen grazed and the ones keeping the three pigs he'd gotten late last fall from straying off.

His neighbors also quit asking why he spent so much time walking over his plowed fields with his head down and his hands behind his back. He had spent every weekend last summer and fall doing that. Walking, walking. Some said he must have heavy thoughts on his mind. Others thought for sure that his war injuries were causing this unusual behavior. Who could predict a man's behavior when he was shot in the head?

Sophia continued staying with him, helping keep the cabin in order, cooking, baking, washing, scrubbing the cabin floor, doing all the things necessary to keep the home spotless. She had even taken on the task of watering the pigs each morning and night, feeding them table scraps along with a few ears of corn stored in a little corn-crib that she had helped Silas build. Justin Meadows and Silas had also built a small chicken coop that housed about twenty-five hens, enough to provide fresh eggs for Silas and Sophia with enough left over to sell a few dozen to the mercantile in Link Lake. Sophia was good with chickens and enjoyed caring for them.

February 22 was Silas's birthday, the same day as George Washington's. Sophia had decided the neighbors should have a birthday party for him, and she made all the arrangements without telling him anything about it. If he knew about it, he probably wouldn't come, she correctly guessed. He seemed most comfortable by himself, sitting by the fireplace on a cold winter night, reading a book. He never said so, but Sophia had concluded that he really didn't like living in central Wisconsin.

Occasionally, Silas agreed to walk to a neighbor's home for a meal, but that was the extent of his socializing. When he drove his oxen to Link Lake for supplies, something he did every two weeks or so, he never stopped at the local saloon, which was a regular hangout for many local men. He might linger a bit at the mercantile, talking with whoever happened to be there, but then he was on his way home.

February 22 dawned clear and cold. Sophia got up, took care of the morning chores, and left right on time for class at Link Lake High School. Her mother had encouraged her to attend. Link Lake High School had only twenty-five students, and she was one of but two young women there. "Waste of time when girls go to school, beyond learning how to read and write and do some figuring" was the mostly agreed upon attitude in the community. Silas was rather pleased with her quest for knowledge; nearly every day when they ate supper, she talked about what she was studying as she shared her lessons and books with him.

When Sophia returned to the cabin from school that Friday afternoon, she reminded Silas that they were eating supper with her folks. She said nothing about this day being Silas's birthday. Of course, he had forgotten. He had been busy mapping out new fields to be plowed the following spring, and even sketching where the fences would go.

Sophia hurried out to feed the chickens and gather the eggs. She also tossed a few ears of corn to the hogs and forked some hay into the manger for the oxen.

"Pull on your coat, Silas; we must go, or we be late," Sophia said when she came in from doing the evening chores.

Silas pulled on his heavy winter coat and cap and the two of them set out walking toward the Reinert farm. The night was clear with a near-full moon. The snow squeaked as the twosome walked along the road rutted with bobsled tracks. Trees, now naked in winter, lined the road on both sides. The bright moon cast tree shadows across the road.

"Look," Sophia said, pointing. "See the blue shadows the moonlight makes on the snow."

Silas, his head down, hadn't noticed. He was intent on arriving at the Reinerts' so he could warm up.

"See," Sophia said. "Blue shadows everywhere. Blue shadows from the tree branches."

"Yes, I see the blue shadows," Silas said with little enthusiasm in his voice.

Sophia was sometimes perplexed about Silas's lack of interest in the beauty around him. To her, he sometimes seemed in another world, with thoughts he didn't or wouldn't share with her. But why should he; she was only his housekeeper. She was also disappointed that Silas never commented on how she looked. He did grunt his approval when she told him about the good grades she was earning in school. But she wondered if there was something wrong with this man who regularly paid for her work at his cabin. Several young men at her school gave her constant attention, invited her to community dances, to ice skating parties, and to cutter rides in the snow. So she knew she was not unattractive. But why didn't Silas at least say she looked nice once in a while? She knew she found him attractive, more so as the days and weeks passed. But she kept her thoughts to herself.

Upon entering the Reinert kitchen, Silas quickly saw that it was filled with people. Besides the Reinerts, his other close neighbors, Justin and Hope Meadows, were there—as well as mercantile owner Owen Davies and his wife, Dorcas, and the Link Lake Blacksmith, Dexter Woodright, and his wife, Prudence.

"Happy birthday!" they all shouted when he came into the steamy room, which smelled of cooking and wood smoke.

"Surprise for you, Silas!" Sophia said.

Silas, his face flushed, hung up his coat and shook hands with each of the men in the room. He nodded to each of the women.

"How old you are today, Silas?" Wolfgang Reinert asked when he shook Silas's hand.

"Twenty-two," Silas said quietly.

"Good age, twenty-two, good age," Wolfgang said.

Soon they were all seated around the dining room table, except for the children, who found places at the kitchen table. Each table had steaming bowls of mashed potatoes, a platter piled high with pork chops, a huge bowl of pungent-smelling sauerkraut, and smaller bowls of home-canned carrots and peas.

"Let us bow our heads for a moment of prayer," Wolfgang said. He folded his huge, calloused hands in front of him.

"Tank you Lord for this day and for neighbor Silas. Silas has birthday today. Bless Silas, and bless this food. Amen."

Soon the platters and bowls were empty. Sophia helped clear the table before Amelia Reinert brought out a big chocolate cake. "For your birthday," she said. A big smile spread across her face. She cut the cake into big slabs, passing the first one to Silas.

With the cake finished, except for a few brown crumbs on the platter, the women left for the kitchen and the dishes, children filed off to a back room, and the men gathered around the woodstove in the dining room, smoking their pipes. Wolfgang excused himself and returned a few minutes later carrying a brown jug in each hand.

"I stop at Link Lake Brewery this afternoon," he said. "I buy beer for tonight."

He placed the two half-gallon containers on the table. "Got more in cellar." He passed around empty pint glasses, which each man filled with the amber liquid.

"To neighbor Silas," Wolfgang said. "He is learning to be farmer."

Everyone raised their glasses toward Silas.

"To neighbor Silas," the group said in unison before each man took a big sip from his glass. Soon the jugs were empty, and Wolfgang brought two more from the basement.

"You bring fiddle?" Wolfgang said to Justin Meadows.

"I did," said Meadows.

"Ve move chairs and table out of the way, and ve have a little dance. Dance a little polka for Silas's birthday," Wolfgang said.

Soon the middle of the big dining room floor was clear and Justin Meadows was tuning his violin. The women, their work in the kitchen finished, came into the dining room, and soon the place was filled with dancers, the children watching on the side and sometimes joining in as well. Polka music, waltzes, even a schottische came out of the battered old violin that Meadows gently held under his chin.

Before he could say he didn't know how to dance, Sophia had Silas on the dance floor and was showing him the steps. His face was flushed from a little too much beer, but he seemed willing to learn the polka.

The dancing and beer drinking went on into the night. Around eleven, Mrs. Reinert prepared a huge meal of sausage, dried beef, brown bread, and dill pickles, with more sauerkraut for those who wanted it.

Sophia and Silas were the last to leave. Sophia had helped her mother clean up while Silas and Wolfgang put the dining room furniture back in order.

"Thank you," Silas said when they left. "This is the first birthday party I ever had. Thank you."

"You are good neighbor, Silas Starkweather. You take good care of our daughter. We are glad you come to Link Lake."

Together the young pair walked along the quiet country road, with blue shadows from the moonlight splashing on the snow in front of them.

"A good name for your farm, Silas," Sophia said.

"What, what name?" Silas muttered.

"Blue Shadows. 'Blue Shadows' is a good name for your farm," Sophia said.

Silas didn't answer, but from that day forward his quarter section of homesteaded land became known as Blue Shadows Farm.

Upon arriving home and being greeted by Rex, Silas threw a couple of logs in the fire and promptly crawled into bed. Even with the cold walk from the Reinerts, his head was still spinning a little from the beer, which he was not accustomed to drinking.

Sophia made her way up the ladder to her sleeping quarters in the loft. But soon she was back downstairs, standing by Silas's bed.

"You sleeping, Silas?" she whispered.

"No," Silas said, groggily.

"I have birthday present for you."

"Birthday present?"

Sophia pulled back the covers and crawled in beside Silas. He quickly noticed that she was not wearing any clothes. Soon she began unbuttoning his nightshirt.

Later, Silas and Sophia slept in each other's arms. Sophia had been assured that there was nothing wrong with Silas. She fell asleep thinking about blue shadows on the snow and of her future.

Silas was still asleep when Sophia got up, started some oatmeal and coffee cooking on the stove, and left for her folks' place to help her mother with the Saturday chores.

February 23, 1867

Don't know how to write this. Almost ashamed to put it in words. I could blame it on the beer. But I won't. I could blame it on Sophia. It's not her fault. She shared my bed with me last night. Said it was a birthday present.

I must gather strength and tell her she must sleep upstairs tonight, in her own bed. What's happening to me?

21

Mixed Thoughts

May 1867

Silas and Sophia's routine continued much as before Silas's birthday, except for the nights. Silas tried to tell Sophia that she should return to her bed in the cabin loft, but he didn't know how, or perhaps he didn't want to. His thoughts were tangled and troubled. He had come to Wisconsin with a single mission, and that did not include spending his nights in a warm bed with a pretty young woman who he now realized loved him deeply.

Silas had vowed when he left the army that he would not become involved with a woman. This would get in the way of his main reason for coming to the wilds of central Wisconsin. And now he was involved, or, perhaps better said, a woman had become involved with him. But he knew he must take some responsibility. He could have sent her back to her bedroom that cold night of his birthday, but he didn't. Silas also tried to convince himself that he had no feelings for Sophia, that she was merely his housekeeper, taking care of cooking, cleaning, washing his clothes, and helping with the chores. He knew what he must do. He must tell her she should return to her bedroom now that spring had come and the long winter nights had passed.

That morning, Sophia, a big smile on her face as usual, had promptly left for school after fixing breakfast and tidying up around the cabin. After finishing his coffee, Silas spent the day digging postholes and setting new fence posts. As he worked, he continued to think about what he had gotten into. He didn't hear the meadowlarks singing, didn't hear the ruffed grouse drumming in the woods to the west, didn't smell the fresh soil his posthole digger turned up. His mind was a muddle and his thoughts scattered. His goal had been to acquire some land quietly, do what was necessary to become a full owner, and then spend full time on his mission. He had not wanted to become a part of the neighborhood and did not want any attention. How differently things had worked out. His neighbors had befriended and helped him in time of need, invited him into their homes, and even saw him as some kind of hero for killing a giant black bear in his yard. He wanted none of this. His purpose for being here was a secret, and he wanted to keep it that way.

When Sophia returned from school that afternoon, she came into the cabin quietly and put her books on the table. She immediately began preparing supper. A short time later, Silas came in from working in the fields and hung his jacket on a peg by the door. He noticed something different about her. Usually she was bubbling with enthusiasm and ready to share her day at school—what she had been studying, what the teacher had been talking about—but tonight she prepared supper without saying a word.

"Are you not feeling well?" Silas inquired.

"I am feeling fine," Sophia said, quietly.

Sophia had fried a big slice of smoked ham, from the meat Silas had gotten when he had helped the Reinerts butcher last fall. She also heated up a big pot of sauerkraut from the crock that stood near the fireplace. And she fried potatoes, some of the few left from their garden harvest last fall. (She had set aside enough seed potatoes for planting in their garden this spring.)

Silas and Sophia ate quietly, so different from other meals, when Sophia talked on and on about her studies, about places in the world she had not known, about famous people who had done important things, about how she wanted to be like these famous people.

Finally, when their meal was finished and Silas pushed back from the table, Sophia said quietly, "I have something to tell you, Silas."

Silas thought it must be about something that happened in school, but he couldn't imagine what.

"Silas," she said, hesitating. She looked down at her hands.

"Yes," he said.

"I have news for you."

"What news?"

"Special news."

"Special news?"

"Ja, very special."

Now Silas thought she surely had won some award at school. But if she had, knowing Sophia, she would have blurted it out as soon as she had seen him.

"I am having a baby," she said, almost in a whisper.

"You what?" Silas said too loudly.

"I am in family way."

"How can it be?"

Sophia smiled.

"What do we do now?" Silas asked, rather dumbstruck by the information he had just gotten.

"Answer easy."

"Easy. You're supposed to be my housekeeper. I promised your folks that you would be fine here, sleeping in your upstairs bedroom."

"But it was cold up there," she said with an impish grin on her face.

"What do we do now?" Silas asked again. "You can't tell your folks. Your pa will run me out of the county."

"Papa not do that," Sophia said.

"Yeah, he will probably point his big double-barreled shotgun at me besides."

"Answer easy," Sophia said.

"Easy?"

"Ja, easy answer," Sophia said, smiling. "We get married."

"Get married!" Silas said. He nearly fell off his chair.

"Ja, we get married."

May 6, 1867

Worst possible news. Sophia says she is having a baby. Now what do I do? My world is collapsing around me. My dreams are dashed. She says we must get married. I didn't come to Link Lake to start a family. It's awful. What have I done to deserve this fate? Nothing has turned out as I have planned. This has been clearly one of my darkest days.

22

Wedding

July 1867

Sophia made all the arrangements. She contacted the famous preacher Increase Joseph Link and asked if he would marry them. He reluctantly agreed. He asked both Sophia and Silas why they had never darkened the doors of the Standalone Church, where he preached every Sunday when he was not on the road spreading his message of saving the land.

"Always meant to stop in," Silas said. "Never got around to it, I guess."

"That will change now that you are getting married?" Increase Joseph said, with the hint of a smile on his face.

"We are German Lutheran," Sophia said, looking the preacher in the eye.

"But there's no German Lutheran church in Link Lake," said Increase Joseph.

"So we go to no church. Silas and I will plan to attend Standalone Church," Sophia said.

Sophia, with her mother's help, made a beautiful wedding dress, with fancy crocheting across the bottom and around the neckline.

Sophia had told her mother about her pregnancy but not her father. "Don't tell Papa," Sophia said to her mother as they worked together on her dress.

Sophia's mother smiled. "I tell you a secret," she said. "Ve tell relatives that Fritz born early. He not born early. He took nine months just like most babies. Ve knew about Fritz coming before ve got married."

Now Sophia smiled as she thought about what had been a family secret. "No problem, babies born early," Amelia Reinert said. "As long as couple gets married. Marriage important. Family important. Nothing more important than family. Family must come first. Never forget, Sophia. Family must always come first. Now you are starting family. You no longer girl. Now you are a woman."

"Yes, Mama," Sophia said as she worked her needle on her wedding dress.

Meanwhile, Silas had gone to the Link Lake Mercantile.

"Always good to see you," Owen Davies, the mercantile owner, said. "What can I do for you on this fine summer day?"

"I . . . I'm getting married," Silas stammered.

"Well, congratulations," Davies said, grabbing Silas's hand and shaking it.

"And who is the lucky bride?"

"Sophia Reinert," Silas answered, smiling.

"She's been your housekeeper since last fall, hasn't she? Guess you must know exactly what kind of a cook she is and what kind of house she keeps," Davies said, chuckling.

"I do," Silas said. He didn't want to hint that he knew more about Sophia than her housekeeping skills.

"Good to have a wife, especially during long, cold, winter nights." Davies winked at Silas. "Well, what can I do for you?"

"I need some wedding clothes. Need a new coat and pants and a new shirt."

"We can fix you up. I'll order just what you need. Be here in a few weeks."

Davies found a tape measure and measured Silas for size. He then wrote down some numbers on a piece of paper. "Well, that ought to do it," he said, tucking the tape measure away in a drawer. "I'll get word to you when your clothes come in."

Early July saw several days of hot temperatures, well into the nineties. Saturday, July 6, Silas and Sophia's wedding day, was no exception. A thunderstorm had rolled through the Link Lake community a couple days earlier, so the crops, the wheat and the corn and the potatoes, too, were doing well. But the moisture had raised the humidity level enough to make the weather nearly unbearable.

Nonetheless, a considerable crowd had gathered at the Reinert farmstead for this important day. Justin and Hope Meadows, Dexter and Dorcas Woodright, and Owen and Prudence Davies were there. And many more. All gathered under the big maple tree that stood in front of the Reinert home. It provided shade from the unforgiving sun, but the shade it cast wasn't near enough for the crowd that gathered for the wedding. At various times people crowded under the tree for shade and then discovered that standing so near to other heavily perspiring bodies made them hotter still.

Preacher Increase Joseph climbed onto a small four-legged table. He handed the bouquet of wildflowers that had been there to Amelia Reinert. Mrs. Reinert wore a bright blue dress that she had sewn from material she bought at the mercantile. Clearly, her dress was one of the finest dresses, if not the finest, worn by anyone at the wedding.

"If I can have your attention," Increase Joseph said, in a voice that carried across the crowd and got the attention of the Reinert milk cows grazing in the pasture across the road. The animals all looked toward the group that had gathered in the yard. One big brindle cow let out a loud "moo."

"You all know why we are here," the preacher said. He was dressed in his usual black pants, black shirt, long black coat, and black hat and holding his ever-present red book. People looked his way, swabbing their sweating brows with an assortment of plain and fancy handkerchiefs. Increase Joseph stood full in the sun but seemed not to perspire in the least.

Dexter Woodright noticed the problem first. The table on which the pastor stood had been placed on a spot where rainwater had rushed from the farmhouse roof and the ground had gotten a bit soggy. The two legs on the left side of the table began to sink slowly, but he continued the ceremony, without seeming to notice that he was standing on a tilting platform.

Silas, wearing his new suit and a shirt that was a tad too tight at the neck, stood next to his bride, who was resplendent in her white wedding gown. Her face was a bit flushed from the heat, but everyone later agreed that she was one of the most beautiful brides they had ever seen.

Little Anna, Sophia's sister, wore a new pink dress her mother had made for her. She stood immediately in front of the preacher. She began giggling as the table on which the preacher stood began tipping. Others close by could also see the precarious situation developing. Increase Joseph went on with his remarks, intoning in his huge voice the benefits of families and the importance of marriage.

"The future of Link Lake, the future of Ames County, the future of Wisconsin, the future of this great country all depend on the family. Committed men and women. Working together. Raising their children. Teaching their children. Showing their children the way," the man in black said.

Sweat poured down the faces of those watching the ceremony. But the famous minister continued, oblivious to both the weather and the fact that the little table had tipped so far that he had begun to lean to the right to stand up straight.

Finally, after several minutes of intolerable waiting, only made easier because everyone now wondered when the table would finally tip enough to toss off the preacher, he completed his message.

"We have before us two young people who seek matrimony," Increase Joseph continued. "Sophia Reinert and Silas Starkweather, would you please step forward."

The couple, already standing only an arm's length from the table with its yet-to-tip pastor, edged forward an additional few inches.

"Would you face each other, please, and take each other's hands."

The group was now silent, listening to the pastor's words and watching the unfolding events. The brindle cow bellowed once more from across the road, a long mournful sound that broke the silence.

"Do you, Sophia, take Silas to be your lawful wedded husband?"

"I do," Sophia said in almost a whisper.

"And do you, Silas, take Sophia to be your lawful wedded wife?"

"I . . . I do," Silas stammered.

"Speak up, man," the preacher said loudly.

"I do," Silas repeated in a firmer voice.

"Then . . ." At this moment the table settled several more inches to the left and the surprised preacher fell into the crowd. Before he hit the ground, Wolfgang Reinert and two other men caught him and helped him to his feet.

Without missing a beat, without saying a word of thanks to those who caught him, without even bothering to dust off his black pants and coat, Increase Joseph raised his hands high over his head and said, "I now pronounce you man and wife."

A slight breeze from the south rustled the leaves of the big maple tree; otherwise there was no sound. Then clapping began at the back of the crowd, and soon everyone was applauding and coming forward to shake Silas's hand. Several of the women hugged Sophia and wished her well.

On the east side of the big farmhouse, in the shade now that the sun had moved further around to the west, stood long tables resting on sawhorses. While the women busied themselves carrying food, the men gathered around a barrel of beer that Wolfgang had gotten from the Link Lake Brewery. Also, a three-piece polka band, friends of Wolfgang's who farmed east of Link Lake, tuned up. The band consisted of a concertina, a bass horn, and a banjo. Polka music wafted over the members of the overheated crowd who had now grabbed glasses of beer and sought whatever shade they could find.

Soon the tables were filled with food: bowls of German potato salad, pork chops, baked ham, sauerbraten, several kinds of sausages, thick slices of rye bread, golden-brown baked beans, peas, radishes and new red potatoes from the Reinert garden, plates of homemade butter, limburger cheese from the Link Lake Cheese Factory, and several pans of rich, dark, German chocolate cake.

Eating and drinking and polka music went on into the night. Finally, about midnight, Silas and Sophia made their way back to their little log cabin. Inside the door, Sophia wrapped her arms around Silas and kissed him hard on the lips. "I love you, Silas Starkweather," she said. "We make a good team for Blue Shadows Farm."

"I . . . I love you, too," Silas muttered.

Sophia snuggled up to him after they crawled into bed. "I am so happy," she said as she ran her hands through his hair and then across his bare chest and flat stomach. "You will be a fine husband."

Several minutes later, the young couple was sound asleep.

"Ka-pow, Ka-pow." Silas jerked awake with the sound.

"Gunfire," Silas said. Sophia, now awake, sat up in bed.

"Ka-pow."

Sophia smiled. "It is a shivaree," she said, smiling.

"Shivaree?" Silas said. He was not yet fully awake.

"It is neighbors. They come for treats."

"In the middle of the night?"

"Ja, that's when they come. I make cookies for them. Mama said to prepare for shivaree. So I bake."

The young couple pulled on some clothes and opened the door. More gunshots, sounds of hammers pounding on metal tubs, cheering and yelling. They carried out platters of cookies, and Sophia started a big pot of coffee. Soon everyone was sitting on the cabin porch and around the yard drinking coffee, eating cookies, and once more congratulating the young couple.

The first signs of sunrise began filling the eastern sky as the revelers slowly trailed off for home.

"Now we are officially married," Sophia said, once more kissing her new husband.

July 7, 1867, Sunday.

I am now a married man. But my mind is a twisted mess. I came to Link Lake on a mission. I had no interest in women or marriage. The last thing I want is a family. Now I am a farmer, married, and soon will be a father. Sophia is a fine woman. But I'd rather she was my housekeeper than my wife. I will never tell her this. I think she loves me. She says that many times. The idea of having a baby. Another major distraction. What have I done to accumulate all these burdens?

23

New Baby

February 15, 1868

A cold spell gripped the Link Lake community for nearly two weeks. Some nights the temperature plummeted to thirty below, and the high temperature stayed below zero. Dan and David, Silas's trusty oxen, seldom ventured from the lean-to that shielded them from the brutal northwest wind. They had grown thick winter coats, and as long as they had water and hay in their bellies they managed well.

Silas spent much of his time chopping wood. He kept both the kitchen stove and the ever-hungry fireplace going day and night as the time for the new baby's arrival was approaching.

Sophia had become increasingly more uncomfortable. "I am waddling like a duck," she said to Silas. Even with her discomfort, she continued to cook and clean. The cabin was absolutely spotless. Silas, with his father-in-law's help, built a pinewood crib that sat at one side of the fireplace, ready for the baby. Amelia Reinert made a special baby quilt for the cradle; it was of blue and red check and filled with goose feathers.

"Baby must be cozy varm," Amelia said, smiling.

A few nights later, Silas was deep in sleep, dreaming about his army days, about the ambush and his wound, about his days recovering in the New Orleans hospital, about his surprise when he learned what he and his fellow Union soldiers were transporting when the Rebs attacked them, about how he had decided to come to Link Lake as a result of that information.

"I think the baby is coming," Sophia said quietly as she shook Silas awake. Silas glanced at the clock over the fireplace. It was two o'clock.

"Go get Mama."

Silas jumped out of bed, lit the kerosene lamp on the table, piled a couple more logs on the still-burning fireplace, and stuffed a couple sticks of wood into the cookstove. He then pulled on his clothes, crawled into his woolen coat, and pulled his cap down over his ears. The thermometer read minus twenty-five as he set out on foot for the Reinert farm. Rex sensed the excitement; he clearly wanted to accompany Silas.

"You stay with Sophia," Silas said. "She needs you."

The big dog looked at Silas, and then toward Sophia.

"Hurry, Silas," Sophia said, her teeth clenched.

The snow crunched under foot as Silas ran the half-mile from his farm to the Reinerts'. The moon was full, and the naked trees cast blue shadows everywhere. But Silas saw none of this. He didn't feel the cold northwest wind tearing at his skin either as he ran with his head down, his thoughts about Sophia and their new baby.

He saw smoke rising from the two chimneys of the Reinert farmhouse, but the house was dark, as he knew it would be this time of night. Upon reaching the back porch, he began pounding on the kitchen door.

"Wolfgang!" he yelled. "The baby is coming! The baby is coming!"

New Baby—February 15, 1868

A flicker of light appeared in the kitchen as Wolfgang touched a match to the wick of the lamp on the kitchen table.

"Silas, you look frozen," he said when he pulled open the kitchen door.

"The baby . . . is coming," Silas said. He was trying to catch his breath. As cold as it was, Silas was drenched in sweat.

"I will wake Amelia," Wolfgang said, quickly disappearing into the back of the house.

In a few minutes, Amelia appeared, fully dressed. She had helped deliver several babies in and around Link Lake, so she knew exactly what to do. She gathered up several towels and some white sheets. Meanwhile, Wolfgang had gone out to the barn and harnessed and hitched one of his horses to their cutter.

"Cold one tonight," Wolfgang said when he returned to the house and began rubbing his hands over the cookstove to which he had earlier added wood. "Horse and cutter ready," he said to Amelia.

Silas pulled on his coat and cap and turned toward the door.

"You not going," Amelia said.

"But I must," Silas said.

"No good to have husband around when baby coming," Amelia said. "You stay here. Wolfgang take me to your cabin. Then he will come back. Everything will be fine."

"But I must go."

"No," Amelia said firmly. "You not needed. You be in the way."

Silas glanced out the window as the horse and cutter headed toward his cabin. He slumped down in a chair by the woodstove, listening to the snapping and popping of the wood as it burned. In a few minutes, Wolfgang returned.

"How is Sophia?" Silas immediately asked.

"Having a baby," Wolfgang said, smiling. "But it will take a while. First one always takes a while."

"I'm going back to bed. Amelia said to drop by after the sun comes up. Baby will be born by then."

"What am I supposed to do?" Silas asked.

"Get some sleep. Sophia will need your help with the baby. Sleep on the sofa over there if you want." A sofa, on which Wolfgang took his noon naps, sat along one wall of the kitchen.

Silas stretched out, but he couldn't sleep. His mind was a clutter of competing thoughts.

"Time to wake up," Wolfgang said, shaking Silas's shoulder. He had fallen asleep, and now the first hints of a cold dawn began appearing in the east.

"Let's go see what happening at the Starkweather cabin," Wolfgang said, smiling.

The two of them set out with Wolfgang's horse and cutter and soon pulled into Silas's yard. Silas jumped out of the cutter, ran up on the porch, and burst into his cabin.

"Quiet," Amelia Reinert said, holding her finger to her lips. "Sophia is sleeping."

"Come here," she added. She pointed to the crib by the fireplace. "See anything?"

In the crib was a very red and wrinkled little baby. It, too, was fast asleep.

"Congratulations. You are father of a baby girl."

"I . . . I am?" Silas stammered.

"Healthy baby girl," Amelia said. "You have nice little family."

With that, Amelia packed up her things and she and Wolfgang turned toward the door to leave.

Wolfgang grabbed Silas's hand and shook it. "Congratulations. You make Amelia very happy. She now has a granddaughter."

For a long time after Wolfgang and Amelia left, Silas sat on a chair and watched his new daughter. The only sounds in the room were the occasional popping of the wood in the fireplace and the ticking of the big clock on the mantel.

Sunday, February 15, 1868

I am a father. A baby girl. The most beautiful thing I have ever seen. I am surprised at how happy I am. The sun is shining brightly.

24

Elsa

April 1872

Silas and Sophia named their new baby Elsa, after Sophia's grandmother who lived in Germany. With Sophia's tender care and the loving attention of grandparents Wolfgang and Amelia, the baby flourished. By the time she was a year old, she was walking and soon was the major attraction of the neighborhood. Wherever Silas and Sophia went, whether it was to church—they occasionally attended the Standalone Church in Link Lake as they had promised—or to Link Lake for provisions, everyone wanted to see that "cute Starkweather baby." The little girl was the spittin' image of her mother, curly blonde hair, sparkling blue eyes, bubbly personality, and independent streak.

One day, when Sophia was busy tending her vegetable garden, she looked up and little Elsa was not in sight.

"Elsa," Sophia called. There was no answer.

"Elsa," she called again. No reply.

Frantically, she ran to the cabin, hoping to find Elsa there. She was not in the cabin. Sophia thought to call Silas to help look, but he was somewhere on the back part of their farm, digging holes for new fence posts.

Sophia looked everywhere, out in the new apple orchard just north of their cabin, in the tall grass just south of the cabin, all the while calling, "Elsa! Elsa!"

Sophia thought to look for their dog to help. "Rex," she called. Usually with one call she heard a quick "Woof," and the dog came running, but not this time. Sophia wondered if little Elsa and Rex had wandered off together. The two were nearly inseparable. Wherever Rex went, blonde-haired Elsa was not far behind.

Sophia walked the short distance to the barnyard, where Dan and David were grazing. There she saw Elsa and Rex together with the oxen. She was aghast. The oxen, although quite docile, were far from being pets. Sophia had seen Dan stomp a coyote to death only a year ago. She wondered what she should do to save her child from this potentially dangerous situation. Her worries were unfounded. Dan, who weighed about two thousand pounds, had his head down and Elsa was rubbing it, babbling words that Sophia could not understand. Rex stood by her side, wagging his tail. A quick movement of Dan's giant head would have sent little Elsa flying. But the huge animal and the little girl were enjoying each other's company. And besides, faithful Rex stood at her side to help if there was but a flicker of danger.

By the time Elsa was three years old, she was following Silas everywhere. What a sight it was! First, slow-moving Silas, then bubbly Elsa, who was skipping and jumping, and then Rex, bringing up the rear. Elsa helped with the chores; by this time the Starkweathers owned two milk cows, which had to be fed and milked each day. Silas and Elsa took care of the feeding; Sophia milked the beasts twice a day. Elsa carried arms full of hay to the cows and to the oxen as well. When Silas set out on one of his regular fence-building jobs, she was with him. The only time she had to stay home with her mother was when Silas worked at the far end of the farm. Sophia thought it would be too tiring for the little girl to walk more than the half-mile to the distant fields.

On those days when Elsa could not accompany her father, Sophia took time to play games with her and tell her stories. Elsa loved her mother's stories, especially those about when Sophia was a little girl in Germany.

One October day, when Silas was working in their potato patch, which was in one of the little fence-enclosed fields at the far end of the farm, Elsa came up missing again. Sophia looked in all the usual Elsa haunts, the cabin loft, the cow stable, the orchard, her favorite climbing tree, but no Elsa. Sophia called and called, with no answer. But she was not overly concerned because Rex was missing as well, which meant the two of them were together.

At suppertime, she looked out the cabin window to see Silas and the oxen team pulling a load of potatoes on the ox cart, with Rex walking beside the huge animals. Looking more closely, she saw little Elsa, her little Elsa, riding on Dan's back. Sophia rushed outside. Elsa was grinning from ear to ear. "I ride Dan," she said, giggling. "He is fun to ride." Silas stood by, beaming.

About once a week, Sophia and Elsa walked to her folks' farm, so that Elsa could visit with her grandmother Reinert. Grandma Reinert always had a ready supply of white sugar cookies in the cookie jar that sat on the kitchen counter.

About the first thing Elsa said when she burst through the Reinerts' kitchen door was, "Cookie for me, Grandma?"

Grandma and Elsa played a little game, the same every time Elsa visited.

"Why do you think I have any cookies?"

"You always have cookies, Grandma."

"Maybe today I have no cookies."

"No cookies?" Elsa would pretend she was going to cry.

Grandma would put the cookie jar on the kitchen table, and Elsa would crawl up on a chair so she could reach it.

"Say please to your grandma," Sophia said.

"Please for a cookie," Elsa said, reaching for the cover.

"A cookie for Elsa," her grandmother said as the little girl lifted the cover, carefully placed it on the table, and reached for a giant sugar cookie. Elsa sat on a chair eating her cookie as Sophia and her mother talked. Soon sugar was all over the face of the little girl, who looked longingly at the cookie jar for another.

"No more cookies 'til next time," Grandma Reinert said.

On Elsa's fourth birthday, the Reinerts invited the entire neighborhood for a birthday party. Everyone marveled at how much Elsa had grown and how smart she was. Of course, Sophia worked with the little girl every day, teaching her to read and write the letters of the alphabet. It was good practice for Sophia, too, as she continued to learn more about the English language. At the birthday party, Elsa sang a little German song her mother had taught her:

> Du, du liegst mir im Herzen,
> Du, du liegst mir im Sinn,
> Du, du machst mir viel Schmerzen,
> Weißt nicht wie gut ich dir bin.
> Ja, ja, ja, ja,
> Weißt nicht wie gut ich dir bin.
>
> [You, you are in my heart,
> You, you are in my mind,
> You, you give me a lot of pain,
> You don't know how attached to you I am.
> Yes, yes, yes, yes,
> You don't know how attached to you I am.]

When Elsa finished her little tune, everyone clapped. Then Grandma Reinert brought out a big birthday cake with four candles. Elsa easily blew them out and began opening her presents. From her mother and father she received a copy of Louisa May Alcott's *Little Women*. "This is one of my favorite books," Sophia said, when her little girl tore off the wrapping and looked at the cover.

She received hand-knitted mittens, a colorful new dress, and three pencils and a pad of paper from her uncle Fritz. "So you can practice writing," he said.

That night, when the Starkweathers were back at their cabin and Elsa was tucked into bed, Sophia said, "What a wonderful family we are, Silas. We lucky to have such a fine daughter."

"Yes, we are," Silas said as he realized he had grown as fond of his little girl as he was of Sophia.

Spring came early that year. By mid-March the snow had melted, and by early April Silas and his trusty team of oxen were plowing and making ready to plant oats and corn—he had planted ten acres of winter wheat the previous fall. Last year's wheat crop had not done well; he hoped this year's would be better.

On an early April morning, when Elsa woke up she said, "Mommy, my throat hurts."

"Let me look," Sophia said.

The little girl opened wide, and Sophia saw the redness that accounted for the child's discomfort.

"You maybe caught a little cold," Sophia said. "You'll feel better in a couple days."

The next day, the child's throat was so sore she could scarcely swallow and she had developed a temperature.

"You stay in bed today," Sophia said. "Rest. Read your books."

Sophia rode one of their new horses to her mother's house and asked that Grandma come by to have a look at Elsa.

Soon Grandma Reinert arrived. "The child is burning up," She said. "And see this rash on her chest and tummy. She's got some kind of sickness. We must go for the doctor."

The nearest doctor was in Willow River, more than twelve miles away. Silas hopped on one of his horses and rode hard all the way there. Luckily, the doctor was in his office, and upon hearing about Elsa's sickness, he immediately harnessed his horse to his buggy and followed Silas back to his cabin.

There the doctor found little Elsa, covered with red blotches, burning up with fever, and unable to talk. He immediately ordered cold well water. He soaked pieces of cloth in the water and put them on the little girl.

All night long the doctor worked on her as her parents and grandmother stood by, helpless. Rex lay near her bed, his head resting on his paws.

As the first light of dawn spilled through the cabin windows, Elsa died.

"I am sorry," the doctor said. "I did all I could. Sometimes it's God's way."

Preacher Increase Joseph conducted the funeral services at the Standalone Church, but Silas insisted that their little girl be buried on the home farm. He labored most of an afternoon digging the grave on the hillside above the cabin. Tears rolled down his face and stung his eyes, making digging difficult. More than one neighbor offered to dig the grave, but Silas insisted that he do it himself. While he labored, Rex lay nearby, watching his every move.

When the tiny coffin was lowered into the fresh hole, Silas slowly covered it, a shovelful at a time. Rex once more was by his side. Sophia stood nearby, quietly sobbing. When the hole was filled, Silas put in place a marker he had made from a hewn piece of pine.

Elsa Starkweather
Born: February 15, 1868
Died: April 15, 1872
Beloved daughter of Silas and Sophia Starkweather

"It's time to go home," Silas said, his shoulders shaking as he sobbed. Sophia turned to walk with Silas, but the big dog would not move.

He laid his head on the fresh dirt of the grave and looked up at Silas with big, sad eyes.

That night, people throughout the neighborhood heard a dog howling, a mournful, eerie sound that echoed through the valleys and rolled up the hillsides. A day later, Rex returned to the cabin and, after some water and food, lay by Elsa's empty bed, refusing to move.

April 17, 1872

My heart is broken. My spirits are dashed. My darling daughter, Elsa, is dead. We buried her today in a special place just up the hill from the cabin. How can I go on living? She brought such joy to this dreadful place. Now she is gone. I don't have words to say how much we miss her.

25

Increase Joseph

Summer 1872

The days following their daughter's death, Silas and Sophia moved as if in a trance. Elsa, with her blonde curly hair, bright blue eyes, and vibrant personality, had been a bright spot in both their lives, a ray of sunshine during days of clouds. Silas plodded through his work, walking behind his oxen as he plowed and smoothing the fields where he would plant oats. He knew the work must be done, but his heart was not in it. He had never wanted to be a farmer and even now hoped that he soon could give up the occupation. With the death of his daughter, his mind was a clutter of confusion and ever-occurring images of his little girl lying in her coffin, her eyes closed as if in sleep. He didn't know what to do, didn't know what to think, so he did what had to be done. He planted his crops whether he felt like planting them or not.

Sophia was even more devastated by Elsa's unexpected death than her husband. Being a mother had made her feel complete, like a whole person. With the birth of Elsa, her longing for travel, desire to meet famous people, and wish to see exotic places she'd read about became far less important. The red, wrinkled, helpless little baby changed her life completely. Filled with guilt about the baby's death, each day she thought about her daughter's illness and what she could have done differently to save her.

Sophia's mother had told her again and again that it was God's will. But Sophia could not accept that God would will the death of a beautiful little girl who had made such a difference to both Silas and her. "What kind of God would do that?" These words Sophia said to herself over and over, day after day. Even more devastating thoughts poured through her mind. Maybe the death of her daughter was God's punishment for her wrongdoing.

Sophia spent her days staring out the cabin window. The garden plot that Silas prepared went unplanted. The cabin, once so clean and tidy, became cluttered. No more pies and cakes and homemade bread appeared, as they had nearly every day since Sophia moved in. Every afternoon, she trudged up the hill to Elsa's grave, where she sat staring over the fields surrounded by fences. When the wildflowers began blooming in May, violets and wild roses and wild geranium, she would each day take a bouquet to the gravesite, where she would place them by the pine marker.

Silas did not know how to help his wife. He felt she was slipping away, becoming a person he didn't know. Moving toward a dark, frightening place. He told Wolfgang about his fears, and his father-in-law said that he, too, was concerned and that neither he nor Amelia knew what to do. They had invited Silas and Sophia to their home each Sunday for dinner, but Sophia sat at the table eating little and saying nothing at all. She had become a shell of her former self. Silas began to fear that soon he would be digging another grave on the hillside where his daughter was buried.

One day when Silas drove his team to Link Lake for provisions, he stopped at the Standalone Church, on the chance that Increase Joseph Link might be there. Increase Joseph had been traveling the Midwest for several years, preaching to enormous crowds as part of his tent ministry.

Although at their wedding Silas had promised to attend church more often, that had not been the case. He, Sophia, and Elsa got there maybe five or six times a year, mostly around Easter and Christmas and a few times in between. So he didn't know how he would be received by the preacher.

Increase Joseph sat on the front steps of the church when Silas approached with his team. He was paging through his red book, something that he carried at all times.

"Brother Silas," Increase Joseph said, standing and raising his hand in greeting.

"Pastor," Silas said.

"So good to see you. I was just now thinking of your tragic loss. What a fine girl Elsa was. Though she is gone, you still have her memories."

"I think of my little girl every day," Silas said quietly, removing his hat.

"How can I be of some help to you, brother Silas?"

"It's Sophia."

"I heard she was having a difficult time."

"I'm worried about her. She may be losing her mind."

"Grief can do that," Increase Joseph said. "Grief can heal, but it can also destroy."

"I don't know what to do. Don't know which way to turn. I've not kept my promise to attend church regularly. I know that." Silas hung his head as he spoke. "So you could send me on my way and I would understand. I would understand completely." He brushed a tear from his cheek.

"Nonsense, my good man. Turn you away in your time of need? Nonsense." The words came out deep and strong. Increase Joseph stepped forward and put his hand on Silas's shoulder.

"You will help me, then?" The tears now flowed freely.

"Tell me how."

"Could you, would you come out to the farm and talk to her?"

"I will," Increase Joseph said in his deep voice. "I am here to help people in need, all people." He moved his hands in a big sweep as he looked skyward.

The next day, when Silas was working in one of the back fields, he saw a buggy with a man dressed in black pull into their farmyard.

When Silas came in for dinner, he asked about the visitor.

"It was Pastor Increase Joseph," Sophia said quietly.

"What did he want?" Silas said, hoping that the preacher hadn't said that he, Silas, had stopped by the church the previous day.

"Oh, he just wanted to know how I was doing. He can be quite a nice man."

"Is that all?"

"No, he wants me to help him with his ministry. Part-time, maybe once a week or so."

"Doing what?"

"Greeting people. Increase Joseph says he needs someone to welcome people when they come to the big gatherings under his tent."

"Will you do it?"

"I will try. Next week Increase Joseph has a meeting planned for Plainfield."

The following week, Sophia traveled with Increase Joseph and his small crew to Plainfield, where they put up the big tent for a three-day meeting. Sophia had not heard Increase Joseph speak outside of the Standalone Church in Link Lake. She was amazed at what she heard. Not only did he have a most commanding presence and a wonderfully loud speaking voice, but his message was one she had not heard before.

He spoke of the land, of how land cared for people and how people must in turn care for it.

"The land comes first," the preacher said in his deep voice. "It's the land I'm talking about, and we must take care of it or we shall all perish."

And, as if he was talking directly to Sophia, he spoke about the land and its spiritual dimensions, about its healing capacity for people in time of need, about how the land gives back in mysterious ways.

After each of these tent sessions, Sophia would return to Silas and their cabin. One day in late May Silas noticed that Sophia was working in her garden, planting seeds, sweet corn and lettuce and radishes and squash and pumpkins, and even some flower seeds that her mother had given her. She gained some weight, and the sallow look on her face began to disappear. A little of her bubbly nature began to return slowly as the warm days of June turned the countryside into the beauty of summer.

After each trip with Increase Joseph, Sophia shared the preacher's message with Silas when she returned home. She began talking about the importance of caring for the land and commended her husband for not plowing large fields that would be subject to wind erosion. Silas listened carefully but said nothing. He didn't say he agreed or disagreed with what the famous preacher was saying. Sophia thought his mind must be in another place; he was listening but not hearing. Of course, Silas had other reasons for making small fields with many fences, but he didn't share these with his wife.

Sophia knew Silas grieved the loss of his daughter, as she did. She still felt the empty place in her heart for little Elsa, who had left them so unexpectedly. Once a week, on Sunday, she stopped by Elsa's grave with fresh flowers. She often took Silas with her, and together they spent a few minutes by the little mound of dirt that now had grass growing on it. Together they quietly remembered their firstborn.

July 15, 1872
These are difficult days. Oh, how I miss my little Elsa. We would be having so much fun together these warm days of summer.

Increase Joseph—Summer 1872

Sophia seems to be getting over the loss. She is working part-time for the famous Link Lake preacher Increase Joseph. The work helps her with her grief. But for me, I go day by day, week by week. Life is difficult. I've once more begun reading Thoreau's book. He wrote: "The mass of men lead lives of quiet desperation. What is called resignation is confirmed desperation." This is me. A man leading a life of quiet desperation. A life of sadness. A life with little future. A life without hope.

26

Going Home

August 1872

*I*n mid-August, Silas stopped at the mercantile. Owen Davies greeted him and informed Silas that he had a letter for him. Silas saw that it was from his mother in Watertown, New York.

He slit open the envelope with his pocketknife and read:

Dear Silas,

I hope you and Sophia are well. Your father and I want to express our condolences for the loss of your lovely daughter and our granddaughter. Although we never had a chance to meet her, we could tell from your letters that she was a wonderful little girl. How awful it is to lose a child. We are grieving with you.

I'm afraid I have other bad news. Your father is not well. He is able to work only one or two days a week in the harness shop and is way behind in completing his orders. It is very difficult to find help. In fact, it is almost impossible to find anyone skilled enough to make quality saddles, bridles, halters, and harnesses.

Going Home—August 1872

Is there any possibility that you might come home and take over the business? I know from your letters that farming hasn't appealed to you, especially in the wilds of Wisconsin where there are few conveniences and much hard work.

I know you sometimes didn't get along with your father, but he has great respect for your work. Your father says you are a natural harness maker and that the skills came to you easily.

I hope you will seriously consider this offer. Your father needs you. I know Sophia will quickly gain friends here in Watertown; as you know there are German families here, too.

Please let me know your decision as soon as possible. Our greetings to Sophia.

Love,
Mother

Upon arriving home, Silas immediately showed the letter to Sophia. He said nothing, waiting for her reaction.

"What is Watertown, New York? Big city? Like New York City? I remember New York City when we first come to this country," Sophia said.

"Watertown is not at all like New York City. In fact it is many miles north and several times smaller."

"Is the harness shop a good business?"

"Yes, quite good. Every horse needs a harness. And the country has many horses."

Sophia sat quietly, her hands on her lap. She looked out the window at her vegetable garden and noticed how well it was doing. She saw the hollyhocks she had planted showing their red blossoms just outside the window. A bit further away she saw the apple trees that she and Silas planted and noted how well they were growing and how they would be bearing apples in but a few years.

She knew that Silas cared little for farming, yet he had learned how to do it with the careful instruction of his father-in-law and his other neighbors. She had yet to figure out his obsession with fences and small fields and his constant digging of yet another posthole to set yet another fence post.

Since the death of their daughter, he seemed a bit less obsessed with his fences, at least she thought that to be the case. He made more trips to Link Lake then he previously had, going at least once a week with the pretense that he needed some piece of equipment repaired, a new supply of nails for his fencing, some tobacco, or to pick up the mail. He did receive a small disability check from the government each month, for his war wound. This small amount of money nonetheless gave them a steady income and some insurance for the times that a crop failed or a farm animal died.

Sophia also noticed that Silas had the smell of beer on his breath when he returned from town. But she said nothing about it. Sometimes he didn't return until late at night. She sat up waiting for him, sitting by the window, reading by the light of a kerosene lamp. She worried about his safety. Some of the men who spent time at the tavern in Link Lake were unpleasant when they were sober. With a few drinks they became obnoxious and often looked for a fight.

As Sophia thought about the letter, she also considered that making a new start in a new place might be good for both of them. There were so many reminders of Elsa that they bumped into every day here, both in the cabin and outside. And, of course, there was the little girl's grave that stood alone on the top of the hill just above the cabin.

Last year Silas had shared with Sophia that they now had clear title to their farm. He had been on the place long enough to meet all the requirements of the homestead law, so the land was his. This meant that he could sell it, and the money would be his, with no requirements to pay the government anything. Sophia had a feeling that her father would probably buy their farm if they wanted to sell it, because with her brothers living at home and wanting to farm he would probably need more land.

Several days passed and Silas did not mention the letter or what he was thinking. With all his good points, one of his shortcomings was not sharing with his wife. She didn't even know the amount of pension money he received each month. A few months ago, he had purchased several milk cows without telling her he was doing it. After the fact, he had said that wheat farming was a dead horse in Wisconsin and dairy farming was the future. Of course, she was expected to help with the milking and with the butter and cheese making. She didn't mind doing it; she merely wanted some say in deciding.

Two weeks later, Silas came into the cabin for his evening meal. He hung up his hat and sat down at the table, Sophia sitting opposite him.

"I have decided," he said.

"About what?"

"About moving home."

"What have you decided?"

"We will stay here in Link Lake," Silas said, reaching for the bowl of new red potatoes that Sophia had dug that morning. "My work here is not done."

That evening he wrote a letter to his mother with the information. Silas did not share the letter with Sophia.

August 21, 1872

The days pass. My mind is a muddle of sadness and despair. I walk by my daughter's grave each day, and the tears flow and my body shakes. I do not share this with Sophia for fear some of my anguish will pass to her. Oh, these are trying times. The worst of times.

My father is not well these days. Ma wants me to come home to work in the harness shop. I should go. But I said no. I can't leave my darling daughter who sleeps in the cold ground on the hill above the cabin. I can't leave this place. This is my home now.

27

Modern Nature Educators, Inc.

Emma
November 2000

As I drove to the high school, I was still thinking about William Steele. He sure thought he was the biggest toad in the puddle. If Modern Nature Educators was anything like him, I doubt I'd want much to do with them.

I was surprised how quickly it got dark these mid-November days. The weather forecast had said snow was on the way, starting this evening and continuing tomorrow. A little early, but not unusual. A haze had gathered around the streetlights in front of Link Lake High School, creating interesting shadows on the brick building. I saw people walking through the doors to the gym. I glimpsed the Reverend Ridley Ralston and several of his followers near the school. One carried a big sign: "The Bible First." I wondered what that was all about.

I had gotten there a little early, as I wanted to see first hand what this Modern Nature Educators group was all about. They sounded good on paper. I especially wondered why they seemed interested in buying my farm. At least it sounded like they were interested. But

I'm a skeptical person. I sure didn't think much of William Steele. Typical "keep your hands clean" city person. But first impressions sometimes prove wrong.

The meeting had been well publicized. I read an announcement in the *Link Lake Gazette*. It was a front-page story with the headline "Modern Nature Educators to Share Development Plans." I'd also heard the announcements on the Willow River radio station yesterday.

The meeting had been set for seven o'clock, and here it was just a little after six and people were already pouring into the gym. When I pulled open the gym door, I spotted several rows of computers, their screens glowing, set up on tables on the right side of the big room. I never bought a computer, expect I never will. Kate Dugan said I'd find a computer useful for sending and receiving e-mail messages. If I have something to say, I write a letter, call on the phone, or talk to the person face to face. I call it talking to people by hand. It's worked for me for as long as I can remember. Can't say it makes much sense to change now. If people want to get in touch with me, they'll find me, seems they always have.

"Folks just don't have time to do that these days," Kate said.

"Well, if they want to talk to me, they need to find some time," I said. That pretty much ended the discussion about e-mails and computers. I noticed that Kate was shaking her head, and I'm sure she thought I'd slipped a couple notches.

Only a few of the gym lights were on, so the big room had an eerie feeling, almost an ominous sense, at least it felt that way to me. The first computer screen I stopped by featured a forest fire game. A young woman from the company stood near it. I glanced at her name tag: "Jenny Abramson."

"Students learn about fighting a forest fire, the equipment used, the risks involved. They learn it all by playing this game," Jenny said. "The game players choose different roles. One is the communication director, another is the pilot of a plane dumping fire retardant, and still another is a smoke jumper. It's fun, but it's also educational. The players cooperate to put out the fire. The game has three levels of difficulty," Jenny said, enthusiastically. "And, need I add," she said, smiling, "it's perfectly safe. No one is ever in any danger. The forest fires portrayed are actual fires filmed on location in Colorado." I must say, I was impressed. I'd never seen anything quite like this.

Three enormous screens stood in front of the gym. Images of frogs, turtles, enlarged views of molds and fungi, a paramecium seen through a microscope, the respiratory system of a mammal, the vascular system of an oak tree, a visual description of the water cycle, the structure of a snowflake, and much more flashed on and off as people found seats.

I noticed scale models of the proposed Modern Nature Educators, Inc. buildings on four tables on the left side of the gym. I joined several others to look at them. A young woman wearing a green blazer with the Modern Nature Educators, Inc. logo on the breast pocket (an oak tree encircled by the words of the company), with a name tag that read "Theresa Thompson," told us about each model. She wore a tiny microphone and she held a long slim silver pointer that she touched to different building models as she talked. She explained which buildings would house the production plant where nature books, computer games, DVDs, and such materials would be produced.

Ms. Thompson went into considerable detail pointing out the various "nature experience centers," as she described them. "In this building we are able to create winter. Children will feel snowflakes on their faces and will experience what it's like to walk in deep snow in the woods. They will be able to see the tracks of wild animals. To identify the tracks, a child needs only point the MNE Remote Sensor to the animal track. The name of the animal will flash on the device's screen. We do all this with high academic expectations. All these experiences are based on state and federal standards of instruction. Our Nature Experience Centers provide the most effective learning conditions possible."

Everyone seemed in awe of this young woman's presentation, except an older man who was smiling broadly. He shook his head slowly back and forth.

Ms. Thompson continued, "With the flip of a switch, we can change this same room into a rainy day in summer, with rain dripping on the wildflowers and falling from the tree leaves, with the occasional flash of lightning far in the distance and the gentle rumble of thunder in the background. Of course, at all times the children will be safe. Very safe. They won't even get wet. There will be no chance for insect bites, contact with poison ivy, or injury from a lightning strike."

I noticed several people nodding their approval. Our guide continued talking as she walked from model to model. "This is our Virtual Nature Campus," she gushed. "This entire room," she explained as she pointed to one of the models, "is devoted to climate change and its consequences. Children will see, and be able to touch, glacial ice—and see how centuries-old glaciers are melting as the earth warms. They will see virtual polar bears and learn how their numbers are dwindling. They will learn how climate change will raise the water level in many low areas of the world, endangering major coastal cities."

"This is our land-history room," Ms. Thompson went on, scarcely drawing a breath, "where children see a simulation of how the great glaciers formed the hills and valleys in much of the Midwest, gouged out the lake bottoms, and caused the rivers and streams to run when the ice melted." She pointed to yet another building. "This building is devoted to soil conservation, where students can watch water erode a stream bank and see how a heavy rain can cut gullies in a plowed field."

"And this is the Charles Darwin room, where children learn how evolution works." Now I understood why the Reverend Ridley Ralston and a handful of the members of the Church of the Holy Redeemed were parading back and forth in front of the school, carrying signs that read, "The Bible First." The Reverend Ralston stood solid against teaching evolution to children.

"Finally," Ms. Thompson said with even more enthusiasm, "in this building looking out over this beautiful virtual lake with a real waterfall tumbling over native stones is our Teacher Education Facility. Here teachers from all over the Midwest will gather to study earth and life sciences from the most noted researchers in the world. These researchers are the leaders in their respective fields and knowledgeable of current and important curricular standards."

Now she pointed to panels on the roofs of all the buildings. "These are solar panels," she said. "Our buildings are heated and cooled with solar energy, the most up-to-date technology. All our buildings are 'green.'" People nodded their heads in approval.

I must say that I was most impressed with what I was seeing. And to think that all of this might one day take place at my Blue Shadows Farm! Yet, a little voice began to whisper in the back of my head, "What is Modern Nature Educators, Inc. really about?"

Part 5

Modern Nature Educators
II

Emma
November 2000

I glanced around the gymnasium and noted that now nearly all the chairs were filled. I just couldn't believe that so many people were interested in nature study, but I guessed that new jobs along with a broader tax base and lower taxes might be the main draw.

Shortly after I found a chair, the gym lights came up and Superintendent of Schools Duncan Gullickson walked to the podium. A gym light reflected from his shiny bald head as he began speaking.

"Thank you all for coming," he said. "These are exciting times, and it appears that Link Lake will be the arena for these out-of-the-box educational ideas. We have the potential for taking environmental education to the next level. We could hit a home run with this one. Score a touchdown. Let me present Jon Jessup, our visionary mayor."

"I'm pleased to see so many of you here," Jessup began. "In my judgment, this is one of the most important meetings to take place in our community for a very long time. Tonight we are being introduced to the future. Link Lake, Wisconsin, has the opportunity to become one of the premier educational leaders in the Midwest, if not the entire nation. We are privileged to have with us this evening business people who understand teaching and learning and who are committed to providing unequaled learning opportunities for our children."

I saw Kate Dugan on the far side of the room with her camera and notepad, taking notes. On the other side of the gym, I spotted skinny William Steele chatting with Ms. Thompson. Jessup continued his introduction, making glowing comments about Modern Nature Educators, Inc. I wished he'd sit down soon so I could hear what the MNE folks had to say. Jessup could be such a windbag.

"Representing Modern Nature Educators, Inc. tonight is Dr. Winston Merrifield," Jessup said. "He is the director of development for MNE, Inc. Dr. Merrifield."

Merrifield, a tall, rugged-looking man in his early fifties, had graying hair and wore a tan sport coat with leather patches at the elbows. His light blue shirt was open at the collar.

"Thank you Mr. Jessup," Merrifield began. He had a deep baritone voice.

"As you all know, we are considering a major investment in your community. It is our policy before we even purchase land to make sure the community understands who we are and what we plan to do. If you haven't had a chance to inspect our building models or to see some of our products in action, I hope you will take a few minutes to do so."

I soon discovered how much I enjoyed hearing this fellow talk. Maybe it was his voice, or perhaps his mannerisms. But he had a way about him that kept people listening.

He continued, "First, let me say that our company is devoted to protecting and improving the environment. Not only do we produce materials to help children learn about biology, science, nature, and the environment, we practice what we teach." He hesitated for a moment to allow his last words to settle over the audience. I'd guess more than two hundred people had gathered on this dark and damp fall evening.

"For example, we invite schoolchildren of all ages to visit our nature center and experience nature in a controlled environment," Merrifield said. "And we provide the transportation from schools within a seventy-five-mile radius of our facility. We have special buses that run on biofuels."

Using a handheld laser device, Merrifield pointed to the screen in back of him where an image of a biofuel-powered bus appeared. He went on to talk about employment opportunities. With the mention of jobs, I could see the majority of the people leaning forward in their seats.

Merrifield continued, "The educational system in this country has many challenges. We are making progress toward meeting these challenges, and we believe our company is making a major contribution. For instance, we support the idea that unless we can measure what a child is learning, we don't know if he or she has learned."

Now what is he talking about, I wondered. Measuring a child's learning? Writing down a number to represent what children learn about something? I don't measure learning. I measure lumber and how many feet of barbed wire I need to fix a fence. Learning for me seems a lot more complicated than something you can measure. How do you measure what a youngster sees when he watches the sun set? Or what she feels and smells when she walks through fallen leaves in autumn?

Merrifield went on. "To start with, every state has academic standards for science. Standards are what children are expected to know and do after learning certain materials. Every single segment of what our company does will result in measurable learning outcomes. When children interact with Modern Nature materials, they learn, and they can demonstrate their learning on tests. We guarantee that the science scores of students will rise from experiencing our learning centers."

Merrifield had lost me. From the looks of the faces sitting nearby, he'd lost these folks, too. Why is it, I wondered, that whenever one of these professional educators stands up to speak, he slides into jargon that the good Lord himself can't figure out? I changed my mind about the guy. He was just like all the rest. He wouldn't know good learning if he stepped in it. He began to sound like one of those education types who didn't know beans when the bag was open.

"Thank you all so much for allowing me to make these brief comments." Merrifield sat down to polite applause.

Once more Jon Jessup took the podium.

"What do you think, folks? Is this a company we'd like in Link Lake?" He sounded like a high school student at a football pep rally, crowing on about this Modern Nature Educators outfit.

"Are we ready for some questions?" Jessup asked. "Who wants to be first?"

Several hands shot up.

"You mentioned jobs, Mr. Merrifield. About how many new jobs do you see coming to Link Lake?"

"Thank you so much for asking," Merrifield said as he once more returned to the podium. "We will add several hundred jobs to the Link Lake community; the exact number will depend on how large a facility we'll build."

I watched Kate hunched over her notepad, scribbling rapidly. Earlier she had stood up and snapped a couple photos of Merrifield when he was talking.

"How much money do you intend to invest in buildings?" someone asked.

Merrifield chuckled. "I suspect several million dollars before we're finished.

"Any more questions?"

"When do you plan to start construction?"

Merrifield smiled. "We are presently in final negotiations and should complete the purchase of land soon."

Final negotiations? He surely wasn't talking about my land. The only contact I had with the company was with that horse's patoot William Steele. They surely must be talking with someone else; I wondered who that might be.

Mayor Jessup once more stood up. "That concludes our meeting," he said. "If you haven't had a chance to inspect the building models and try the science computer games, please do that before you leave."

When Kate saw me leaving, she walked over.

"So, what do you think? Pretty cool, huh?" Kate said.

"It's the cat's meow," I answered. "Sure different from when I went to school."

"Different from when I went to school, too," Kate said, laughing. "These MNE folks make you an offer, yet?"

"No, they haven't. Sounds like they're looking at some other property."

"I doubt that," Kate said. "Will you sell if they make an offer?"

"I'm thinking about it. Suspect it'll depend on the offer."

"Sounds to me like these folks have money," Kate said. "This little presentation tonight cost them a bundle. Talk to you later."

I left through the gymnasium doors into the wintry night. The Reverend Ridley Ralston and his followers were handing out little folders. "Evolution no. The Bible yes." Their coats and caps were white with new snow. One of the young women handed me a pamphlet. She was shivering.

29

Greed

Summer 1874

*T*wo years passed quickly. Sophia continued helping Increase Joseph with his tent ministry, especially when he set up in such nearby towns as Pine River, Grand Rapids, Waupaca, and Coloma. She had become convinced by Increase Joseph's message, about how saving the land was as important as saving souls. Most preachers spent their time with soul saving and the afterlife; few talked about the importance of preparing a place on earth for future generations.

"Good people," Increase Joseph would intone as he addressed a group. "Think of your grandchildren, and their children. Think of their future when you misuse the land, when you plow up huge acreages that the wind will tear apart. Think of your grandchildren's future when you plow up and down hills, allowing the rains to wash away the rich topsoil. You are destroying the future of your grandchildren when you do such things."

Sophia found it remarkable that people would sit quietly and listen to this preacher chastise them and scold them for how they treated their land. Perhaps it was his way of speaking with his large, booming voice. Perhaps it was his manner of telling stories with deeper messages. Sophia, like everyone else, enjoyed hearing Increase Joseph's stories, even though she was quite certain most were not true but merely the result of the famous preacher's vivid imagination.

She remembered one in particular.

"I knew a man who lived south of here, a good man in many ways," Increase Joseph began. "But like all of us he had faults. Success became his problem. Ah, you are thinking. How can success be a fault? Aren't we all seeking success?" The famous preacher paused to allow the words to settle over the audience of several hundred who sat crowded in a too-hot tent with the sun beating down on the canvas. Its sides had been rolled up to allow a breeze to enter, but there was no breeze on this warm day.

"Success becomes a person's fault when it is contaminated with greed," Increase Joseph continued. Then he repeated himself, "Success becomes a fault when it is contaminated with greed." He paused for a moment, with his long, thin arms hanging at his sides.

Then he continued, "This man, this once good man whose name I will not divulge, lost his soul to greed. To greed. Greed!" He said the words so loudly that some later said the canvas tent began shaking as the words rolled out over the crowd.

Increase Joseph stopped speaking for a moment and fished in his pocket for a white handkerchief, which he swiped across his sweaty brow.

"This once good man started with a modest farm. A quarter section, it was. One-hundred-sixty acres of land. With his family, he cleared these acres. He chopped down the trees. He sweat behind a breaking plow with three teams of oxen strung out ahead of him. He sowed wheat on these rich virgin acres. At first twenty acres, then forty acres. Then he bought his neighbor's farm. His neighbor was another good man who lost his wife and had to sell out and move back East. The man continued planting more and more wheat until he was growing a hundred acres. His enormous fields stretched from horizon to horizon." The preacher made a huge sweeping motion with his left arm.

"The money rolled in when he harvested his crop and hauled the wheat to the mill for grinding into flour. He bought yet additional acres and a new reaper. Then another new reaper. Old Cyrus's invention.

"Then it happened. Greed has its consequences. Almost always the greedy will suffer." Once more Increase Joseph paused to allow the words to settle.

Someone seated directly in front of the preacher, hanging on every word he spoke, blurted out, "What happened?" He couldn't help himself. Increase Joseph had that kind of effect on people. They became a part of his stories as he told them.

"My good fellow," Increase Joseph said, looking the man straight in the eye but talking in a voice that could be heard in the far corners of the massive tent and beyond.

"This once successful farmer. This good man once respected by his neighbors and loved by his family. This model farmer. This example to follow."

"So what happened to him?" another impatient man toward the back blurted out.

"Today he is a broken man. Ruined. Destroyed. Without friends." Increase Joseph said the words more quietly so people had to strain to hear, but hear they did.

"Remember a couple years ago, when the rains didn't come as often as they might?" Increase Joseph asked. Heads were shaking up and down.

"And remember the wind? The dust. The dirty black clouds that rolled across central Wisconsin."

More heads were shaking in agreement.

"This man lost his land that year." Increase Joseph paused. "He lost his farm to the winds that blew across his vast acres of plowed land, tearing up his fragile wheat crop and leaving him but a few stalks here and there, not enough to harvest." From the looks on people's faces, it was obvious that most remembered that dry year and what it had done to their crops.

"He also lost his land to the bank because he couldn't make his mortgage payments. Yes, this man is a broken man today. He and his family live in a little shack in town; I won't tell you what town. He helps out in the blacksmith shop and at the local mill, and his family suffers. And he suffers because they suffer.

"And what did he do wrong? He let his ambition become contaminated with greed. 'Bigger will be better,' he thought. 'If a few acres of crops can provide a reasonable living, many acres can provide an even better living.'

"Greed!" Increase Joseph thundered the word. "Look out for it. It comes quietly in the night, like the bear that steals your hogs."

After hearing that story—he had several versions of it that he shared as he moved his tent from town to town—Sophia knew she would never forget the words. But she knew she didn't have to worry about her husband opening up huge fields and planting them to wheat. Silas was content with tiny little five-acre fields, and he seldom planted more than twenty acres of wheat. In recent years, since that droughty year that Increase Joseph referred to, he planted even less wheat. He had begun switching to more hay crops as he increased his dairy herd to ten cows and now needed pasture and hay ground.

After a trip with Increase Joseph, she shared the preacher's message with Silas. Silas listened carefully but said nothing. Sophia wanted to discuss what the preacher had said, to get Silas's opinion. She wanted to discuss with Silas what Thoreau had written and make comparisons to Increase Joseph's message. But he showed no interest in such discussions. She knew he continued to read Thoreau's *Walden,* but he was secretive about this book. She couldn't imagine why.

June 10, 1874

I don't know what I would do without my dear Sophia. My most sincere thanks to that strange preacher called Increase Joseph. He has helped my Sophia so much during these challenging times. It has been two years since we lost our darling Elsa, and Sophia is nearly back to her old self. She is a wonderful woman. How fortunate I am to have found her.

Today, when I visited my darling daughter's grave, the lupines were in full bloom. How beautiful they are. Deep blue, rising from a bed of green leaves. Like the flowers of the garden pea, but larger, and more colorful. I also saw tiny little blue butterflies flitting about. They are no larger than my thumbnail. But so blue they are. I caught one and saved it in a little box. I don't tell Sophia about these things.

30

Borrowed Hay Mower

Summer 1874

*E*ach spring Silas, who had now lived eight years in the Link Lake community, wandered his freshly worked fields in the evening after supper with his head down. Occasionally he would kick at a clod of dirt, sending up a little puff of dust. Or he would reach down and pick up a little stone and then toss it aside.

When Silas learned of the invention of barbed wire, he began buying it by the roll and stringing it around his fields, even though wooden-rail fences already surrounded the fields. Rather than replace the rails that he had painstakingly installed, a few every year since he homesteaded the place, he built the new barbed-wire fence a few feet away from the old fence, with all new posts. Whenever Silas wasn't attending to his crops or walking his fields, he was digging postholes, setting posts, and stringing barbed wire.

Sophia had learned by now not to ask Silas why he seemed so obsessed with building fences or why he rather aimlessly walked his fields hour upon hour, until darkness forced him inside. Neighbors observing this rather unusual behavior continued to ask Sophia about it. She answered that she did not know. That she could not understand it either.

Those who passed by the Starkweather farm marveled at the strange arrangement of fields and fences. Looking straight back from the country road that trailed by the farm, one could make out three rows of five-acre fields, with a pair of travel lanes separating them, stretching back a half-mile to the end of the farm. Twelve little fields totaled sixty acres of crops. Most farmers divided their fields into ten- or twenty-acre plots, with twenty acres being the most common. But not Silas Starkweather. The farm totaled 160 acres. The hundred acres not cultivated were wooded, steep, and stony. In the midst of the big woods, which consisted of white pine, burr oak, black oak, and black locust, one found a five-acre pond. Near the pond, in addition to some giant oaks, cottonwood and willow trees grew, with a side hill of maple and another side hill of aspen that turned a brilliant yellow in fall.

Increase Joseph preached what he called "crop rotation." This meant not planting the same crop on the same piece of ground year after year. Most farmers planted their fields to wheat every year, since the first year they broke the soil. Sophia had shared the idea of crop rotation with Silas, and although he did not say he agreed with the preacher, he began practicing this new approach to farming.

Many farmers slowly began adding milk cows to their livestock inventory, a few more every year. By 1874, Blue Shadows Farm had twelve cows housed in a log stable that Wolfgang and his sons helped Silas build.

As his cowherd grew in number, Silas found it nearly impossible to cut enough hay with a scythe to provide the quantity of feed needed for the cattle to survive the long Wisconsin winters.

His father-in-law offered Silas the use of his new mower, a machine pulled by horses that cut a five-foot swath of hay while the farmer rode on a seat and did nothing more than hold the reins and guide the team. The team of young Percherons that Silas had recently purchased was spirited and some times a bit difficult to control. Not at all like Dan and David, his trusted but slow, plodding oxen that now spent most of their days grazing with the cows in a pasture. The difference between oxen and horses, aside from their temperaments, was speed. The Percherons, Bill and Pete, moved twice as quickly, no matter if they were pulling a plow or hauling a wagonload of corn and oats to the mill in Link Lake for grinding.

On this beautiful June morning, with robins and meadowlarks singing, and a red-tailed hawk soaring high overhead in a cloudless sky, Silas guided Wolfgang's new hay mower, pulled by his horses, around and around the five-acre hayfield. Spring rains had come regularly so the hay crop of clover and timothy stood tall and lush. Silas dozed as the hot sun warmed his back and the sweet smell of fresh-cut hay engulfed him. He thought how easy farming had become with this new equipment that required so little effort by the farmer. The horses and the machine did all the work.

Silas had hated farmwork. And he thought by now, after these several years on his homesteaded place, he would have accomplished what he had come here to do. But something about his farm was touching him in ways he couldn't fathom. He had a wonderful wife who he knew loved him. But his feeling about farming went well beyond Sophia and the other people living in the Link Lake community. True, everyone had treated him well, indeed beyond anything he had ever expected. But there was something more about this place that was affecting Silas, something even deeper than the people he'd come to love and respect. He couldn't put his finger on what it was, but the feeling was there, growing in intensity. As strange as it sounded, it was as if the land was talking to him. The sounds came on the wind. He also heard them on still evenings and in the quiet of morning with the birdsongs, and on snowy days when the snow pelted the cabin windows and he crowded closer to the fireplace.

Silas didn't see the badger hole. He had been daydreaming and should have been looking for such obstructions. One wheel of the mower fell into the hole, jerking the machine to a near stop. Almost simultaneously, a very angry badger emerged from its nearly destroyed den, hissing loudly and running alongside the horses.

Upon seeing and hearing the badger, both horses reared and then took off on a gallop across the hayfield, the cutter bar chattering loudly.

Silas, now jerked awake and, not quite sure what had happened, began yelling "Whoa, whoa!" while he sawed on the reins. But there was no stopping the frightened team.

"Whoa, whoa!" He continued yelling, but to no avail. Just when he thought he might be gaining some control over the runaways, the back wheel of the mower struck a stone. Silas flew off the seat, landing in the newly mown hay while the runaway team charged for the narrow field gate as they headed for home on a gallop. The new mower bounced along behind them, the sickle bar still chattering. The team made it through the narrow field gate without incident, but not the mower. Its right wheel struck a fence post on one side of the gate and snapped it off like it was kindling wood. The sickle bar, ordinarily lifted when passing through a gate, struck three more posts and snapped them off. The broken posts tangled with the new barbed wire.

The frightened team galloped down the narrow lane toward the stable, their sides heaving and sweat dripping from their bodies. Silas watched them run, the occasional fence post flying into the air as the sickle bar struck it. He got up, intent on running after them, but discovered that he had injured his ankle, so he limped along, watching the flight of broken fence posts and tangled barbed wire.

The horses stopped when they arrived at the barn. When Silas finally got there, Sophia had tied them to the barnyard fence and was talking to them quietly.

"What happened?" she asked when she saw her husband limping toward her.

"Damned team ran away," Silas said. He felt for his hat, which was missing, realizing that it was lost in the hayfield. "Badger scared them. Came out of its den and they bolted." Silas didn't say that he had dozed off and it was likely his fault that the team ran away.

"You hurt?" Sophia inquired.

"Sprained my ankle," Silas said.

"Horses seem not hurt. I calmed them down," Sophia said.

"What about your dad's new hay mower?"

"Not new anymore," Sophia said, smiling.

July 15, 1874

Can I do anything right? Today I smashed Wolfgang's new hay mower. Broke it beyond repair. I expected him to yell at me. He didn't. Calmly said that horses sometimes run away. I wish I could be more like Wolfgang. He takes each day as it comes. Lately I've been trying to enjoy farming. Something about it that I can't put words to is moving me. But now this. One step ahead for me and three back.

31

Tornado

August 1875

Sophia couldn't believe that three years had passed since the death of their beloved Elsa. She thought of the little girl every day as she cleaned the cabin, helped care for their growing herd of dairy cows, and tended her garden. She remembered the little girl's giggle, her bouncy personality, and how she loved working with her daddy. Once a week Sophia visited her grave and placed some freshly picked wildflowers on the little mound.

In early June she left a bouquet of blue lupines on the grave. A couple years ago she noticed this beautiful wildflower growing in a little open area just north of the cabin. In her spare time, of which she had precious little, she cut out some of the hazel brush and scrub oak that grew nearby. With the area cleared, the lupine patch grew larger until nearly a half-acre was covered with the beautiful flowers.

She learned the name of the blue flower from her friend Henrietta Bakken, who ran the *Link Lake Gazette* with offices on Main Street in Link Lake. She had gotten to know Henrietta when they both traveled with Increase Joseph's tent ministry. Henrietta had said how she enjoyed seeing lupines. "Beautiful flowers. Bees like them. Butterflies like them, too," Henrietta said.

Henrietta was so right about the bees and butterflies. When the lupines were in full bloom, the air was abuzz with wild honeybees and bumblebees gathering the sweet nectar. Sophia also noticed several blue butterflies, tiny ones, no larger than the tip of her thumb, flitting from flower to flower. When she looked at them closely—she had to get down on her hands and knees to do it—she saw a row of yellow spots on the outsides of the butterflies' wings.

By the end of June, the lupines had finished blooming, but other wildflowers took their place. Sophia walked for the cows each morning and kept track of the new wildflowers she saw each week. She spotted orange-red butterfly weeds and noted the butterflies of many sizes and colors clustering on them. She saw leadplant, a mysterious kind of flowering shrub that grew along the ground and displayed blue flowers. She stopped to look at the blue spiderwort and the delicate pink columbine and the deeper-pink wild geraniums. And as the summer days passed, she saw a new kind of wildflower nearly every week. Goldenrods, wild strawberry, butter and eggs (a plant with a flower resembling an egg frying in a skillet), goat's beard, and wild raspberry. Sophia did not know the names of these many wildflowers, but she nonetheless enjoyed them. She stopped to smell their fragrance, looked closely at their blooms, and sometimes picked a few, which she displayed on their kitchen table. She especially enjoyed the wild roses that grew along the fencerows, out from among the stones that Silas had piled there when he cleared his fields before planting each spring. She noted how subtle was the fragrance of the wild rose, a treat for someone who would stop and smell the blossom.

When she saw a new wildflower blooming, she would collect two or three specimens, bring them home, and put them among the pages of one of her many books to dry. During the long, snowy, wintry months, she would often go to her wildflower book and look at the dried flowers, remembering where she picked them.

The spring of 1875 had been wet and warm. Sophia's garden had come up quickly and never suffered from too little moisture, which was a problem almost every year. She and Silas enjoyed fresh lettuce and radishes in late May; they ate fresh peas in mid-June and new red potatoes in July. And now, in August, the tomato crop was ready for canning.

For several weeks Sophia hadn't felt well, especially in the mornings. She at first thought she was having some kind of stomach flu, but by August she was quite certain that she was pregnant. She hadn't told Silas yet. She wasn't sure how he would take the news, especially since he had taken the loss of their first child so hard.

Sophia had asked her mother if her sister, Anna, who was now thirteen, could spend the day helping preserve the bumper crop of tomatoes. In many ways, Sophia saw Anna, who was now beginning to blossom into a young woman, as she had seen herself at that age. Anna enjoyed reading, wrote poetry, and pencil-sketched wild animals she had seen. Her drawing of a raccoon was especially good; she had given it to Sophia as a Christmas present last year, and Sophia had placed it in a little frame and hung it on the wall near the fireplace.

Sweat poured from Sophia as she picked ripe red tomatoes that hot, humid, August morning. Not a hint of a breeze. Anna arrived in time to help with the picking; the two sisters working side by side, sharing stories from their lives, although Anna did most of the talking.

Within an hour, they had picked more than enough tomatoes to start processing. Sophia had earned a reputation in the neighborhood for her tomato soup, and that was the main project for the morning. As Anna washed and sliced the fresh tomatoes, Sophia prepared the canning jars by boiling them in hot water.

Soon a mixture of tomatoes, onions, and other seasoning bubbled in a huge pot on the woodstove. The heat of the stove along with the already hot day made the temperature in the cabin nearly unbearable, but the two sisters continued working.

At noon they took time to enjoy a brief lunch on the cabin porch, which was a bit cooler than inside the cabin, but not much.

"Pa says it feels like a storm is coming," Anna said as she glanced at the sky to the west. The hot August sun bore down on the little log cabin, and not a cloud appeared in the sky.

"Pa's usually right," Sophia said. "But I sure don't see any signs of a storm."

"Don't wanna argue with Pa; he's right more than not," Anna said.

Soon the two were back cooking tomatoes. By midafternoon several pints and quart jars of tomato soup stood on the kitchen table.

"We did a good job," Anna said, looking at the filled jars.

"Ja, we did," said Sophia. "We make a good team." Sophia had never felt closer to her little sister than at that moment. For the first time she saw her not as a little girl but as someone she could talk to and share secrets with.

Just as Anna prepared to leave for home, they both heard the low rumble of thunder and saw a menacing bank of clouds building in the west.

"Better hurry, Anna," Sophia said. "Seems that Pa's storm is coming."

"Bye, Sophia," Anna said as she set off down the dusty road for home.

Sophia looked to the west, toward the twelve little fields that Silas had so carefully developed and fenced. On this hot, muggy day, Silas was repairing a fence in a distant field. A nosy cow had broken the wire as she looked for greener grass on the other side.

The dull rumble of distant thunder became louder, and Sophia saw the huge bank of black coming ever closer. The air was close, and there was not a sound. No birds, no animals. Nothing was moving in anticipation of the storm. Sophia hoped Silas would make it home before the rain began falling, and she hoped her sister would arrive home before the storm broke.

Sophia walked toward the barn with the intention of closing its doors in case the storm had wind in it. Before she got to the barn, she saw Silas and the team and wagon galloping down the narrow lane. At first she thought it was another runaway, a reminder of the day when the team smashed her father's new hay mower. But this time, Silas seemed in full control of the horses, in fact, urging them on, slapping them on their rumps with the reins and yelling "Hi-yah, hi-yah!"

He sawed on the reins as the team galloped toward the farmyard, the steel-wheeled wagon bouncing when it struck the occasional stone in the lane.

"Tornado coming!" Silas yelled when he saw Sophia near the barn. "Tornado coming!"

Silas quickly unhitched the team and turned the horses loose in the barnyard without taking off their harnesses. They stood, lathered with sweat, panting just inside the barnyard gate.

"We must find a place to be safe," Silas yelled as he grabbed Sophia by the arm and ran with her to a spot near a huge rock in the fencerow by the nearest field. Together, they hunched down as the roar of the storm grew to the intensity of a freight train passing through their yard.

In but a few seconds, the twister passed, sparing their buildings and livestock. Now a downpour of rain drenched the couple as they made their way to the cabin porch, where they stood watching the rain pour off the cabin roof.

"I think the funnel cloud moved south," Silas said. "Hope the storm spared your home place."

"We must go see," Sophia said. "We must go see right now."

Silas hitched the team to the wagon and they set out for the Reinert farm. The rain had let up some and in the west they could see patches of blue sky.

About halfway to the Reinert farm, they saw where the tornado had touched down. It had ripped up trees and tossed them like kindling wood from one side of the country road to the other. The storm was no wider than a couple hundred yards, but within its path, nothing was standing except for a few naked tree trunks stripped of their leaves and branches.

"Hope Anna made it home ahead of the storm," Sophia said.

"I'm sure she did," Silas answered as they made their way through the broken branches and then on to the Reinert farm.

Wolfgang came out to meet them when they drove into the yard. All their buildings were standing, as were the trees in the yard. Besides the rain, there was little evidence of any storm at all.

"Anna not with you?" Wolfgang asked.

"No," Sophia said. "She started for home just before the storm hit."

"She's not here," Wolfgang said as Amelia joined him on the porch of their farmhouse.

"Fritz, Emil," Wolfgang yelled. "Anna is missing!"

"Amelia, you stay home," Wolfgang said. "You stay with her, Sophia. We go look for Anna. We sure she is all right, maybe still hiding somewhere to stay dry."

The four men jumped on Silas's wagon and they headed north toward where the storm had struck.

"Whoa," Silas said when they came to where the broken branches cluttered the road.

"Boys, you look on one side of the road. Silas and I look on the other side."

Silas tied the team to a broken tree branch and they began searching through the mess of downed limbs and smashed trees.

Then Silas heard a scream like he had never heard before. It came from the side of the road where Fritz and Emil were searching.

"It is Anna!" Fritz screamed. "Anna is dead! Anna is dead!"

The young man carried the limp, broken body of his sister from the tangle of downed trees. A broken tree branch protruded from her chest; green leaves still remained on the jagged stick. A slow trickle of blood dripped from the fatal wound.

"The storm killed Anna," Emil sobbed. "The storm killed our sister."

Wolfgang took the limp, rain-soaked body from his son and gently placed it on the wagon, covering it with his jacket.

"We take Anna home now," Wolfgang said.

August 10, 1875

Another sad day. A tornado killed Sophia's beloved little sister.

"An accident," someone in town said. But accident or no, Anna is dead. Once more Sophia is grieving. And I am grieving, too. How much more is it possible for us to endure?

32

Silas and the Arrowheads

Summer 1876

*P*reacher Increase Joseph was once more of great help to the Reinert family, following the loss of their beloved Anna. Although the Reinerts had not attended his church, in fact had attended no church, the famous preacher made all the arrangements for Anna's funeral, including burying her in the Standalone Cemetery, located on a hill just back of the Standalone Church in Link Lake. Sophia had come to know Increase Joseph well, having been a part of his traveling ministry several times. She had asked the preacher if he would help her family and he had readily consented.

Now, the following April, Sophia sat by the window of her cabin, looking out over the still brown and bare fields and thinking of her sister who had died such a horrible death. Her new baby boy lay asleep in the handmade wooden crib that sat near the fireplace. Abe Starkweather had been born on February 12. Silas insisted that they name the baby after Abraham Lincoln, who had been born on that same day. And so Abraham Lincoln Starkweather it was.

"He will grow up to be an important person," Sophia said.

*E*ven though baby Abe was but four months old, Sophia wanted to attend her friend Henrietta Bakken's wedding. She was marrying Preacher Increase Joseph's son Joseph Jr., commonly known as "Little Joe" in the Link Lake community.

The wedding was set for June 17. People came from many miles away for the celebration, as hundreds of people knew Increase Joseph and his tent ministry. Many also had met his son Little Joe and Henrietta, who often traveled along and helped the famous preacher.

Silas hitched the team to the wagon; Sophia wrapped little Abe in a blanket, and they were off to Link Lake. Once there, Silas was surprised at how many people wanted to see his new son. Many of the men shook his hand in congratulations while their wives gazed fondly at the little one who slept through the entire event, including the trip to town and the trip home.

Sophia had become increasingly concerned about Silas in recent months. She thought that with the birth of little Abe, Silas's broodiness and melancholy would disappear, but it didn't. It became worse, if anything. He scarcely looked at his little boy, never held him, and mostly had nothing to do with the little one. When people congratulated him on the birth of a son, he didn't smile, didn't say thank you, but had a sullen look on his face, like his mind was somewhere else.

Not long after Henrietta's wedding, Silas returned home one afternoon, after spending much of the day digging postholes for a new barbed-wire fence to surround one of the fields on the far end of the farm. For the first time in many months, he was smiling.

"Look what I found," he said. He handed Sophia a greenish piece of material. It was about an inch and a half long and a half an inch or so wide.

"What is it?" Sophia held the object up to the light and felt its rough edges.

"It's an arrowhead," Silas said. "A special arrowhead an Indian must have lost."

"Special?"

"Very special. Most unusual. It's made of copper."

"Copper?"

"Pure copper. See where it was formed to fit on the shaft of an arrow?"

Once more Sophia inspected the little piece of copper; she could see where the edges had been bent upward.

Silas walked to the woodbox that stood alongside the fireplace. He pulled it out from the wall, reached behind it, and brought out a little metal box with a hinged cover. He opened the rusty little box and showed the contents to Sophia.

"Arrowheads," Silas said. "Arrowheads that I have found on our farm. But none as special as the little copper arrowhead I am holding now."

"You found these on our farm?" Sophia asked, surprised. She had never seen Indian arrowheads before. Besides, she wondered why Silas had never told her about them. Were there other things he wasn't sharing with her?

Silas took the arrowheads from the box and placed them on the table, side by side. They were of various shapes and sizes, and several colors, too. Some were nearly white, several cream-colored, and some reddish brown. All of various types of hard stone that had been meticulously chipped to form points and sharp edges.

"Indians have traveled over our fields for many years," Silas said.

Sophia sat at the table, picking up one arrowhead after the other, turning it over in her hands. Her mind was racing. Now she had the answer to why Silas spent so much time walking his fields in the spring and doing so much digging—he was searching for arrowheads. Sophia would have an answer for her neighbors and friends who continued to inquire about Silas's strange habit of spending hours strolling over his newly worked fields nearly every evening until dark. And digging holes and setting unending fence posts.

"May I show these to Henrietta?" Sophia asked. She expected to receive a "no" answer, as Silas had been so secretive about his arrowhead collection and his unending search for them.

"Sure," Silas said.

Sophia was surprised by the answer. Even though the two of them had been married for nearly ten years, Silas remained a mystery to her. There was so much about him that she didn't know and so many secrets he seemed to hold.

The following day, Sophia, Silas, and baby Abe drove to town with their team for groceries and to the Link Lake Mill, where the miller would grind some oats and corn for cow feed. Sophia stopped at the newspaper office, where Henrietta was busy working at her desk just inside the door.

"Sophia, so nice to see you. And how is that little Abe—growing like a weed, I see," Henrietta said.

"He is growing for sure. Seems to spend most of his time eating and sleeping," Sophia said, smiling.

"Nice of you to stop by. Always nice to chat a bit."

"I have something for you to see," Sophia said, placing the rusty little box on the desk.

"What have we here?" Henrietta asked as she took the box from Sophia.

Sophia opened the cover, revealing a heaping pile of arrowheads, with the new copper arrowhead on top.

"Whew, bunch of arrowheads. Where'd you get these? Never saw so many in one place."

"Silas. Silas found them. Reason he spends so much time walking his fields," Sophia said.

"Didn't know he was collecting arrowheads," Henrietta said.

"Nor did I," Sophia said, smiling.

"One of the best collections I've seen. Think Silas would mind if we put them on exhibit here in the office and I wrote a little story about the collection?"

"Do it. People will know that Silas has reason for his behavior. Some think he is a little strange."

"That they do," Henrietta said.

The headline of a front-page story in the *Link Lake Gazette* that week read, "Local Farmer Finds Unusual Arrowhead." The story continued, "Silas Starkweather, Civil War veteran and local farmer, has amassed a collection of Indian arrowheads, including one made of copper. He found all the arrowheads on his farm, located south of here. We are privileged to have an amateur archaeologist in our midst."

The story went on to explain that Silas's collection was on display at the newspaper office and everyone was invited to stop by and see it. Many people did, and several asked what an amateur archaeologist did. They said they thought Silas Starkweather was a dirt farmer.

Old-timers remembered when Silas shot a bear attacking his oxen; for them he now had another claim to fame—arrowhead collector.

Sophia thought Silas would be put off by all the attention he was getting, but he said little about the article or the comments of people who saw the exhibit at the newspaper office. He continued walking his fields and building fences, often now with a smile on his face.

September 9, 1876

I am so busy these days. Taking care of the farm. Keeping my fences in order. Trying to be a decent husband. Abraham, our new son, takes so much of Sophia's time. She has little time to help me with the cows and the farming. But I don't mind. Maybe I'll be a farmer yet. Farmwork seems a lot easier than I remember it when I first got here. Newspaper office is showing off my arrowhead collection. Enjoying the attention. Didn't think I ever would.

33

Kate Dugan

November 2000

After the meeting at the high school and hearing Modern Nature Educators tout their wares and wow the public with their electronic gadgetry, Kate Dugan had more questions than answers. Her biggest concern—all of this sounded too good to be true. She had a notebook full of facts. In her mind, there were three kinds of facts: those that people wanted you to know, those that they didn't, and those that weren't facts at all but downright lies. It was the latter two categories she set out to explore.

What seemed to be facts in the first category: (1) Modern Nature Educators has its eye on little Link Lake, Wisconsin. (2) They want to build a multimillion-dollar facility devoted to science and environmental education. (3) They plan to hire several hundred people. (4) Their fancy buildings would increase the tax base of the community beyond anything Link Lake had seen in its history.

But long ago, Kate had learned from her father that a reporter has to do some digging, has to probe beneath the surface to find out the real story. She spent much of the morning studying the material she had accumulated about the organization. Just before noon, she decided to call Dr. Winston Merrifield in California. She was surprised how quickly she was able to reach him.

"What can I do for you?" he asked, after Kate introduced herself.

"I've got a few questions for you."

"Shoot," he said.

"Might's well get right to it. Has your company made an offer for Emma Starkweather's farm?"

Merrifield laughed. "You reporters have a way of cutting right to the quick. The answer is no, but you can write that we are seriously interested in buying property in the Link Lake community."

Kate asked him a few more questions about virtual education, and he repeated much of what he said the other night at the high school about how the future of schools was tied to virtual imagery, the power of the Internet, and the ability to control and measure what children learn, no matter the topic.

"What about your interest in environmental education?" Kate asked.

"The future of the planet depends on how well we teach children about caring for the environment; no question about it. It may sound a little extreme, but the survival of the human race depends on our children having a firm grasp on all dimensions of the environment. That, you can write down."

"Well, thank you for your time," Kate said in concluding the interview. When she hung up she wondered what Dr. Winston Merrifield hadn't told her. His tone of voice suggested he was being upfront and truthful, but she had thought that about other people she had interviewed, and sometimes she had been proven wrong.

Kate didn't know a whole lot about virtual education. She decided that in order to write her story she needed more background information.

With a quick Internet search, she discovered several schools in Wisconsin using virtual teaching approaches in their classrooms.

She called the curriculum coordinator for the relatively small Berry-town School District in the northeastern part of the state. She talked to a Ms. Smithwright, who described in tedious depth the school district's virtual science education curriculum.

"It starts in kindergarten," Ms. Smithwright said, "and continues on through high school. We have carefully developed learning objectives."

"Such as?" Kate asked.

"I'll read the objectives for kindergarten science: 'Students will develop observation skills, and they will learn about the five senses and the basic needs of plants and animals.'"

"Yes," Kate said by way of response.

"One way the kindergarten children will meet these learning objectives is to study life in a pond, with computer models and interactive computer simulations."

"Oh," Kate said as she scribbled notes on her pad.

"And if you want to learn more, go to our website. It's all there. Detailed learning objectives and virtual activities for all the grades," Ms. Smithwright said.

"Thank you," Kate said. "And I will have a look at your website."

Kate spent several minutes studying the details of the Berrytown School virtual science curriculum.

Next she called her friend Joe Crawford, at the school.

"How'd you like a cup of coffee after school today?"

"Got anything stronger? Been a long day," Crawford answered.

Kate laughed. "Not handy, and besides, I've got a bunch of work to do."

"Sure, a cup of coffee will be just fine. See you at the Eat Well about three-thirty?" Joe said.

Joe Crawford was waiting in a back booth at the Eat Well Café when Kate arrived.

"Hi, Kate. He's back there," J.J. said, pointing to the booth. The place was nearly empty, except for a couple of older men sitting at the counter nursing their coffee, talking politics, and solving the world's problems.

"Let's get right to it," Kate said as she slid into the booth and took out her notepad and pen.

"How are you, anyway? Haven't seen you since the other night."

Kate smiled. She knew one of her faults was being too serious, too concerned about the newspaper and its success.

"I'm OK," she said, reaching across the booth and touching Joe's hand.

"Just wondering," Joe said. "What was it you wanted to talk about?" he teased, as he had a good idea what was on her mind. "Thought maybe we could talk about us for a minute or two."

Kate pulled back her hand. "I've got a story to write," she said, smiling. "But how about tomorrow night? Come over to the house, and I'll fix you dinner."

"Never pass up a good meal. So, what was it you wanted to talk about?"

"It's this Modern Nature Educators outfit that I think wants to buy Emma's farm. Lots of hype about MNE. Mayor thinks they're the next best thing to sliced bread."

"It would be a mistake to sell to them," Joe said. His playful self quickly disappeared and a worry line crossed his brow.

"Why is that?" Kate had her pen at the ready.

"Because Link Lake needs a place like Emma's Blue Shadows Farm just the way it is, some land where people can raise a garden, walk in the woods, look for birds and wildlife—a place where kids can get acquainted with nature firsthand. A place where parents and their kids can do things together."

"Families can do all that at one of Ames County's parks," Kate said, looking up from her notes.

"Not really. Parks are mostly ball diamonds and soccer fields— not many nature trails. And a family certainly can't grow a garden in a county park."

"I guess that's right, but why should anyone want to grow a vegetable garden?" Kate asked, playing the devil's advocate, as she'd long supported Emma's community garden efforts.

"Don't get me started," Joe said. "You just can't get acquainted with the land without getting your hands dirty, planting seeds, pulling weeds, hoeing, harvesting."

"But you can buy everything you grow in a garden right at the Link Lake Mercantile," Kate continued, pushing her friend.

"Of course you can, but where was it grown—Florida, California, Brazil? And who knows what pesticides have been dumped on it."

"You got a point there, Joe. But what about Modern Nature Educators? They sound reputable. I talked by phone to this Merrifield fellow earlier this afternoon. He makes a lot of sense."

Joe took a deep breath and a long sip of coffee.

"Where can I start?"

"Anyplace you want," Kate said.

"Do you want to know what I think, no holds barred?"

"I do. That's why I'm buying coffee this afternoon."

"I'll start with the positives."

"Please do." Kate turned the page of her notepad.

"They seem to be believe in what they're doing. I think they want kids to learn about the environment. They make a good product. Their materials are professionally done. Their publications are accurate and well edited. Their computer games are creative and clever. Their videos cover everything from what you see looking through a microscope at pond water to glacial action in Alaska. And they'll surely help the economy in Link Lake."

"Okay, Joe. What's the rest of the story?" Kate said, resting her pen on her pad and taking a drink of coffee.

"First, they talk about hiring people. They won't hire many from around here," Joe said.

"And why is that?"

"Because most of the people who work for them are design art-ists, video experts, editors, and biologists, many with graduate de-grees. We don't have many people like that around here. People they'll hire from here are janitors and security guards—low-paying jobs."

"Point taken," Kate said as she scribbled in her notebook. "So, it doesn't sound like you have too many negatives," Kate said as she waved to J.J. to bring over more coffee.

"I haven't gotten started. Modern Nature Educators thinks they can do more than it is possible for them to do."

"Huh?" Kate said.

"What they do, they do well. But they can't replace what kids learn when they are outdoors."

"Joe, you're losing me. What's the point?"

"Okay. Here's an example. Modern Nature Educators wants to build a building where kids can go on virtual nature hikes and not go outside."

"So?" Kate said. "I thought that was one of their selling points. No more kids frightened by lightning strikes, no more sunburns and mosquito bites, no more bruised knees."

"Imitation can never replace what is real," Joe said firmly. "To understand the environment, children need to be outdoors."

"Alright, Joe, what do kids learn on an actual nature hike that's so special, that's better than an imitation one?"

"Well, they learn how to use all their senses."

"Such as?"

"Oh, seeing a bird hidden in the underbrush or a hawk soaring high overhead, or listening to the sound of the wind in the treetops, or feeling the bark of an old oak tree, or smelling pine needles."

"Good point," Kate said. She was writing down almost every word.

"Kids can learn patience on a nature trail. If they sit quietly in the woods for a half-hour or so, the place comes alive. And at another level," Joe continued, raising his voice just a little and gesturing with his right hand.

"Now you sound like you're standing in front of the school board," Kate said.

"Once a teacher, always a teacher," Joe said, smiling. He sipped his coffee and continued. "When we're out in nature, no matter how alone we may feel, we are not alone. Other living creatures are all around us."

"You're starting to sound philosophical," Kate said, looking up from her pad, where she had been writing furiously.

"Maybe so, but if we want adults caring about the environment, then we gotta get our kids outdoors. Take them fishing and hiking, show them how to garden. Help them learn how to see in new ways."

"You feel rather strongly about these things, don't you?" Kate asked.

"You noticed?" Joe replied, relaxing a little before continuing his speech.

"When I was a kid growing up on a farm in northern Wisconsin, I belonged to a 4-H club. 'Learn by Doing' is the motto of 4-H. And it's a good one. I take it one step further. You learn best by doing something real, not something simulated, which is what computer games are all about."

"So I should write something about 4-H clubs?"

"Why not? Our most important learning comes from discovering something on our own, figuring something out by ourselves."

J.J. stopped by the booth with his coffeepot in hand. "You two want any more coffee?" he asked. "The way you're going at it, looks like you need some more."

"No thanks," Kate answered. "I've got a story to write." To Joe she said, "Any chance you could take me on a nature hike at Emma's place? So I can see firsthand what you're talking about. I've never hiked at Blue Shadows Farm."

"Sure," Joe said. "How about tomorrow after school? I'll pick you up. And I'll take you out for dinner afterward, save you cooking."

"Deal," Kate said. "I also want to see where the lightning struck the tree. What got Ashley Anderson's panties in a twist."

"Parents will be parents," Joe said, laughing. "I deal with them all—the good, the bad, and the ugly."

"See you tomorrow," Kate said.

Part 6

34

Hiking Emma's Farm

November 2000

*J*oe stopped at the newspaper office promptly at three-thirty the next day. Kate was on the phone when he came into the office; she waved a hand at him as she wound up her conversation.

"Okay, I'm ready," she said.

A few minutes later they arrived at Blue Shadows Farm and headed out on the trail that the middle school children usually took when Joe and Emma led hikes.

The pungent smell of fall was everywhere. They walked through a scattering of dead leaves on the trail. The afternoon was cool, and the sky was clear without a cloud in sight.

"Trees have about lost their leaves," Joe said. He pointed to a hillside of aspen and maples above the sparkling blue waters of the pond. A few remaining bright yellow and scarlet leaves remained on their mostly bare branches.

"It's beautiful today," Kate said. So far she had said little as she hiked along the trail, kicking her boots through the dead leaves.

"Anything in particular you'd like to see?" Joe asked.

"The lightning-struck tree, of course."

"Almost there," Joe said. They walked another hundred yards, and he pointed to a tree standing at the edge of the trail.

"See that big pine tree?"

"Yes."

"Well, look close; see that scar up near the top?"

"No, I can't see a scar."

"Let's get a little closer, and I'll show you."

They walked up to the big pine, the scar now easily visible, along with a ragged furrow that led from the top of the tree to the ground where the bark had been torn off. Pieces of pinewood were scattered all around.

"Wow," Kate said. "Never saw anything like this before."

"Lightning is powerful. You don't mess with it. Ask anybody who plays golf. A thunderstorm comes up, and you'd better hightail it off the course."

"Were the kids in any danger, as Ashley Anderson argued?"

"Nah. We were way back down the trail. Kids could see the tree though, and of course the sound of the thunder was deafening."

"Turned out to be a good nature lesson," Joe said.

"I guess Ashley Anderson doesn't agree with you."

"Guess not, but it's no reason to quit having nature hikes. Like I told you yesterday, you can't learn about nature without being out in it. And sometimes we're surprised. Can't always predict what nature will do."

"So you don't think the kids were in any danger?" Kate asked again.

"Definitely not," Joe said as he picked up a piece of wood that the lightning had torn from the tree. "But I have another worry."

"What's that?"

"Ashley Anderson makes me wonder how many more parents out there agree with her. Probably a lot more than I think. She's got me thinking. I'll give her that."

They continued hiking to the top of a little hill that overlooked the pond in the valley. The blue waters of the pond, with the mostly bare branches and gray tree trunks surrounding it, contrasted with the bright blue, cloudless sky. A late flock of Canada geese winged high overhead, their calls filling the quiet of the afternoon.

"It's beautiful," Kate said, breathing deeply. "I understand why you like hiking in the woods."

"Do it every chance I get."

They sat together on a little bench that overlooked the lake, neither of them saying anything. The bench itself was special, one that Joe built following the Aldo Leopold bench plan. Just when Joe was about to explain its history, he caught a movement near the pond.

A buck deer emerged from the shadows to the north, walked to the pond, and dipped his muzzle in the water. Sunshine reflected off the massive horns as he lifted his head, big brown ears flicking back and forth, listening, always listening.

Joe held his finger to his lips and pointed toward the big buck. He felt Kate shiver when she saw the animal.

"Isn't he beautiful?" Joe whispered.

"Can we leave now?" Kate said, standing up quickly and turning to walk the trail back to the farmstead.

"What did I do?" Joe said.

"Nothing, you didn't do anything," Kate responded. Joe could see that she was crying.

"Aren't you feeling well?"

"I feel fine," Kate said as she fished for a handkerchief in her pants pocket.

The twosome walked silently back to Joe's car. By the time they got there, Kate had regained her composure.

"What happened out there?" Joe asked.

"I . . ." Kate began crying again.

"Do you want me to take you home?" Joe asked.

"I thought you were taking me out to eat," Kate said. She wiped her eyes with her handkerchief.

That night, over dinner, Kate shared why she reacted to seeing the deer as she had.

"It was four years ago this month," Kate began, "when Fred hit a deer with our car. Just like the one we saw at Emma's place. Fred died in the accident." She began to cry again.

"I'm sorry," Joe said. "I didn't know."

"You deserve to know," she said, dabbing her eyes. "Life goes on."

She reached over and took his hand.

The next day Kate was back in her office, working on her story about Modern Nature Educators, Inc. She was reading through her notes but had difficulty concentrating, as her mind kept jumping back to Joe Crawford and the afternoon and evening they'd spent together.

In fairness, she knew she must call Mayor Jessup for his perspective. She already knew it, but she needed a quote for her story. When she reached him on the phone, he gushed on about how the MNE development would solve many of Link Lake's problems in addition to becoming a showcase for a "cutting-edge" approach to environmental education. Kate had heard him at the meeting talking about "bottom-line" budgeting, "goal-oriented measurable objectives," and "behavioral outcomes" (whatever they were). She listened to him go on and on about how wonderful this opportunity was for Link Lake and how it was a gift from heaven that their little town should even be considered by such an important national organization that was "quickly developing a leadership role in environmental education."

Kate felt like blurting out, "You are so full of it." But she resisted. She scratched down his words as he spoke them. She would include some of them in her story, and many people would say how simply wonderful was their mayor. On a whim, she decided to call the newspapers in St. Paul and Omaha, where Modern Nature Educators had built facilities several years ago.

35

Abe and the Kittens

May 1880

Silas and Sophia celebrated Abe's fourth birthday in February. He was becoming a difficult little one, clearly with a mind of his own and often avoiding direction from either of his parents.

His favorite saying had become "No, I won't do that." One day, Sophia looked out the cabin window to see little Abe walking up and down the dusty road in front of their cabin, wearing no clothing, not a stitch of anything. When the Reinerts drove by with their team and wagon on the way to Link Lake for provisions, Abe waved and flashed a big smile. Wolfgang smiled at his grandson; Amelia frowned and motioned for him to return home. Abe didn't move, but when they passed and had their backs turned, he picked up a stone and hurled it at the team, hitting one of the horses on the rump. It jumped, which frightened the other horse, and the team took off at a gallop with Wolfgang yanking on the reins, yelling "whoa, whoa" and not knowing what had spooked the team. Abe stood laughing and waving his arms as the horses galloped down the road, stirring up a considerable dust.

Throwing stones at passing teams had become one of Abe's favorite pastimes, until one day, neighbors Olaf and Ella Hanson drove by. At least on this day, Abe was wearing clothes because it was a bit chilly and uncomfortable being outdoors in the altogether. Olaf caught him pitching a rock at his team. This time the rock hit the wagon with a dull thud. Olaf handed the reins to Ella, jumped off the wagon seat, and ran after little Abe—who took off running down the road.

Abe was no match for the long-legged Norwegian, who quickly caught up with him and grabbed him around the waist. Abe kicked and screamed as Olaf carried him to the Starkweather cabin, where he knocked on the door.

Sophia answered. "My God! Is Abe hurt? Has my little boy been hurt?"

"He . . . is . . . not hurt," Olaf said.

Abe screamed, "Olaf is a bad man. Olaf hurt me. He ran after me on the road."

Olaf let go of Abe, who ran to his mother, sniffling.

"What happened?" Sophia asked, looking squarely at her neighbor.

"Your son . . . he was . . . throwing stones at my team," Olaf said.

"That right, Abe? Did you throw stones at Olaf's horses?"

"I was throwing stones at a rabbit. Not at Olaf's skinny horses," Abe said defiantly. "I missed the rabbit and hit his old wagon."

Sophia turned her attention to Abe, grabbing him by his collar and turning him toward her neighbor.

"Say you're sorry for hitting Olaf's wagon with a stone," Sophia instructed.

"I am not sorry," Abe said. He had stopped sniffling.

"Abe," Sophia raised her voice a bit.

"I'm . . . I'm sorry," Abe said as he looked at the floor.

"Too bad this happened, Olaf," Sophia said. "I take care of it."

"Ja, boys . . . will be boys," Olaf said, smiling. "I be on . . . my way to town."

After Olaf had gone, Sophia said, "Abe, you stay in the cabin. Look at your books."

"I don't like my books. They're boring."

"Look at them anyway," Sophia said as she returned to her bread baking.

Later that afternoon, when Silas came in from doing the barn chores, he asked Abe to accompany him to the barn.

"I don't wanna go to the barn," Abe said.

"I have a surprise for you," Silas said, reaching for the little boy's hand.

"The barn is smelly; I don't like it out there."

"You'll like my surprise."

"Why?"

"You'll see."

"But I don't want to," Abe said. He started to sniffle.

"Go with your father," Sophia said. "Go see his surprise."

Reluctantly, the little boy followed his father to the log barn that sat some distance from the cabin. It was a two-story building, with room for horses and cows on the ground floor and a second-story loft where Silas stored hay for the animals.

Abe shuffled along behind his father, kicking at the occasional little stone that lay in the path. Arriving at the barn, Silas pulled open the door and turned to the ladder that led to the barn's loft.

"I'll give you a boost up the ladder," Silas said.

"Don't need help," Abe grumbled as he quickly crawled up the rungs of the wooden ladder. "It's dark up here," Abe said when he had reached the loft. His little feet had stirred up some hay dust, and he sneezed. "I don't like it up here, I'm coming down."

212

By this time, Silas had climbed the ladder and stood in front of him, preventing him from descending the ladder.

"Stand still for a minute. Allow your eyes to adjust to the darkness," Silas said.

"Don't want to. Bad place up here. Makes me sneeze."

After a couple minutes, Silas asked, "Can you see now?"

The little boy didn't answer but followed his father as he walked to a corner of the hayloft and peered behind a clump of hay.

"Quiet now," Silas said as he took his son's arm and pulled him closer to the hay. "See," Silas said, pointing. "See the little kittens." Five little kittens lay in the nest, staring back at the two intruders.

"Kittens," Abe said.

"Here, hold one," Silas said as he gently picked up a little yellow one and handed it to his son.

Abe reluctantly accepted the squirmy little animal, which accidentally scratched him on the finger during the transfer. He immediately dropped it into the hay.

"Don't hurt him," Silas said.

"He's a bad kitten; he scratched me," Abe whimpered.

"It was an accident," Silas said. "The kitten didn't mean to scratch you, and besides, it's just a tiny little scratch."

"The kitten is mean; he don't like me."

Once more Silas picked up the little yellow kitten and began petting it; soon the little kitten was purring.

"See," Silas said. "He is purring. See how nice he is?"

"The kitten is not nice. The kitten is mean," Abe repeated.

*S*everal days later, Silas returned from afternoon barn chores with a sad look on his face.

"I have bad news," he said. He looked like he was about to cry. Sophia immediately wondered if one of the cows had become ill or maybe had died. Or even worse, something had happened to one of the horses.

"What is it?" Sophia asked. She was wringing her hands as she usually did when she was nervous. Abe stood by her side, looking at his father.

"It's the little kittens. The cute little kittens."

"What about the kittens?" Sophia asked.

"They're all dead. Every one of them," Silas blurted out. "Dead. Their little heads twisted off from their bodies. There in the hay. A bloody mess of dead kittens. Awful. Just awful."

"Some wild animal kill them?" Sophia asked.

"I don't know. I just don't know," Silas said. "They were the cutest little kittens." Silas was shaking his head.

"Too bad. We need more cats—too many mice," Sophia said.

Silas turned to his son, "Abe, do you know what could have happened to the kittens?"

Abe turned and walked away, not answering his father.

May 13, 1880

I am worried about my Abraham. I don't trust him. I believe he killed a nest of baby kittens. But he won't own up to the deed. I know he doesn't like me. He hates this farm. How can anyone dislike this place? The air is clear, the sun is bright, and wildflowers grow everywhere. Abe has fields to run over, woods to explore, a pond to inspect. Yet, he seems to be a very unhappy boy, with a mean streak. What can I do?

36

Quilting Bee

November 1885

*E*ach winter the neighborhood farm women living on this side of Link Lake gathered on several Saturdays to sew on their quilts. They took turns hosting, moving the quilting bee from farm to farm; this month they worked at Silas and Sophia's cabin. Although it was a bit small for this sort of activity, they found room to put up the quilt frame on one side of the cabin and leave it there for several weeks, until they had completed new quilts for each of the women. They supported the frame on the backs of four chairs, so they could work around the quilt, pulling the yarn through two layers of cloth with a thick filling between. They tied the yarn, usually a color that contrasted with the quilt's many colors, into neat knots every four inches in each direction. Quilt tying was time-consuming work—all of quilt making, from cutting out the patches and sewing them together to finishing off the quilt with a carefully sewn border, was meticulous work.

But this was also an artistic activity, a way for women to demonstrate their creative abilities and at the same time make something that was practical and much appreciated during the long, cold,

Wisconsin winters. Their husbands never complained when they made quilts; these practical men may not have understood artistic creation, but they knew the value of a warm bed on a cold winter night. The women of the quilting bee included Sophia's mother, Amelia Reinert; Hope Meadows; Ella Hanson; and Sophia. Ella Hanson brought along her eighteen-month-old daughter, Faith, and, because it was a Saturday, nine-year-old Abe was also home.

Abe had a little rubber ball and he rolled it toward Faith, who giggled when it hit her. He repeated the game again and again, much to the amusement of the baby.

"Will you look at that?" Ella Hanson said as she glanced toward Abe and her daughter playing on the floor. "Quite a young man he is becoming." She remembered when but a few years ago he ran naked along the country road, flinging stones at passing teams and wagons.

Sophia remembered those times; she also recalled the incident with the kittens but did not mention it to her friends, especially when Abe was present. Besides, she and Silas had not completely agreed that Abe had done the terrible deed. "I just don't think our little boy is capable of such an act," Sophia had said. Silas didn't agree.

As they worked, the women talked. Beyond the creativity and the practical outcome of their work, a quilting bee was a social event. Farm life for women could be terribly lonely, especially during the long, dark winters. The men saw each other regularly, on their weekly trips to the gristmill in town, and daily at the Link Lake Cheese Factory, where they delivered their milk. While they sat in line to unload their grain at the mill and when they waited to dump their cans of milk at the cheese factory, the men chatted. About the only time women saw each other was every two weeks in winter, when they and their husbands came to the mercantile to trade their eggs for groceries.

"I see your husband . . . has built more fences," Ella Hanson said. She talked with a Norwegian accent similar to her husband's, with the word inflections moving up and down as she spoke.

"He likes fences, I guess," Sophia answered.

"But . . . so much work," Ella said.

"He never complains, just keeps at it whenever he can."

"Do you think it has anything to do with his war injury?" Hope Meadows asked.

Others had asked Sophia this same question many times. She resented the implications—that somehow her husband, her beloved Silas, may have a mental problem caused by the confederate minié ball that creased his head many years ago.

"I don't think so," Sophia said, coldly. "He is still finding arrowheads."

For a moment the room was quiet, except for the crackling of the wood in the fireplace, and the laughter of the children playing on the floor.

"How's Wolfgang . . . feeling these days? Heard he's been . . . under the weather," Ella Hanson said.

"Ja, ja, he had a bad cold. He's better now. Ornery when he's sick. Nobody can do anything right when he's not feeling well."

On this Saturday they worked on Sophia's quilt, a beautiful creation made of many blocks that Sophia had been sewing since late summer. She had cut up worn-out clothing: her old dresses, Silas's shirts, and even his worn-out bib overalls. They all found their way into beautiful designs that Sophia had created.

"This should . . . keep you warm this winter . . . in case Silas isn't able to do it," Ella Hanson said, a broad smile spreading over her face.

"Silas does well," Sophia said, blushing red as she said it. Amelia Reinert and Ella chuckled upon hearing Sophia's statement.

"Look over there," Hope Meadows said in a near whisper. Abe was asleep on the bearskin rug in front of the fireplace, as was little Faith. The little one used Abe's tummy as a pillow.

"Vonderful," Amelia said as she looked approvingly at her grandson, about whom she had heard several negative things over the years. "The children get along so well."

At day's end, with the neighbor women on their way home and Abe outside playing, Sophia sat at her table with a cup of coffee. She was pleased. It had been a good day. A day to remember. She picked up a corner of her new quilt that lay folded on one side of the table. The neighbors, including her own mother, had said what a beautiful job she had done. A little praise goes a long way on a winter day with many more to come.

And she thought about her son, Abe. He had worried her with his behavior, but today he acted as a perfect little gentleman. She smiled and took another drink of coffee. Silas would be home from the gristmill soon; it was time to start supper.

37

School Days

October 1886

*M*a, Teacher wants to talk with you," ten-year-old Abe said as he burst through the cabin door upon arriving home from school. He was in fifth grade. "Got anything to eat?"

Sophia was busy preparing supper, working over her stove where she was boiling a pot of freshly dug potatoes and rutabagas from the garden.

"Help yourself to a cookie, but just one. Don't spoil your supper. What does Teacher want?"

Abe lifted the cover of the cookie jar and took out two sugar cookies. He had his back to his mother. "I don't know what Old Lady Emerson wants to talk about," Abe said, curtly.

"Abe, Miss Emerson is not an old lady."

"She acts like an old lady. Nobody can do anything right when she's around. Can't get away with nothin'."

"'Anything,' Abe. It is 'anything.'"

"That's what I said; we can't get away with nothin'."

"Oh, Abe," Sophia said, tousling his hair. "Go do your chores; supper ready in a little while."

"I hate chores," Abe said as he started munching on his second sugar cookie. Flecks of sugar appeared on each side of his mouth.

"You know what your pa will say if you haven't fed the chickens and carried in wood."

"Other kids don't have chores to do," Abe grumbled.

"Bet they do," Sophia said as she pulled three loaves of fresh bread from the oven and placed them on the table to cool.

Abe slammed the door as he retreated to the granary, where he got a pail of oats, which he took to the chicken house and scattered on the floor for the layers to eat. Then he walked to the woodpile of freshly split logs, loaded his arms with them, and carried them into the house, dumping them in the woodbox as noisily as possible.

The next day Sophia walked the mile to the Link Lake one-room schoolhouse to meet with Miss Emerson. The school was a rather shabby building, once painted a bright red but now faded to a light shade of pink. A bell tower was perched on the roof—Sophia could often hear the eight-thirty warning and nine o'clock starting bells' "dong, dong" that echoed through the community on a still morning. All eight grades met in one room, with Miss Emerson in charge of all the classes.

Sophia arrived at the school just after classes were dismissed for the day. She met Abe trotting down the road, swinging his lard-pail lunch bucket.

"See you at home, Ma," he said to his mother by way of greeting.

"Come in, come in," Miss Emerson said when she spotted Sophia in the doorway. The teacher, tall, thin, and with a rather pointed chin, wore her black hair in a bun. Her long skirt brushed the school seats as she walked to the back of the schoolroom to greet Sophia. This was Miss Emerson's first year teaching at Link Lake School; the previous teacher had left the community at the end of the last school year without a word as to why she was leaving and where she was going.

"I think she got herself knocked up," one of the school board members said, but that piece of gossip had never been confirmed.

"So nice of you to come so promptly," Miss Emerson said. Sophia guessed the young woman was still in her twenties. "Let's sit here in the back of the room, where the seats are a little larger." The seats in the school, lined up in three rows with a narrow aisle between them, were smallest at the front—for the first and second graders—and got progressively larger as they moved toward the back. The largest seats of all were in the far back, for those students, some of them well into their teens, who were trying to finish eighth grade.

"I want to talk about Abe," Miss Emerson said. She had a grayish book in front of her, her grade book.

"Ja," Sophia said, leaning forward.

"Your Abe is a very smart young man." Miss Emerson glanced down at her grade book. "He is the best reader in his grade; in fact he reads better than some of my eighth graders."

"That's good," Sophia said.

"And he's really good with numbers. He's doing seventh grade arithmetic problems."

"Is that right?" Sophia said, a bit surprised, as she hadn't been aware of his arithmetic interest or his ability.

"But there's a problem. What I wanted to talk with you about."

"Yes," Sophia said. With the rather glowing academic report she'd just heard, she couldn't image what the difficulty might be. Abe seemed to have outgrown his other problems.

"Well, there're really two problems," Miss Emerson said. She closed her grade book and looked directly at Sophia. Sophia noticed that she had the darkest eyes she'd ever seen, almost black.

"First, Abe, who, as you know, is big for his age, can be a bit of a bully," Miss Emerson said.

"Bully?"

"Yes, I've seen him more than once trip a first grader and then walk away smiling. Just yesterday he hit one of his classmates and gave him a bloody nose. I'm sorry, but I can't condone that kind of behavior."

"No you can't," Sophia said. "I will speak to Abe about this, so will his father. What is the second problem?"

"This one is more delicate. How can I say it? . . . He curses."

"Curses?"

"Swears, swears like a drunken sailor."

"What does he say?" Sophia asked, surprised.

"Swear words."

"What kind of swear words?"

"Ones a fifth grader shouldn't even know."

"Such as?" Sophia pressed. She had grown up around boys and thought she knew quite well the swear words used these days.

"I . . . I don't want to repeat them," Miss Emerson said. She had begun twisting a handkerchief that had mysteriously appeared.

"I've heard swear words before," Sophia said.

"He says 'damn' and 'hell.' And even 'goddamn,' and 'go to hell.'"

"He does?" Sophia asked, a bit astonished but also surprised Miss Emerson had such difficulty spitting out the words.

"And that's not all," Miss Emerson said. "I heard him just this week take the name of the Lord in vain."

"How did he do that?"

"He said 'Jesus Christ.'"

"Said 'Jesus Christ'?" Sophia was having a hard time not smiling from this exchange. She knew it was serious, and she didn't want her son to curse. But Miss Emerson seemed more than a little prudish.

"And I also heard him say 'son of a bitch.' He said it under his breath when he broke the lead in his pencil. I heard it; the other kids heard it, too, and they all began giggling. I just can't keep order in this schoolroom with such language being used." Miss Emerson had raised her voice and become red in the face.

"I'm wondering where he learned these words," Miss Emerson said, once more looking directly at Sophia. "Does your husband curse?"

"I . . . I suspect he does, once in a while. Every man swears on occasion."

"Christian men do not swear," Miss Emerson said. "Christian men do not take the name of the Lord in vain. You must talk with your husband."

"I've never heard Silas swear in front of Abe. In fact I've never heard Silas swear, period."

"Well your little Abe learned those words somewhere," Miss Emerson said. She had elevated her long nose into a position of pious judgment. "And I will expect you to take care of this problem."

"I'll do my best," Sophia said. "But I have no idea where Abe has collected all these swear words."

"Thank you for coming in, Mrs. Starkweather. I know you and your husband will correct this situation. Now I must return to preparing for tomorrow's lessons." The young woman stood up and walked toward the front of the room, leaving Sophia sitting by herself.

Sophia slowly walked home, a new set of challenges facing her. Now this, just when she thought Abe's behavior had improved.

Christmas Program

December 1886

Sophia told Abe about her meeting with Miss Emerson. She was a bit surprised that he hadn't asked about it when she returned home. Abe had begun his evening chores without being asked. He carried in stove wood and quietly placed the sticks of split oak in the woodbox. His usual style was to stomp into the house, drop the wood into the box, and sulk back outside, leaving no doubt how much he hated doing it. Same with feeding the chickens and picking the eggs. This evening he did these tasks without grumbling and complaining about how much he hated chickens and the sharp smell of the chicken house in winter.

His behavior did not go unnoticed. "Thank you for doing your chores so well, Abe," Sophia said when he placed the basket of eggs on a chair near the table.

"You're welcome," Abe said.

Sophia couldn't remember her son ever using the words before.

She smiled, knowing that Abe was expecting the worst when he heard the report from his mother's meeting with the schoolmarm.

"Well, what'd the teacher have to say?" Silas asked.

"Miss Emerson is quite strict," Sophia began.

"I don't like her," Abe said. "None of the kids like her."

"Just wait, Abe, you'll get your chance to talk. Let's hear what your ma has to say," Silas said. He picked up his cup of coffee and leaned back in his chair. For supper they ate mashed potatoes, baked squash, and fresh pork chops fried in a cast-iron skillet.

Silas had butchered one of their pigs a couple of weeks earlier, and they were enjoying fresh pork once or twice a week. Sophia had warned Abe to stay away from the pig butchering, that it might upset him. But he was right there, leaning on the fence when Wolfgang and Fritz arrived to help. Wolfgang had a long, sharp knife in his hand when he crawled over the fence. Fritz and Silas caught the hog in a corner of the pen. Fritz reached for one of its front legs and quickly upended the animal, with Silas helping to hold it down. The pig's squeals of terror echoed through the valley in back of the Starkweather farmstead.

Quickly, Wolfgang stuck the knife in the animal's neck and twisted the razor-sharp blade. Dark red, nearly purple, blood spurted from its neck as it returned to its feet, staggered a few steps before falling down. It kicked its legs a few times and then lay dead.

All the while, Abe stood at the fence looking, watching every move as the men made short work of killing the animal. Silas had earlier started a fire, over which he had hung a huge black cast-iron caldron, filled with boiling water, on a steel tripod. The three men dragged the dead pig near the fire, preparing to remove its wiry hair by scalding it with boiling water and scraping it off with a metal scraper fashioned for the purpose.

Abe continued watching, fascinated with the process. With the hair removed from the dead animal, Wolfgang cut slits in each back leg, through which he pushed a heavy oak stick with a metal eye screwed in the center of it. To the eye the men attached a tackle block—a series of pulleys and ropes—that allowed them to pull the pig up into a nearby tree.

With his sharp butcher knife, Wolfgang cut a slit in the animal's belly from top to bottom, and a pile of intestines, lungs, and other body organs spilled onto the ground in a cloud of steam and heavy smells. He carefully saved the liver, as everyone enjoyed eating fresh fried liver and onions.

Abe continued his interest in the process, now asking his father what various body organs lay on the ground as poked around in the gut pile with a stick.

Miss Emerson had lots to say," Sophia began. Abe sat quietly, his eyes downward, for he surmised what he was about to hear.

"First, she told me how impressed she was with your reading, and how you know arithmetic beyond your grade."

"I like reading and arithmetic," Abe said, quietly. He knew what was next would not be so laudatory.

"Miss Emerson said that you start fights," Sophia said. "That you sometimes are a bully."

"I only hit somebody when they hit me first. Isn't that what I should do, Pa? When somebody hits me, I should hit them back."

Silas looked at his son but didn't say anything.

"And that isn't all. Miss Emerson said that you use swear words in school."

"All the kids use swear words, the boys anyway. The older kids teach us the words. They tell us that's something we gotta learn before we leave school."

"Abe, you know that's not true. You don't hear your pa and me swearing. Swearing is for people who aren't smart enough to come up with real words."

"But swear words are real words," Abe protested.

"Well, I don't want to hear another word from Miss Emerson about your swearing," Sophia said. Her son was looking down at his cleaned plate.

"You look at me when I talk, Abe Starkweather," Sophia said as she grabbed her son's arm and shook it. Abe looked up.

"Did you hear me?"

"Yeah, I heard you, Ma."

"Well, what'd I say?"

"You said I shouldn't swear whenever Miss Emerson was around to hear me."

"Abe Starkweather, that's not what I said." She was shaking his arm. "I said you will stop swearing at school, no matter if Miss Emerson is around or not."

"Yes, Ma," Abe said.

"You listen to your ma," Silas said. "We don't want to hear about any more fighting or swearing."

"Yes, Pa," Abe said.

Both Silas and Sophia thought their little talk with Abe had made a difference, as they received no more notes from Miss Emerson. November sped by, as did the first weeks of December. One day Abe announced that the school was once more putting on a Christmas program and that he had a part in it.

"I'm happy to hear that," Sophia said, smiling. She and Silas had attended the school programs each year since they were married and enjoyed them immensely. The school Christmas program had become the top entertainment for the community. Everyone attended, no matter whether they had children in school or not. The program consisted of singing, skits, and individual performances by various students.

For several weeks prior to the program, Sophia heard Abe practicing his piece. From what she heard, it was about winter, snow, cold weather, and the coming of the Christ Child at Christmas.

When the Starkweathers arrived at the school on the night of the program, the building was already nearly filled with parents and others from the community. They immediately saw Miss Emerson, who was dressed in a long red skirt and a white blouse that came up to her neck. She welcomed them, as she greeted everyone who came into the school.

The program took place on a little stage in the front of the school building. The stage consisted of wooden planks placed across saw-horses. A wire over the front of the stage held bed sheets that served as curtains.

The big, black woodstove in the back of the school created con-siderably more heat than necessary for a room packed with over-dressed people. Soon the curtains parted, and the program began. A little first grader stood up, said his piece without a flaw. He smiled and ran off the stage, and everyone clapped loudly. Next, six girls sang "Away in a Manger," followed by a skit that was supposed to be humorous, but Silas either wasn't paying attention or he completely missed the point.

There was a moment of confusion backstage with loud whispers and people scampering about before the curtain parted once more. It was Abe's turn. He stood alone in the middle of the stage, wearing a new pair of bib overalls that Sophia had purchased from the mer-cantile. His hair was combed, and Sophia thought, "How hand-some, my little man."

For a long time, longer to Sophia than it actually was, no words came from Abe's mouth. He began fidgeting, shuffling his feet back and forth, and looking toward the ceiling.

And then he said in a loud, clear voice that even those in the far back of the room could hear clearly, "Son of a bitch, I can't remem-ber a goddamn word." He slowly walked off the stage.

The room was deathly quiet. Miss Emerson, who stood off to the side in the front of the room, about collapsed. Her face turned as red as her skirt. Then, from the back of the room, the laughter began. Loud, raucous laughter. Knee-slapping guffaws.

Silas and Sophia, more than a little embarrassed, knew they had some further work to do on Abe's cursing problem.

December 21, 1886

Whatever will we do with Abraham? He made a fool out of Sophia and me at the Christmas program. Stood on the stage and cursed when he couldn't remember his lines. Everyone laughed. But not the schoolmarm. She was furious. I could see it in her eyes.

39

Picnic

July 4, 1895

*T*he years sped by. The Depression of 1893 had its grip on the country, especially in the cities, where many people were out of work. Thousands of urbanites were hungry and near destitute by 1895. As farmers, Sophia, Silas, and Abe always had enough to eat, but they, too, felt the sting of low prices and knew about the terrible problems in the cities. Even in good years, farming the sandy soil of central Wisconsin was unpredictable. Crop yields depended on the weather. Periodic rains determined whether farmers grew adequate crops or not. In 1895, ample spring rains resulted in a hay crop that had grown tall and rank, one of the best in years. At the breakfast table, Silas announced, "It's the Fourth of July. Let's stop haying and spend the day at the lake."

Both Abe, who was now nineteen, and Sophia had been waiting for this, because Silas said the same thing each year. And he always added, "We must celebrate the birth of our country."

Sophia spent the morning preparing a picnic lunch of cold-beef sandwiches, strawberry pie, German potato salad, and lemonade. On the way to Link Lake Park, Silas stopped at the newspaper office and bought a newspaper. (The office had a sign: "Closed at noon for the holiday.") Once at the lake, Abe went swimming, Sophia laid out the picnic lunch, and Silas read the newspaper.

A lead article reported that the depression had caused hundreds of the country's banks to close and thousands of workers to lose their jobs. He thought how fortunate he and his family were to be farming, especially now that he owned the farm after long ago meeting the homestead-law requirement. He had no mortgage payments on his land; he did have taxes to pay, but by selling a few pigs, he could usually meet this obligation without difficulty.

Even though the World's Fair in Chicago had opened back in 1893, the paper continued to carry extended articles about its great success. Silas read about George Ferris's big wheel that stood 264 feet high and had thirty-six cars, each with a capacity of sixty people. He couldn't imagine such a creation turning around and lifting its load of fairgoers high into the air for a view of Chicago and Lake Michigan. He read about the electrical exhibits and the inventions of Thomas Edison and George Westinghouse and how the buildings at the fair were illuminated with electric light. He couldn't fathom what it must be like to have electrical lighting. He remembered how great it was when he and Sophia bought their first kerosene lamp and put aside their smoky candles with their dim light. And now this. No kerosene. No matches. No open flame.

Silas smiled when he read about Buffalo Bill Cody's stunning success at the fair or, better said, just outside the fairgrounds, because the fair officials had not allowed his famous Wild West Show inside the six-hundred-acre lot. The officials had claimed it was too "western" to fit the theme of the fair. I guess old Buffalo Bill showed those city slickers, Silas thought as he continued reading.

"Lunch is ready," Sophia announced. "Yell for Abe to come out of the water." Abe, who had become quite an accomplished swimmer, had been swimming back and forth from the shallow water to the diving raft anchored in about fifteen feet of water.

The Starkweathers gathered around the picnic table that

overlooked the lake, with Abe still in his wet bathing suit. It was a hot, humid day, the kind of weather rather common to central Wisconsin in July. Families from throughout the area gathered at the park on Sunday afternoons and summer holidays. Because of the warm sunny day, the park and the bathing beach were even more crowded than usual.

About halfway through the meal, everyone heard a loud scream and then a series of screams coming from the direction of the beach. A young girl came running toward the Starkweather table. They immediately recognized her as the neighbor girl Faith Hanson.

"It's Bertha! Bertha Walters! She's drowning! She's drowning!" Faith screamed.

"Where?" Abe asked as he jumped up from the table.

"Out there, just beyond the raft." Faith pointed toward where she had seen her friend yell for help, go under, and come up and yell for help again.

Abe ran to the beach, dove in, and swam rapidly toward where the young girl was struggling in the water. Just before he reached her, she sank beneath the surface, causing a loud gasp from the group assembled on the beach, watching. Meanwhile someone had found a boat and was rowing toward where she was last seen.

Upon reaching the spot where he had last spotted Bertha, Abe dove beneath the surface. For what seemed an eternity to those on shore, especially to his father and mother, Abe remained under. The man in the boat had stopped rowing, not knowing exactly where to go.

Then Abe's head broke the surface. He had found Bertha and was swimming toward shore, pulling her along. To those watching, she seemed like a lifeless rag. Upon reaching shore, he picked up the girl and carried her to a shaded, grassy area and gently laid her down. In a moment or so she began coughing, and in a few minutes she was sitting up, smiling, surrounded by her parents and friends.

"Was that Abe Starkweather?" someone asked. "Was he the one who saved young Bertha?"

Meanwhile, Abe had returned to the picnic table where his parents sat smiling.

"I think I'll have a piece of that strawberry pie," Abe said when he sat down at the table.

Sophia patted him on the arm. "How about two pieces, Abe?" she said.

*H*eadlines in the next issue of the *Link Lake Gazette* proclaimed: "Abe Starkweather, Local Farm Boy, Saves Drowning Swimmer." The article went on:

> In a daring Fourth of July rescue, Abe Starkweather, 19, dove beneath the waters of Link Lake to pluck Bertha Walters, 12, from the watery depths. Without Starkweather's quick and skilled response, the Walters girl would surely have met her Maker. Amos Skidmore, 72, found a boat and rowed out to the place where the Walters girl had gone under, but he said, "There was nothing I could do. She'd slipped beneath the surface. I was sure she was a goner."
>
> No one seems to have been aware of Starkweather's superior swimming skills. Starkweather, found after the rescue with his parents, refused an interview. He sat quietly at a picnic table eating strawberry pie. "It's good pie," he said. "Ma knows how to bake a good pie."

July 5, 1895

I am so proud of Abraham. He saved a girl from drowning. The newspaper wrote about his rescue in glowing terms. What a fine young man he has become. I only hope he will develop a liking for farming as I have.

I've come to love this farm. I didn't think I would ever say it, but I think I've become a farmer. There's something about being close to nature that's gotten under my skin. I haven't written much about Thoreau in recent years, but I've never stopped reading *Walden*. I read it over and over again. Each time, I learn something new. Recently I read, "There can be no very black melancholy to him who lives in the midst of Nature and has his senses still." How right he is. I've never told anyone this. Not even Sophia. But it's spending time walking my fields, listening to the birds, gazing at the wildflowers, feeling a cool breeze of summer on my sweating brow that lifts my spirits and makes life worth living no matter what problems are thrown my way.

Thoreau doesn't talk much about neighbors. But I must. To a love of nature must be added a love of mankind. Without my neighbors, I would have failed, perhaps even died. They help me. I help them. It means so much to be a part of a community. Lately I've been repairing my neighbors' horse harnesses. For a long time I let no one around here know that I knew harness making. Now I do it, not to make money–Lord knows I could use more money–but to repay my neighbors for all that they have done for me since I arrived here many years ago. It is also very fulfilling to be working with leather again, doing the things my father taught me back in Watertown.

40

Skinny-Dipping

August 1900

*T*he Starkweather family hadn't been much for churchgoing. Especially since the passing of the Reverend Increase Joseph Link back in 1893. Sophia had taken a real liking to that strange preacher who always wore black and seemed to gather his inspiration from a red book he always carried with him. She especially liked the message that threaded through all his sermons—they were more than typical church sermons because he didn't talk about saving people's souls; he preached that people should save the land.

Increase Joseph cared about people, too, more than most people realized. Sophia never forgot how he had helped her recover from the deaths of her little daughter, Elsa, and her sister, Anna. And she remembered fondly the times she had traveled with the famous preacher when he took his ministry on the road and preached from a big tent in cities around Wisconsin and throughout the Midwest. His message of caring for the land was one she had never forgotten.

But Silas, Sophia, and now Abe had never gotten into the habit of attending regular weekly services—Sophia didn't quite know how to explain it. Maybe it was because she felt a lot closer to God when she sat on the cemetery hill above the cabin with blue lupines spill-ing out in front of her. Or when a thunderstorm boiled up in the west, with lightning splitting the black sky. Or when the trees turned color in the fall, marking the end of another season on the farm.

It wasn't because Link Lake lacked formal religious opportunity. Last summer, the Reverend Jacob John Jacobs rode into town on a bolt of lightning and a cascade of fiery words. At first preaching in a ratty tent on the shores of the lake, he moved his congregation, which he called the Church of the Holy Redeemed, into an old abandoned building just off Main Street, where he preached hellfire and damnation. "The world is filled with sinners," he yelled from the pulpit. "All of you are on your way to hell—unless you heed my word." He was against taverns and drinking, down on card playing, and opposed to dancing. And he spoke out against swimming, a popular activity for local young people. After all, the people of Link Lake had some of the most beautiful sandy beaches in all of central Wisconsin.

When the Reverend Jacobs heard that young people regularly skinny-dipped in a secluded bay half a mile from his church, he devoted an entire sermon to what he called the greatest of all sins—allowing one's unclothed body to be seen by others. He concluded his sermon with words often repeated later by those who attended church that day: "If God had meant for you to run around naked, you would have been born that way." The good reverend even volun-teered to accompany the village marshal, Shorty Lightfoot, on warm summer evenings when they patrolled the beach searching for the sinning skinny-dippers. Marshal Lightfoot, who himself had skinny-dipped when he was a kid, hadn't been too keen on the midnight patrols, but he knew better than to express that to the preacher. The last thing Shorty wanted was to be the subject of one of Preacher Jacobs's sermons—if that happened, he would surely lose the next election, because a bunch of people in Link Lake had trouble seeing the difference between enforcing the law and enforcing morality. Shorty had even checked the village statutes, and in no place had he found any reference to skinny-dipping as an illegal activity.

Of course the young people in the Link Lake community, both boys and girls, paid little heed to this preacher or any preacher. They enjoyed skinny-dipping and during the warm days of summer often participated in this time-honored activity. Abe Starkweather was a regular; not only was he a good swimmer, but he also was quite proud of his muscular body.

Faith Hanson knew about Abe's skinny-dipping, and she, now at age sixteen, hoped she might find him alone in the water some night. She thought it would be fun to join him, although she had never skinny-dipped before.

Abe Starkweather was a local hero since he saved the Walters girl from drowning a few years ago. About every young woman in Link Lake had a crush on him, none more than Faith Hanson. She had dreamed what it would be like to be with him, to have his strong arms around her, to kiss him passionately. Even though they were neighbors and saw each other on occasion, Abe had expressed no interest in Faith whatsoever. She wanted to change that, and skinny-dipping might be the way.

On a warm August night, Faith told her mother she was walking to a girlfriend's house for a visit, but instead she headed for the lake, hoping this might be one of those nights that Abe had chosen for a swim.

Upon arriving at the secluded beach where she knew he often swam, she sat down under a big tree deep in the shadows and waited. Soon, she heard a horse coming along the beach road, and she saw Abe as he tied his mount to a tree. Faith remained in the shadows, watching him strip off his clothes, first his shoes and socks, then his bib overalls, and finally his shirt. She had never seen a man naked before, even though in the darkness she could not see every detail of his body, everything she wanted to see, she saw enough to make her feel something she had never felt before. She sat quietly as he stood up and stretched, his muscles rippling, before he ran into the water and then dove head first into the light chop caused by the evening breeze.

Now she began taking off her shoes, her dress, her underthings. She stood up and walked toward the water, hoping Abe wouldn't see her, but also wishing he would. She wanted him to see her bare breasts and long legs. To see how well she had filled out in the last couple of years. To see how available she was.

Faith began swimming toward Abe, who sat on the swimming raft, his feet dangling in the water.

"Who's out there?" Abe yelled when he saw someone swimming toward him.

"It's Faith, Faith Hanson."

"What are you doing out here?" Abe asked, covering himself with his hands.

"I thought it was a good night for a swim," Faith said. She continued swimming toward the raft, her body shining in the near darkness. Upon reaching the structure, she climbed up the ladder and sat down by Abe. He continued covering himself with his hands but couldn't help but look at Faith's naked body sitting so close to him on the raft, too close.

"You don't have to cover yourself," Faith said. "I've seen a man before," she lied.

She took his hand to pull it away.

"Out there on the raft." Both Faith and Abe heard it at the same time.

"This is Marshal Lightfoot. Who is on the raft?"

"Let's slip into the water," Abe said quietly.

"Preacher Jacobs and I are here, and we see you," Marshal Lightfoot yelled again.

"Give me your names," the marshal yelled.

"Follow me," Abe said as he began swimming further down the lake, away from the prying eyes of the marshal and the pious preacher. Beyond the sight of the intruders, Faith and Abe waited in the deep shadows on shore until they knew Preacher Jacobs and the marshal had given up and had gone on to correct other errors of the night.

They found their clothes, each dressing quietly in the dark. "When are you going swimming again?" Faith asked.

"I . . . I don't know," Abe stammered.

41

Abe Farming

May 1901

The spring sun bore down on Abe Starkweather's back as he guided the team of Percherons across the newly plowed field where he would plant corn in a few days. A meadowlark sitting on a fence post sang its spring song, its yellow breast reflecting the sunshine of the morning. Bluebirds, with their brilliant blue backs and orange breasts, flew about, and the occasional thirteen-stripped gopher sunned itself on the rock piles that Abe's father had made as he re-moved the ever-present stones from the fields. A red-tailed hawk made big circles in the sky as it caught the thermals of the sun-warmed soil, its call a loud-pitched "kree, kree." A red fox resting on a hill looked down on the plowed field with interest. But Abe neither saw nor heard any of this. He rode on the seat of a disk har-row that bounced along on the rough plowed surface, occasionally hitting a stone, which made a sharp sound, like a hammer pounding on a piece of steel. And he hated every minute of it.

Abe had turned twenty-five in February; he still lived with his parents, Silas and Sophia, working this miserable farm that his father had homesteaded. The land was stony, sandy, and hilly—three characteristics that would turn even the most dedicated farmer against the place. He figured his father also hated farming, although the two didn't talk about it. They didn't talk about much of anything. He and his father simply didn't get along; they never did. About the only words the man spoke to his son concerned work he wanted Abe to do. He had paid little attention to the lad when he was growing up. Silas had seldom attended any of Abe's school events, except when Sophia insisted that he go along, such as when the school held the annual Christmas programs and the end-of-school-year picnics.

Abe couldn't wait to leave the home farm, but he didn't know how he could do it. He had no money, and though he could read and write and figure well, he had had many disciplinary problems as a student. More than once his mother had been summoned to the school to talk with his various teachers over the years. Abe seemed to have been born with a chip on his shoulder, so fighting became common for him at school. And bullying young kids had also been one of his shortcomings. All of this showed up as black marks in the "Deportment" column on his report cards.

Without the careful intervention of his mother, Abe would not have fared as well as he had in school—in fact, on more than one occasion, the teacher had threatened simply to kick him out once and for all. "It would be good riddance," Miss Emerson had said in disgust to Sophia at one of their several meetings. Sophia promised Miss Emerson that Abe would behave himself in the future, which he did for a couple weeks before returning to his old behavior.

As Abe worked his way across the sandy field, he gave the horses occasional slaps on their rumps with the leather lines when he thought they weren't pulling hard enough or walking straight. Silas had warned Abe more than once about striking the horses, but the boy didn't listen. Why should he listen to his father now, after all these years, when he felt ignored by him? Besides, these were merely horses and not very good ones either. If they had more money they could afford better horses, could afford better everything, including a better house than the house they lived in. They still lived in a log cabin, the same one that Silas and his neighbors built back in 1866.

When Abe got to the end of the field, he jerked on the lines to turn the team and started back in the direction from which he had just come. Every time he worked in these little five-acre fields he cussed his father for making them so small. What a nuisance to keep turning and watching out so the team and the implement they pulled didn't run into one of the fences that surrounded each field!

For Abe, farmwork was mindless activity, with no future in it. He detested the dust and dirt, the heat and the sweat that poured down his back, and the nasty smell of the horses that swirled around him. There was not only the sour smell of horse sweat, but the team seemed to break wind constantly, filling the air with the pungent smell of stomach gas.

As Abe drove the team, he let his mind wander. He thought of his grandparents Wolfgang and Amelia Reinert, who had farmed up the road. He had liked his grandmother, who cooked special dishes for him and had kind words for him. Not so his grandfather. When he spoke to Abe, Wolfgang usually emphasized something he had done wrong at school.

Now both grandparents were dead, Grandpa in 1888, and Grandma in 1893. His uncle Emil and Emil's son Mort now ran the farm. He had never gotten along with Emil and especially Mort, and he still didn't, although as neighbors they had to share work such as grain threshing and silo filling.

Abe also thought about the old preacher, Increase Joseph Link, who had traveled around the state shouting about saving the land. What did that old fool know about the land? Everyone knew he was the world's worst farmer. Abe could never see what his mother saw in the old preacher. He had died back in '93, the same year his grandmother did. Good riddance, Abe thought. What the world needs less of is preachers, shouting and shooting off their mouths about the sinners in their midst. He thought that especially of the Reverend Jacob Jacobs, who had nearly caught him skinny-dipping a few years ago. He'd liked to have pulled that old Bible-thumper into the lake and given him another baptism, one he wouldn't have forgotten.

When Abe once more arrived at the end of the field, he saw his mother walking up the lane, carrying the water jug for him. She waved, and he lifted his arm for a half-hearted wave back.

About all he could think about these days was how to get away from this old, boring farm. He had read in the *Link Lake Gazette* about life in the big cities, Milwaukee and Chicago, and how they now had electric trolley cars that people rode in. He'd read that some people even owned horseless carriages, little machines that carried them around without so much as a horse in sight.

Abe wished he had a special talent. He had read about Harry Houdini, who had grown up in Appleton, Wisconsin. Houdini did what he called "escapes," with performances in big theaters across the country and even in London, England. Abe wished he could do something like that, something that would make him famous, pay him lots of money for no hard work, and allow him to live in a big city.

He also read in the paper that the Prohibitionists were gaining attention, standing up and yelling about how terrible saloons were and the disastrous effects of beer and whiskey. Spending Saturday nights at the Link Lake Tap had become the only exciting thing in his life. So what that he got drunk once a week? He was usually ready to go back to work on Monday morning.

Drinking became the topic on which his mother and he differed most. She, since working with Increase Joseph, had taken up the tee-totaling cause that was sweeping the country.

"It's only once a week," Abe pleaded with his mother.

"And that's once too often," she said.

"Whoa," Abe said to the team when his mother approached with the water jug, stopped with a corncob. She handed it to her son, and he pulled out the cob and took a long drink, wiping the back of his hand across his mouth when he finished.

"Smile pretty," his mother said.

"What?" Abe said. His mother held a little box, which she was staring down into.

"I'm taking your picture."

Her son smirked at her; he had never had his picture taken, nor had he seen a camera.

"Came in the mail today," Sophia said. "I ordered it from the Sears and Roebuck catalog."

"Got to get back to work," Abe said as he shouted "Giddap!" to the team and tugged on the lines.

Sophia stood staring at her son, a cloud of dust swirling around him as the team plodded across the field. She turned and walked slowly down the lane toward the cabin, carefully carrying her new Kodak camera.

42

Ole Brothers Circus

July 1902

One day the following year, in July, the Ole Brothers Circus showed up in Link Lake for two performances, one in the afternoon and one in the evening. The circus moved from town to town by horse-pulled wagons. It was quite a sight to see the circus moving down the road, a string of fifteen circus wagons with an elephant walking in the midst of the entourage.

The Ole Brothers Circus didn't amount to much. True, it had an elephant. Circus-goers said that if a circus didn't have an elephant, then it shouldn't be called a circus. The elephant's name was Nan; she was a huge beast that had grown old and slow but was mostly docile and seemed to enjoy the crowds of people that came to the circus and mainly just gawked at her as she stood tethered just outside the big top.

The Ole Brothers—Karl, Otto, and Ole—were brothers all right, but their last name was really Gulbrandson. They considered calling themselves the Gulbrandson Brothers Show, but finally settled on "Ole" for a name. "Ole" was short and to the point and didn't require as much paint when they made signs announcing the show's arrival. Besides, Ole Gulbrandson was the oldest of the three and had the final say involving decisions of some import.

Abe rode his horse to Link Lake in time to watch the circus put itself together on a warm, early July morning. As he stood gaping, one of the head guys asked if he'd like to help out, drive some stakes, stretch the canvas, put up the big top.

"Sure," Abe said. At age twenty-six he was tall, strong, and accustomed to hard work on the farm. With a little practice, he was soon pounding stakes as well as the experienced roustabouts who traveled with the show.

When Ole Gulbrandson learned that Abe knew how to drive horses, he took him off to the side.

"How'd you like to spend the summer traveling with our show?" Ole asked.

"Nah, Pa expects me to work on the farm."

"Tell you what, you come with us and I'll teach you how to drive our six-horse team, and that's all you'll do, no more pounding stakes and stretching canvas. Besides that, we'll pay you $3 a day, with free meals and a cot to rest your head." What he didn't tell Abe was they mostly traveled at night and sleep was a rare commodity.

Abe explained all of this to his mother and dad, who were dead set against the idea but agreed when he said he'd give them half of what he earned. So Abe Starkweather was away from home for the first time and traveling with a circus. And he was off the farm. His dream had been fulfilled.

By the third week with the circus, he had mastered driving the six-horse team in parades and down the road at night when they traveled to the next town. He fell into the routine of the circus, which was repeated day after day, night after night, as the Ole Brothers Show made the rounds of Wisconsin's small towns and cities.

When the circus arrived at a town where they were to show, usually in the predawn morning, Abe would unhitch his team, water and feed them, and allow them to rest before the late-morning parade. One day while he was unharnessing the horses, the young aerialist from the show stopped by to watch and chat. Soon she was doing this every day. She said her name was Augusta Meier, although her show name was Jenny Lou Norton. The visits were a bit unusual. Ordinarily, the show people had nothing to do with the workers. But maybe, as a teamster, Abe might be considered a cut above the ordinary workers. Maybe that's why she was hanging around. It didn't matter; he began to enjoy her company.

When he wasn't working with the team, he would sometimes stop by to watch her perform in the big top. She wore the tiniest little costume, leaving not much to a man's imagination. She had long white legs and a narrow waist and bulged in just the right places. She flew through the air like a butterfly. Abe got dizzy just watching her. She performed with her brother and her father, a huge, broad-shouldered man who would catch her when she flew from trapeze bar to trapeze bar.

Abe hadn't paid much attention to the circus advertising, but he was aware that Jenny Lou Norton was one of the show's featured performers. Men especially would flock to see this scantily clad young woman perform. Of course, this was a time when women wore long dresses and blouses that came clear up to their necks. To see legs and the tops of breasts was simply not possible, except in the circus.

"Do you like what you see when I'm performing?" she asked Abe one day, while he was brushing down his team.

"I do," Abe said, blushing.

"Stop by my dressing tent when you finish with the horses," Augusta said. "I've something to show you."

Abe did as he was asked, after stopping to wash off some of the horse smell and comb back his black hair. He stopped outside the dressing tent that had her name hung on one of the tent poles.

"It's Abe," he said quietly.

Augusta pulled open the tent flap and Abe slipped inside. She wore a dressing gown that came up to her neck and reached to her ankles. Abe saw a big wooden trunk standing on the ground with the words "Jenny Lou Norton" emblazoned on the side. He also saw a washstand and a dressing table with a mirror above. A folding cot stood alongside one wall.

"Sit there," Jenny said, directing Abe to one of three folding chairs. She sat on the cot.

Neither of them said anything for a time.

"Do you like me?" Augusta asked. She was fidgeting with her hands.

Abe cleared his throat. "Yes . . . yes, I like you," he said haltingly. He could feel his face turning red.

"How much do you like me?" Augusta unbuttoned the top of her dressing gown.

"Quite . . . quite a lot," Abe stammered.

"You want to sit with me here on the cot?" She patted her hand on a spot next to her.

Abe moved over and sat beside her, his big, calloused hands on his lap.

"You been with a girl before?" she asked in a near whisper.

"Sure . . . sure," Abe lied. He could feel the red in his face moving around to the back of his neck, and he began to perspire. He remembered the time when he'd been skinny-dipping and Faith Hanson showed up, naked as a jaybird. And he remembered what had happened just a year ago when they were threshing at Olaf Hanson's farm. The crew had eaten supper and gone home, and he had stayed behind to do some cleaning up around the strawstack. He was forking loose straw up onto the stack when Faith showed up. Abe wondered what she wanted; he figured she had some message from her pa. Before he could open his mouth to ask, she had her arms around him and was kissing him hard on the lips. He dropped the pitchfork in surprise, and before you could say "roll in the straw," she was unbuttoning his bib overalls and loosening her dress.

Just about the time things began to get interesting, Abe heard her pa coming from the barn. He was whistling some strange tune as he was prone to do on occasion. About as fast as she had appeared, Faith disappeared around the other side of the strawstack while he hustled to hitch up his overalls and find his pitchfork.

"You're doin' . . . a good job there, Abe. But why don't you . . . go on home. I'll finish up," Olaf Hanson said, apparently not at all aware of what almost happened behind his new strawstack. That's as close as Abe had been to "being with a girl."

But thoughts of Faith Hanson flashed through Abe's head as he sat next to Augusta Meier who had now wrapped her arms around him and was kissing him. He discovered that she wore nothing under her dressing gown. She took one of Abe's hands and placed it on her bare breast.

Abe became a regular visitor to Augusta's tent, sometimes twice a day between her aerial performances. Of course, his fellow teamsters began teasing him and wondering what he had that they didn't. He merely smiled and went on caring for his horses.

One day, in the midst of one of his visits to Augusta's tent, the tent flap burst open and Augusta's father stormed inside. He was carrying a double-barreled shotgun and pointed it straight at Abe's head.

"You got my daughter in family way. Marry her you will, or dead you will be," Meier said.

"I . . . I," Abe stammered as he looked for his overalls. Augusta had put on her dressing gown and walked in back of her father. Her face was without expression.

"This weekend will be wedding. You will be there." Meier hesitated for a moment. "Or I blow your head loose."

Augusta's father wheeled around and left the tent. He said not one word to Augusta, who was now sitting on a chair, crying.

"I'm . . . I'm sorry," Abe said. "I . . . I didn't know. You didn't tell me."

"I thought you wouldn't want me if you knew," she said.

"Oh, I do want you, Augusta. I do want you," Abe said.

"You better get back to your horses. We'll talk tomorrow," Augusta said.

Back at the horse tent, Abe shared what had happened with his friend Tony.

"The old man had a shotgun to my head," Abe said.

Tony laughed. "That's the third time this has happened in the last two years."

"What?" Abe said.

"Yeah, the old man wants his daughter married and will do anything to make it happen. My guess is she's no more in the family way than I am."

"What?" Abe said again. "What should I do?"

"You ain't got much choice. The old man probably means it when he says he'll shoot you if you don't show up for your wedding on Saturday. What the other guys did was to skedaddle out of here as soon as they could."

During the evening performance, when Augusta was flying through the air like a butterfly into the strong arms of her father, Abe Starkweather slipped away from the show lot and started the long walk home. He hadn't even stopped to collect his back pay, as he didn't want anyone to know what had happened. In three days he was back at the home farm in Link Lake.

"What happened, Abe?" his pa asked when he came shuffling up the driveway with nothing but the clothes on his back.

"Got tired of circus life and thought I'd best come home," Abe said. He had been thinking of Faith Hanson the entire trip, trying to wash his mind of anything related to the circus. He thought he'd pay Faith a visit once he got a good night's sleep and some home cooking in his belly. Farm life began to look better.

New House and Barn

Spring 1903

Abe heard birds singing outside the bedroom window when he awakened. It was Sunday morning; his head felt like a horse had kicked him. His mouth tasted as if he'd been chewing on horse manure. He rolled over and went back to sleep. Faith, his wife of not yet a year, had been up since dawn, tending to the cattle, feeding the chickens, and even doing a little weeding in the garden that grew just to the east of their new house.

As a wedding present, Faith's parents, Olaf and Ella Hanson, hired a carpenter to build the young couple both a new wood-frame two-story house and a new post-and-beam barn with a haymow in the upper story and room for twenty milk cows in the lower one.

"Need some modern buildings these days," Olaf said. He and his family had come to Link Lake from Norway in 1861, and they had done well with their farm. They had become among the most prosperous farmers this side of Link Lake.

Olaf wasn't especially impressed with his new son-in-law, who had problems getting up in the morning, seemed to avoid work at every turn, and was overly interested in the bottle. But whatever faults Abe had, Faith made up for them. She worked hard and long and clearly was in charge of the farm.

Silas and Sophia continued living in the old log cabin. Sophia took care of a small flock of chickens and her garden, and Silas, although suffering from arthritis and a host of other maladies, continued working on his fences and, when he felt up to it, walking the fields as he had done since he moved onto the place.

Silas and Sophia were most pleased with Faith, especially her gumption, hard work, and knowledge of farming. She had obviously learned well from her father. The Starkweather farm crops and cattle had never been better. Farmers at the mill in Link Lake talked about how the farm had changed since Faith Hanson had taken over. They gave no credit to Abe, for his reputation was that of a Saturday-night drunk and all-around loser. In fact, people wondered how Faith, as smart as she seemed to be, had made such a bad choice for a husband.

As is often the case in small towns, people sometimes accused Abe of more than he was due. But he was surely no Sunday-school boy. For instance, back in early May, he had been in town on Saturday night, drank too much, and started a fight with George Polanski, a huge Polish fellow who farmed near Heffron, north of Link Lake.

Abe had called George a Polack. At first George laughed it off, said to Abe that he had too much to drink and should go home and sleep it off.

"I ain't drunk, if that's what you're sayin', you dumb Polack," Abe said. He was weaving back and forth, and his words were slurred.

"Well you sure look drunk to me," George said, laughing. George Polanski was about six and a half feet tall, weighed more than 250 pounds, and was generally quite a good-natured fellow. Abe Starkweather, when he was sober, scarcely came up to George's chin.

"Nobody accuses me of being drunk. Nobody. 'Specially no damn Polack," Abe said as he tried to stand up straight. He took a roundhouse swing at George, who stepped aside and watched Abe fall in a heap on the saloon floor.

"You're lucky," Abe said, staggering to his feet. "If I'd hit you, you'd be out cold."

George laughed and turned away, back to nursing the bottle of Blatz beer he had in front of him.

Abe grabbed an empty beer bottle off a table—George did not see him do it. Before anyone could stop him, Abe struck George Polanksi in the back of the head. George rolled off the barstool onto the floor, unconscious, blood streaming from the cut in his scalp.

Abe had never been very lucky. Marshal Lightfoot entered the saloon just in time to see him clobber George.

"Put your hands on the bar," the marshal ordered in a loud voice, drawing his pistol and pointing it at Abe.

"Me?" the surprised Abe said, blinking his eyes.

"Yeah, you. I'm talking to you; you're skunk drunk."

Abe put his hands on the bar, and the marshal promptly clamped handcuffs on them.

"You get to spend the night in jail," the marshal said.

"Somebody take care of George here; he's got a nasty cut on his head," the marshal said before dragging Abe off to the Link Lake jail, two little rooms with iron bars in the basement of the village hall.

After locking up Abe, the marshal called Faith, something he had done several times before on Saturday nights. (Shortly after they built their new house, she had insisted they have a telephone put in.)

Faith was fast asleep when she heard the phone ring. She made her way through the dark hall to the first floor of their house, where the phone hung on the wall in the dining room.

"Hello," Faith said into the mouthpiece.

"This the Starkweather residence?" the marshal asked.

"Yes," Faith replied, rubbing sleep from her eyes. She had heard the marshal's voice enough in the past to know who it was.

"Afraid I got bad news for you, Mrs. Starkweather," the marshal said. "Got Abe locked up in jail for the night. He's skunk drunk, and besides that, he hit big George Polanski over the head with a beer bottle."

"Oh my gosh!" Faith said. Usually she heard he was drunk, but he hadn't hurt anyone.

"You can come pick him up in the morning. He'll be sobered up by then. Doubt George will file any charges, so this should be the end of it. Oh, see if you can talk to that husband of yours; if he isn't careful he'll pick a fight with the wrong guy and get himself killed."

Faith hung up the phone and went back to bed. But there was no sleep for her that night.

44

End of an Era

1905

*F*aith continued doing most of the farmwork, and Abe, although he did manage to plow and plant the fields each spring and do some of the harvesting, kept drinking. His problem had gotten worse, if anything. Faith had recently brought up the situation with her mother-in-law. The two of them had become close friends. They shared a cup of coffee several times a week, along with discussions about farming plans, gardening challenges, and the like.

Faith had avoided talking about Abe; she knew that he and his mother still talked regularly, which was more than could be said for Silas, who seldom talked to his son at all. When he did, it was usually about some scrape Abe had gotten into in Link Lake on a Saturday night.

"What can I do about Abe?" Faith asked quietly. She was holding her cup of coffee with both hands and looking down. Many people had commented on how much Faith had aged since she married Abe. She was now only twenty-one years old, yet some had said she looked forty. Her once bright eyes had lost their sparkle; her beautiful brown hair hung limp. Lines had formed around her eyes, and the radiant smile that everyone remembered about her had mostly disappeared.

"I've talked to him," Sophia said. "Many times. He doesn't listen."

"It's as if he has a sickness that has grabbed him and won't let go. Like a giant snake that's wrapped its coils around him," Faith said.

"I don't know what to do," Sophia said. "I know how hard it is on you. And I know how hard you work to make this a good farm. I want you to know that Silas and I appreciate what you're doing."

"Thank you," Faith said. "Thank you so much. Abe never says a word of thanks. In fact he doesn't say much of anything anymore. Mostly he just mumbles and cusses."

"I'm sorry," Sophia said. "But remember—whenever you want to talk, just come over."

"Thank you. Thank you." Tears were running down Faith's face as she turned to leave the little log cabin and head back to the farmhouse where she and Abe lived.

That afternoon, Sophia walked quickly across the short distance to Faith's house and knocked on the door.

"Sophia, come in. Come in," Faith said.

"I am worried about Silas," Sophia said. "He didn't come home from the fields this noon for dinner. I'm afraid he may be hurt, or sick. He's not been feeling well lately."

"Abe," Faith yelled into the other room. "Your mother is here. She's worried about your dad."

"Abe," she yelled again.

Finally, a faint "What?" came from the other room.

"Your mother is here."

"What the blazes does she want?"

"It's about your father," Faith said.

"What about the old man?"

"He didn't come home for dinner this noon."

257

"Maybe he ain't hungry," Abe said.

"Can you come out here?"

"I'm taking a nap."

"Your mother is here. Talk to her."

"Tell her I'll stop over later this afternoon."

"She wants to see you now."

In a few moments the door to the back room opened, and a disheveled Abe appeared, rubbing his eyes.

"Whadda you want, Ma?" Abe said.

"It's about your pa. He didn't come home this noon. Can you go look for him?"

"Ah, Ma. It's hot out there. He probably wanted to set a few more fence posts before he came home for dinner."

"It's not like him," Sophia said. "He always comes home for his noon meal."

"It's too blamed hot for hiking to the back of the farm," Abe said, scratching himself under the arm.

"Would you do it, Abe?" his mother pleaded.

He pulled on his well-worn straw hat, pushed open the kitchen screen door, allowing it to bang shut, and slowly headed up the lane toward the back of the farm.

As he walked slowly along the path the cows had made in the lane, he stepped around the occasional cow pie covered with big blackflies. He thought about his dad and why the old man insisted on working on his blamed fences no matter how hot and uncomfortable the day might be. He even worked on them in the rain. About the only time he didn't work on his fences was when he walked his newly worked fields. Abe knew about the old man's arrowhead collection, but how many arrowheads does a person need? Besides, Abe didn't think arrowheads were all that interesting. He could think of two dozen things more interesting than digging around looking for arrowheads. Once Abe got halfway up the lane, he began yelling "Pa!" every few minutes, but there was no response.

"Pa!" he yelled again. He could never figure out his old man, or why he stayed on this godforsaken farm with its droughty soil and limited crop production.

"Pa!" Abe yelled again. He could see their herd of dairy cattle grazing in one of the former hayfields. He walked by one of the cornfields, which was doing reasonably well, although it could certainly use a good rain. He hiked by the two oat fields; the crop was turning from green to a golden yellow, and in a few weeks he'd be hitching the team to the grain binder and cutting the crop. He dreaded the harvesting work and his old man's usual reminder of how he had once cut grain with a cradle and how much easier it was now with a team and grain binder.

Abe thought of his brief experience with the Ole Brothers Circus. Maybe he would try circus work again, with a different show. At least with a circus, you got to see the country and weren't tied down with a bunch of smelly dairy cows that needed constant attention, and you didn't live in a community with a gaggle of nosy neighbors who kept track of your every action and had some comment about it, usually negative.

"Pa!" he called again.

This time he heard a faint, "Over here."

"That you, Pa?"

"Over here." Abe heard the faint sound again.

Abe turned off the lane and followed a fence line down a little hill to a valley that ran up to the big oak woods to the north.

There, on the ground by a freshly dug posthole, Abe found his father. The old man was stretched out, one arm hanging limp on his side.

"I'm sick," Silas said. "Can't get up. Leg won't work. Arm won't work. Can't breathe." The old man's words were slurred.

"Too hot to be out here," Abe said. "You should be home."

"Can't hold up my head," Silas said. "Feeling dizzy." The whispered words came slowly.

"Come closer, Abe," Silas said.

Abe leaned near to his father, closer than he had physically been to him since he was a little boy. He smelled vomit and sweat.

"Listen to me," Silas whispered haltingly. When he finished talking, he closed his eyes and said not another word.

The funeral was a simple one. Increase Joseph's son Little Joe conducted the service at the Standalone Church. They buried Silas next to his daughter, Elsa, on the hilltop back of their log cabin.

Abe had insisted on digging the grave by himself, to the surprise of the neighbors who had volunteered to do the job.

"I wanna do it," Abe said as his shirt soaked through with sweat.

After the burial, Abe, Faith, and Sophia stood by the gravesite. The simple tombstone read:

Silas Starkweather
Born: February 22, 1845
Died: July 5, 1905

45

Gravel Pit

1906

One promise Abe had made to his father was to keep the farm's many fences in order, replace the posts when they rotted, buy new wire when it became rusty, and put up an entire new stretch when a tree fell on it or a winter storm smashed the fence flat. In April, the year after his father's death, Abe worked at restoring a stretch of fence destroyed by the past season's more than average snowfall. As he dug hole after hole to replace the broken fence posts, he discovered that the soil was filled with gravel. Abe wasn't usually one to come up with a new idea, but this day a thought struck him like an unexpected kick from a horse. When he had been in Link Lake the previous day with his team and wagon, he came upon a shiny new touring car stuck in the mud along the way. He had stopped, unhitched the team from the wagon, and pulled out the car. The owner thanked him profusely and offered him a dollar for his efforts. He stuffed the dollar in his pocket.

Now, as Abe dug postholes in his gravelly soil it occurred to him that spreading some of his gravel over those stretches of muddy road would make the road passable during the spring thaw. And likewise, spreading it on the sandy hills would make them easier to climb in summer. It was even worse for an automobile to become stuck in sand than in mud. But as the old-timers said, "When you're stuck, you're stuck. Don't matter much if it's mud or sand or deep snow."

That evening, Abe climbed on one of his horses and rode to the town chairman's farm to share his new thought. As it turned out, the town chairman, Gunther Fosdick, was open to his idea. "Been thinkin' of doin' somethin' like that," he said. "Didn't know where we could latch onto any gravel."

"I got me a whole hill of gravel," Abe said, smiling. "Got maybe five acres of gravel, don't know how deep it goes, but when I dig postholes, I never get through the stuff."

"You wanna sell some of it?"

"You bet I do," said Abe. The two of them dickered for a time about prices, until they agreed that Abe would receive so much per wagonload and that he would help with the shoveling. In fact, Abe insisted not only that he help with the shoveling but that he inspect every load of gravel before it left the premises. Fosdick thought this request was a little odd—a load of gravel was a load of gravel—but he agreed to it.

Later that week, several teams and wagons appeared at Abe's place, and they threaded their way up the long lane to the area that Abe had now deemed a gravel pit. The men, township farmers that the town chairman had hired, began shoveling back the thin cover of sod and loading gravel on their steel-wheeled wagons. The township was six miles square, with roads running about every mile, so the road-graveling project would take more than a year to complete.

The gravel wagons arrived in early morning and continued coming until suppertime, every day but Sunday. Abe helped some with the shoveling, but he mostly watched carefully what went on every load.

By fall and freeze up, the gravel diggers had dug an immense hole in the side of the hill on the back of Blue Shadows Farm. Abe had more money in his pocket than he had ever known, enough so that one day, to Faith's surprise, he came home from Link Lake driving a new Oldsmobile touring car. His new car was the first one in his neighborhood; none of his neighbors made enough money from their cows and hogs to buy such a fine machine.

On Saturday night, Abe drove his new Oldsmobile to Link Lake and parked smack-dab in front of the Link Lake Tap, where all his drinking friends could see it. That night he bought several rounds for everyone in the saloon, showing off that he had a little extra money. Of course, as usual, he drank too much. He was not completely familiar with his new car, as he cranked the machine until it finally started. He climbed on the seat and pointed it toward home, on the newly graveled road. On nights like this, when he wasn't too sure of what he was seeing or hearing, he gave his horse the lead and the horse took him home and stopped by the barn door. Along the way, Abe usually fell asleep and left the trip to the horse.

Now behind the wheel of his new car, Abe fought sleep as he tried to steer the Oldsmobile down the middle of the road. He constantly pulled on the steering wheel as the machine veered from one side of the road to the other, chugging merrily along at a top speed of ten miles per hour.

On one of the little turns in the road, Abe misjudged just where the road was. Abe yelled "Whoa!" several times, but when he got out the last "whoa" several strands of barbed wire lay across the hood of the car and a broken fence post dangled by one of its front wheels. Abe was hopelessly stuck in the ditch, with the front end of the Oldsmobile in his neighbor's cow pasture. Several Holstein cows wandered over to see what all the commotion was about. One of them let out a big "moo."

"Ah, shut up," Abe said as he pushed open the car's door and fell on his face in the ditch.

He grabbed the fender of the car, pulled himself to his feet, and staggered the half-mile home. He struck a match and looked at the clock in the dining room, one o'clock.

He walked up to the bedroom, holding onto the stairway banister for support.

"Faith," Abe said quietly as he gently shook Faith's shoulder. "Faith, are you asleep?"

Slowly, she opened her eyes.

"Abe, you're drunk," she said.

"Got a little problem," Abe said. His words were mangled.

"You bet you do. Go sleep downstairs. You smell like a brewery."

"New car is in the ditch."

"In the ditch?"

"Couldn't control the son-of-a-gun. Yelled, 'Whoa,' but she wouldn't stop."

"What do you want me to do?" an exasperated Faith asked.

"Need you and the team to pull the thing outta the ditch."

Reluctantly, Faith dressed and went to the barn. She harnessed the team while Abe stood leaning against the side of the barn door.

It was nearly three o'clock before the considerably less than new looking Oldsmobile was parked in front of their house, its shiny paint badly scratched by the wire fence.

Merrifield Visits the Farm

Emma
November 2000

As I probably said earlier, I always keep a big pot of coffee going on the woodstove, no matter what season of the year. It gets a little strong by late afternoon, and when that happens, well, I just add a little water and thin it out some. Of course, first thing every morning, before I do any chores, I start a fresh pot. Some folks I know just add grounds and more water and keep the brew cooking. Now, if you want miserable coffee, that's how to do it.

I remember it being only a couple days after Modern Nature Educators put on the big show at the high school. I was still thinking about what I'd seen and heard and trying to wrap my mind around what that big company was planning to do here in Link Lake, maybe on my farm. Of course, I wondered if they still were interested in buying. I hadn't heard a word from them.

It was a chilly morning, but the snowflakes that fell the other night had all melted. It's like that here in central Wisconsin in the fall. One day it's sunny and warm, the next it's cloudy and damp. It may snow a little, then a day later the snow melts. Winter comes slowly, but it comes. It always comes; I suspect it always will. You can count on old Mother Nature.

I was reading the *Milwaukee Journal Sentinel* that's delivered to my mailbox every morning long before I get up—and enjoying a second cup of coffee after finishing a big bowl of oatmeal. I like oatmeal, always have. My mother said, "Oatmeal will stick to your ribs. Not like that stuff that comes in a fancy box."

I didn't hear the green sedan pull into my driveway until the driver slammed the door. I glanced out the window to see a tall, trim man walking up to the house carrying a small leather folder under his arm. Without hesitating, he stepped up on the porch and rapped on the kitchen door.

"Come in," I said. I stood up from the table and walked toward the door, carrying my coffee cup in one hand.

"How do you do?" the tall man said. "My name is Winston Merrifield. I'm with Modern Nature Educators, Inc."

"Yes, yes, I remember you from the school meeting," I said. "Come in, come in. A little nippy out there."

"Not bad at all," Merrifield said, pulling off his black woolen cap.

"Here, let me take your coat," I said. I put down my coffee cup and reached for the coat. I saw the L.L. Bean label.

"I'll just hang it on the back of a chair," Merrifield said. He ran his fingers through his salt-and-pepper hair, which was on the longish side, at least according to Link Lake standards.

"Would you like a cup of coffee?" I asked. "It's a little strong."

"Stronger the better," Merrifield said. He walked over to the woodstove and rubbed his hands above the black iron top. "Don't see many of these around anymore."

"No, you don't," I answered. "Not many this old anyway. My grandfather Silas Starkweather bought this stove more than a hundred years ago."

"You don't say," Merrifield said as he continued rubbing his hands over the hottest part of the stove.

"Yes, sir, Grandpa Starkweather was quite a guy, a mysterious fellow."

"How so?"

"See those fences out the window? Grandpa Silas built them. Seems every five acres of cleared land has a fence around it," I said.

"Maybe he liked small fields," Merrifield offered.

"Don't think that was it. He wasn't much of a farmer. My grandma Sophia was the farmer in the family. She was born in Germany and came here with her folks when she was a little girl. Reinert was her maiden name. Reinerts were farmers, good farmers." I took a sip of coffee and wondered why I was running on about the history of my family. Must be a nervous thing.

"Here, have a seat," I said, a little embarrassed that I had not offered sooner. I pulled one of the chairs out from the kitchen table. Merrifield sat down, and I sat on a chair opposite him.

"I grew up on a farm in Minnesota," Merrifield said. "We had a few milk cows, a pen of pigs, and a small flock of chickens. We grew some wheat, up to a hundred acres some years. Made our money on the wheat."

"So you're a farm boy. Thought you might be when I heard you talking the other night. I can usually tell who grew up on a farm. Something about how they walk and how they talk."

Merrifield laughed. "You've got me pegged. Once a farmer, always a farmer. Home farm is where I got interested in nature. Learned from my dad. He knew about wild animals, trees, birds, even wildflowers. Pa was interested in everything." Merrifield hesitated for a moment, staring out the kitchen window. "My older brother took over the home place when Pa died. I went off to college and never came back."

"Lots of young folks left the farm," I said. "Not much room in farming anymore—the way it's done these days with thousands of acres and hundreds of milk cows."

Merrifield took another sip of his coffee.

"Hear you've got this place for sale. One hundred and sixty acres, right?"

"That's right, quarter section that Grandpa Silas homesteaded when he was discharged from the Union army."

"Land's been in your family a long time," Merrifield said. He seemed to enjoy the black coffee I'd offered him. "Why do you want to leave?"

"Comes a time to make a change. I'm not so young anymore, getting a little long in the tooth," I said.

"We're all getting older," Merrifield said, chuckling. "Suppose I could look around a little, have a peek at the buildings, see the lay of the land?"

"Sure, let me pull on my boots and coat, and I'll give you a little tour." Already I could see that Merrifield had quite a different approach to things than that skinny, into-himself William Steele who had been out here before and said an aerial map had all the information he needed. I grabbed my walking stick.

I first took Merrifield to see Grandpa's log cabin, where in later years my hired man, Jim, had lived. We walked past the garden plot used by the Link Lake families. I told Merrifield how much gardening meant to these folks.

"I grew up helping my mother with the garden," Merrifield said. "Learned a lot, gardening."

"This is Grandpa's cabin," I said as we stopped in front of the little structure. The logs had aged to a deep gray, contrasting with the reddish brown of the new cedar-shake shingles I'd hired a guy to put on last fall.

"Looks kinda old," Merrifield offered.

"It is old—the oldest building on the farm. Grandpa Silas built it in the spring of 1866, when he was but twenty-one years old. He and Grandma Sophia lived in that little one-room cabin all their lives. When my dad and mother married, Ma's folks built the house I live in now."

"Very interesting," Merrifield said. He made some notes in a little notebook he carried in his pocket.

"See up the hill? That's the family cemetery. That's where my grandparents and my folks are buried," I said, pointing to the top of the hill above the cabin. "And that entire hillside leading up to the cemetery is covered with lupines. You know about lupines?"

"I do," Merrifield said. "We had them in Minnesota. Beautiful flowers."

Next I took Merrifield to the wagon shed with the corncribs on either side and the middle storage space, where I still keep the horse-drawn buggy my dad used before he bought his first car. Merrifield scratched down some more notes.

We walked up the steps to the granary door. It sagged a bit but still opened quite easily. "Here's where my dad and granddad stored their grain crops. In these bins." The air was filled with the musty smell of old grain. Dust-covered cobwebs hung everywhere. I saw a mouse hole in the corner of one of the bins, but I don't think Merrifield saw it.

Next we stopped at the chicken house, its big windows facing south to catch the sun. Even without going inside, I caught the sharp, acrid smell of chicken droppings from the twenty-five chickens that kept me supplied with eggs for eating and baking and enough to give to friends and neighbors. The laying hens were making clucking noises and scratching in the litter on the chicken-house floor.

We walked over to the big barn, also empty and unused since I'd sold the milk cows many years ago. I showed Merrifield the cow stalls, lined up in a row, and the place where a team of horses once stood, and the pen where the calves romped in fresh straw that had been my responsibility to bring into the barn each evening when I was growing up.

The last stop was the pump house, a smallish building that housed the well. I pulled open the weathered door, and Merrifield peered inside. Two little windows, covered with dust and grime, offered mediocre light. He saw a singletree hanging on one wall, and a neck yoke on another, both left over from the days of farming with horses. On a little workbench that stood in front of one of the windows, he spotted an empty Hills Brothers coffee can, filled with rusty nails, and a hammer, and a couple of rusty wrenches.

"I don't come out here much these days. Not since I had a new well put in a few years ago. One of those fancy ones with the pump down inside the pipe. Never have to worry about it. Something was always happening to that old pump jack when we used this well."

Merrifield wrote a few more notes. "Heard you have a pond on the place?"

"I do. Not a big one, only five acres or so. But sure attracts lots of wildlife."

"Can we hike to it?"

"Sure, it's just down the hill."

We walked by the tree that had been struck by lightning, but I didn't comment about it. We hiked along the trail that had been a field road and by some of the fences.

"You're right about the fences," Merrifield said. "Never saw so many fences on a farm." He wrote something in his notebook.

Once at the pond, we gazed across the water, a light breeze rippling the surface.

"Nice pond," Merrifield said. "Reminds me of Minnesota."

"The pond will be one of the things I'll miss most when I sell," I said. "In a typical spring, we'll see a pair of sandhill cranes nest here, a pair of Canada geese, several nests of ducks—mallards and wood ducks especially. And that says nothing about the deer and wild turkeys and raccoons and birds, hundreds of birds, that depend on this pond during a dry summer."

We walked back up the trail to the farmyard, neither of us saying anything. When we got to Merrifield's car, he said, "We're definitely interested in your place. It would make a great location for our manufacturing plant and destination nature center. Any idea what you want for it?"

"Nope" I said. "I do know that land prices have been climbing the last several years."

"They sure have," Merrifield said, chuckling. "Of course they're not making any more land. What's here is what there is."

"Ain't it the truth," I said.

"If we decide to buy, we'll offer you a fair price, probably more than you might get for the place if you sold locally. You'll hear from us in a couple weeks."

With that, Merrifield got in his car, and drove off. I walked back in the house and poured another cup of coffee.

Part 7

How Dry I Am

1919

*F*or the next few years, Abe Starkweather's gravel business continued to bring in money, but not at nearly the same pace as earlier. By 1919, all the roads in the area had been thoroughly covered with Starkweather gravel, including the main streets of Link Lake, Willow River, Plainfield, Almond, Pine River, Poysippi, Waupaca, and more. Unfortunately for Abe's business, the villages had begun to hard-surface their streets and thus needed far less gravel.

Abe continued driving his Oldsmobile with the wire-fence scratches across the hood until 1915, when he bought a spanking new Model T Ford touring car. A Ford dealership, Link Lake Motors, had opened in town. Abe paid $440 for the machine, which was quite an improvement over his old, beat-up Oldsmobile.

If you wanted to find Abe, especially on a Saturday afternoon and evening, you looked for his Model T parked in front of the Link Lake Tap. In recent years, he stopped working—if you call his part-time fencing activity and supervision of his gravel pit "work"—by noon on Saturday so he could spend the afternoon and evening in town.

Abe continued reading about the growing strength of the Anti-Saloon League in the state. He couldn't believe that a good German-Irish-Polish state like Wisconsin would ever close its saloon doors. His drinking friends agreed with him. How could life go on without a bottle of beer or two or three or perhaps even a stiff snort of the harder stuff? Abe couldn't see making it through the week without his Saturday saloon visit.

Yet, even the *Link Lake Gazette* carried regular stories about the evils of drink. A year or so ago, Henrietta Bakken, editor of the *Gazette,* had placed on the front page of the paper this poem:

> It was not on the field of battle,
> It was not with a ship at sea,
> But a fate far worse than either
> That stole him away from me.
> 'Twas death in the ruby wine cup,
> That the reason and senses drown:
> He drank the alluring poison,
> And thus my son went down.

Abe couldn't believe that such an inflammatory piece of writing would appear right here in Link Lake. To add to the insult, Abe's wife, Faith, cut out the poem and thumbtacked it to the wall, right by the telephone, so he would see it every day. She didn't say a word about it, didn't mention the poem once. She didn't need to; there it was, rubbing him the wrong way every time he went to the telephone.

To make matters even worse, his mother, who was now in her late sixties, had done the same thing. She, too, said nothing about it but put the poem right where Abe hung his hat when he came to visit her.

But poems in the newspaper were nothing compared to what the politicians had been doing. Abe read that the U.S. Senate had passed a Prohibition resolution in the summer of 1917. And the House of

How Dry I Am—1919

Representatives had done the same thing in December of that year. These lawmakers, apparently under great pressure from a bunch of ill-advised Christians, prissy women, and those who didn't know the great value of beer, liquor, and the sociability of saloons, wanted an amendment to the Constitution of the United States.

Abe was horrified to learn that state after state began ratifying the amendment. Among other things, didn't these misinformed people know that we were fighting a Great War in Europe, trying to bring down the mighty kaiser? When these soldiers come home from war, will we deny them a drink? The very thought of it put Abe in a sweat.

Locally, women who were members of the Women's Christian Temperance Union began marching back and forth in front of the Link Lake Tap every Saturday night. He usually ignored them when he came to town for his regular weekend bender. But he couldn't ignore the wife of the new preacher from the Church of the Holy Redeemed. She and her husband, the Reverend Clarence William Spotsworthy, were both holy terrors—in Abe's mind at least.

Abe remembered well the Saturday night when he first met Mrs. Spotsworthy; "confronted" would be a better way of saying it. He'd parked his Model T in its usual place, crawled out, hitched up his pants, and strode toward the open door of the tavern. Mrs. Spotsworthy jumped out of the shadows and stepped right in front of him.

"You scared the bejeebers outta me," Abe said.

"My good man, such language is not called for," Mrs. Spotsworthy said. She was dressed in black from head to toe; her face, with deep wrinkles, looked like a dried-up prune.

"Pardon me," Abe said, lifting his hat in a mocking kind of way.

"And where would you be headed?" the woman asked.

"Madam, I don't believe that would be any of your business."

"If it's that den of iniquity that you have on your mind, then it's my business."

"What?" a now befuddled Abe spat out.

Mrs. Spotsworthy pulled out a sign she had been holding behind her back. It read, "Close the saloons."

"Stand aside, woman," Abe said, now that he'd learned the reason for the woman's interruption. "Stand aside, or I shall push you aside," Abe had found a little backbone, or perhaps his thirst had reached a new level.

"Touch me, and I shall yell for the police," Mrs. Spotsworthy said as she stood aside for Abe.

Once in the saloon, Abe shared his experience with his friends. "What a bitch that woman is!" Abe said. "What's the world coming to when you're stopped because you're stepping into a saloon?"

The *Link Lake Gazette* opined that with a sufficient number of states ratifying the Prohibition amendment, it would go into force on January 16, 1920. And on that date, every saloon in the United States would be forced to slam shut its doors and turn its thirsty customers out into the street.

Little did Abe realize that matters were moving even faster. Abe knew that the war had ended with the Armistice of November 11, 1918—the eleventh hour of the eleventh day of the eleventh month. But nonetheless, to his horror, he read that the foes of the devil drink snuck an amendment into an agricultural appropriations bill, making it illegal for breweries to use food materials for making beer. They argued that these foodstuffs were needed for the war effort. Of course, food materials, barley especially, were used in beer making. But to Abe's way of thinking, these politicians were completely out of their minds. The war had ended ten days before the law passed. What each of these politicians needed was a stiff drink to set their thinking straight, thought Abe.

This new law said Prohibition was to go into effect on July 1, 1919, well ahead of the Constitutional amendment's specification.

How Dry I Am—1919

Here it was, already June 1919, and the Link Lake Tap owners prepared to close the place at the end of the month. Their beer supply had begun to dwindle by midmonth, and try as they might to receive emergency shipments from the big Milwaukee breweries, they couldn't. Soon they were out of Schlitz, out of Miller, had no more Blatz, not a bottle of Pabst. They had a small supply from the Berlin Brewery, a lesser amount of Point Special from Stevens Point, and a modest quantity of La Crosse's Heileman. Tucked in the back, the owners found a couple barrels of Fauerbach from Madison; it had not been one of their bestsellers. Now, with the imminent closing, customers drank anything: good beer, bad beer, it didn't matter, as long as it was beer.

On Monday night, June 30, 1919, the Link Lake Tap was filled to capacity. Of course Abe's Model T Ford was parked out front, as he had been there since noon.

By eleven o'clock, someone, no one clearly remembered who it was, got up and said, "We all should stand and sing a song."

"A song?" Abe asked. He had never been known for his singing ability, and at the moment he was quite certain he would not be able to stand either.

As best they could, the crowded room full of drunks and near drunks staggered to their feet and, in as lusty a voice as each could muster, sang,

> How dry I am, how dry I am.
> Nobody cares or gives a damn.
> I'd sell my hat.
> I'd sell my shoes,
> For one good bottle of any booze.

48

What Now?

Summer 1919

The rest of the summer of 1919, Abe Starkweather crawled out of bed each morning with no direction for the day. His head was clear, and his headaches had disappeared, especially the headache he had every Sunday morning after an all-night drinking bout at the Link Lake Tap.

Faith tried to cheer him by baking his favorite wild-berry pie and cooking meals fit for a threshing crew. But nothing seemed to pull Abe out of the dregs of despair and disbelief. Well into August, he had not yet accepted the closing of the saloon. People talking to him, which happened seldom as he spent little time in Link Lake, thought a close relative of his had died since he seemed deep into grieving and loss. In a way, that was the case. He and a bottle of beer, well, several bottles of beer, had become close friends; they were closer to him than his own wife.

Abe continued to fix fences, dig postholes, and supervise the occasional load of gravel he sold from his pit. Those who came for the gravel, now with Model T trucks, wondered why he wanted to inspect every shovelful of the material. But he did. It seemed an obsession. Some, who knew of his previous drinking habits, whispered to each other that this strange behavior resulted from being cut off from drink. When someone asked him why he inspected it so closely, he snarled, "My gravel, ain't it?"

A few people, those who knew of his father's interest in Indian artifacts, thought maybe he was looking for arrowheads. But those who thought about it for a minute knew there were likely no arrowheads twenty feet underground—which was the depth of the gravel pit in many places.

Abe did meet occasionally with his old drinking buddies—they tried gathering for morning coffee at the Link Lake Eatery. Somehow, coffee seemed a poor substitute, or no substitute at all, for a good stiff drink of bourbon or a tall glass of Blatz beer from the tap.

At one of these morning gatherings, Abe's old friend Noah Stringfellow said, "I just heard from my uncle Joe in Illinois. He said you can make beer out of potatoes."

"Is that right?" Abe asked, trying not to show too much interest. "You happen to have the recipe?"

"Well, I do. You want a copy?"

"I might. Never can tell when it might come in handy," Abe said.

Noah Stringfellow, a rather heavyset man who helped out at Link Lake Motors, pulled a stub of a yellow pencil from his pocket, wet the end with his tongue, and scratched some words on a paper napkin.

Abe glanced at the napkin, then stuffed it into his pocket without comment. The group went on talking about other matters.

When Abe got home he said to Faith, "Think I'll wander out to the potato patch to see if them early spuds are ready for diggin'."

"Don't you think it's a tad early?" Faith said.

"Well, we've had good rains. They been growin' good, and you've done a good job hoein' out the weeds. Think I'll try 'em."

Abe had never shown much interest in their ten acres of potatoes. True, he assisted with the planting. But Faith was in charge of the potato patch, as she was of all the rest of the farming operation. Faith didn't remember that he had ever offered to do any potato digging without her first nagging him to get at it.

"Where's the six-tine fork?" Abe said when he got up from the dinner table.

Faith smiled. She, of course, did most of the work around the barn, forking the hay, forking out the manure, forking oat straw for bedding. Of course she knew where to find the fork.

"Hanging just inside the south barn door," she said.

Abe wandered off to the barn, found the fork, and headed up the long lane to the potato patch. He dug potatoes that afternoon until several bushels lay on the ground, waiting to be put into boxes and hauled to the farmstead.

"Wonder if you could give me a hand with the taters?" Abe said when he returned home. He had a pleasantness to his voice that Faith hadn't heard for a long time.

"How many you got?" she asked. She expected he would say a bushel or two.

"Got a few bushels; we'll need the team and wagon."

Abe went to the barn, harnessed the team, and hitched them to the steel-wheeled wagon. They drove to the potato cellar, a building they had constructed some years earlier, which was partially underground. Here, in the underground part, they stored their potato crop each fall. A stone wall about eight feet high surrounded this lower section of the building—with a door to the outside on the exposed end. The upper part, of wooden construction, was where they kept machinery. Faith had stacked fifty-some bushel-sized wooden potato crates in the upper part of the building, waiting for the fall harvest.

"How many crates do we need?" Faith asked. She grabbed up a cluster of three piled together.

"Ten or fifteen should do it," Abe said, smiling.

Faith couldn't remember that they had ever harvested this many potatoes this early in the season. In fact, she wondered about the wisdom of it all. With a few more growing weeks, the yield would be much greater, and besides, she didn't know what the market for potatoes would be in late August.

Faith helped Abe pick twelve bushels of medium-sized potatoes—they would have been larger if Abe had waited a month to dig them. Soon they were back at the potato cellar, dumping the potatoes into one of several potato bins.

"Where you gonna sell these potatoes?" Faith asked.

"I got a market in mind. But it's kind of a secret."

"A secret?"

"You'll soon see that I know what I'm doing," Abe said.

"Well, I hope so. We need the money, since our gravel business has dwindled down to near nothing."

"Be patient, Faith," he said, smiling. He had the recipe for potato beer in his pocket.

For several weeks, he spent much of his time working in the potato cellar. Faith heard pounding, saw Abe carrying water from the well, and wondered why he had fired up the woodstove in the building that they used only in winter to keep the potatoes from freezing.

"What are you doing in the potato cellar?" Faith asked one day.

"Give me a little time; I want it to be a surprise," Abe said.

Curiosity got the best of Faith. One day when Abe was in town, she walked to the potato cellar, pulled open the door, and looked inside. Without windows, the place was damp and dingy. She lit a lantern that hung on a nail near the outside entrance and made her way to the back of the structure, where she saw a wooden partition with a door. A big padlock hung on the door latch so she couldn't get at or see what was behind the partition. She smelled something unusual, kind of a sweetish aroma mixed with that of cooking potatoes. When Abe returned home, she didn't inquire about the wall or the door. But now she was more than a little curious. She also knew that Abe had made no attempt to sell any of the potatoes they had dug, even though now the potato bin was less than half full. In early October, when he should be digging the rest of the potato crop, as well as cutting corn and doing a host of jobs in preparation for winter, he was still spending an hour or more a day in the potato cellar.

On a warm October Saturday, Abe said at the dinner table that he had invited several of his friends over for a little party that night and that she should not be concerned with fixing anything because they would be gathering down by the potato cellar. Faith thought the potato cellar was about the last place where she would invite her friends, but she didn't say anything.

With a full moon, it was a beautiful October evening. Abe's friends began arriving around nine, several carloads of them. They parked their cars and gathered near the cellar, as per Abe's instructions.

"I've got a surprise for you," Abe said. He had several corked bottles of clear liquid on a little table in front of him.

"What you got there, Abe?" one of the men asked.

"This here is potato beer," Abe said. "And pretty blamed good, too. Made it myself."

"Potato beer, huh?" another fellow piped up. "Didn't know you could make beer out of potatoes."

"You can make beer outta most anything," Abe said. "Noah Stringfellow, I want you to try the first bottle. Got the recipe from you. You deserve to be my first customer."

Stringfellow, a big grin on his face, stepped up to the table. Abe handed him one of the corked bottles.

"Don't look like beer," Stringfellow said.

"It's the taste that matters, not the looks," Abe said.

Stringfellow struggled with the cork for a bit, then it popped out of the bottle, followed by a geyser of clear liquid that shot out on the ground.

"You gotta move faster," Abe said. "You yank the cork then pop the bottle into your mouth."

Stringfellow slowly removed the cork from another bottle.

"Quick, pop it in your mouth," Abe said when the cork came lose.

Stringfellow did as he was told and immediately a stream of potato beer shot from each of his nostrils.

The group broke into hilarious laughter that went on for several minutes.

"Well, who's next?" Abe asked when the laughter died down.

Not one person stepped forward.

"It's good stuff," Abe said. "Lot's of power in it."

"A little too much power—about blew off Stringfellow's head."

Soon, the disgusted and disappointed group climbed into their cars and headed back toward Link Lake. Abe was left with a powerful batch of potato beer, that, in a few days, began exploding by itself. The little room in the back of the potato cellar became the most dangerous place in Ames County until all the potato beer bombs had blown up.

Abe was depressed for days. He never did tell Faith what he had been up to, but she surmised. She also heard the explosions, which confirmed her thoughts about homemade booze going bad.

Abe once more drifted into a haze of depression and despair.

49

Visitors

Summer 1920

Abe's former drinking buddies spent the winter discussing his potato beer and how it almost blew off the top of Noah Stringfellow's head when he tried it. A couple of them also heard about the explosions that went on for more than a month, at all hours of the day and night at the Starkweather place. People who heard the loud noises said they figured Abe was firing his shotgun at critters trying to molest his wife's chickens. But those who knew about the potato beer surmised correctly that the overly active brew had simply exploded, sounding like a ten-gauge shotgun going off right beside your head. People who'd heard the explosions also wondered why Abe was firing his shotgun at three in the morning. Dr. Cleever said he had been out delivering a baby and drove by the Starkweather place about that time when he heard a shotgun go off—that's what he reported anyway.

The explosions at the Blue Shadows Farm became the talk of the town. If it wasn't one thing about that place that sent tongues wagging, it was another. Many remembered Abe's father and how he'd wandered around his plowed fields walking with his head down and his arms behind his back, apparently searching for arrowheads. When he wasn't searching his fields, he was digging postholes and setting more fences. Always making fences, it seemed. Nobody had made as many fences as Silas Starkweather.

And Abe, well, everyone knew him as one of several town drunks who avoided work at every turn and seemed committed to one hare-brained idea after the next. People did say that his gravel-pit idea had paid off and earned him a tidy sum, besides providing a real service to the auto drivers in the community, who by now included just about everyone.

Most of the local women had nothing good to say about Abe Starkweather. They remembered his drinking bouts and even more could not believe he opposed the right of women to vote. He spoke out against the Nineteenth Amendment to the Constitution right up to the day it was ratified—August 18, 1920, and he continued to rail against it even after its passage. His behavior was unbelievable, especially considering both his wife, Faith, and his mother, Sophia, had been strong proponents of women's suffrage.

Why Faith put up with this man, no one could understand. She did the majority of the work and did it well, as Blue Shadows Farm had never grown better crops nor had a better herd of dairy cattle since she'd essentially taken over the operation. But Faith had another side that most people didn't know about. She liked to have nice things: a nice house to live in, up-to-date furnishings, a good automobile, the best of everything. It took money to have these things, and she got a taste of the good life when Abe's gravel pit brought in more money in a month than income from the milk cows did in a year.

The story of Abe's potato-beer experiment spread widely among those seeking an alternative to the golden liquid that they had come to love so much and was not now available since Prohibition had reared its ugly dry head—at least not legally available.

Several men secretly tried various recipes for homemade brews, with varying degrees of success. Abe's closest friends, although laughing at the volatile potato beer, encouraged him to try something else. After all, he had most of the necessary equipment in the locked room at the back of his potato cellar.

"Nope, no more potato beer," Abe said.

"We don't mean potato beer. Something else. You thought of moonshine?" one of his better-informed friends asked.

"Thought about it. And that's where it ended," Abe said. He continued digging postholes, wandering his cultivated fields, and exploring every square foot of his gravel pit, which was little used these days.

A few days after the comment from his friend, who told him he didn't know how much longer he could live without a drink, a big black Packard pulled into Abe's yard. The long black car had Illinois license plates and dark windows so you couldn't see inside. Two men, a tall one and a short one, wearing dark suits and fedoras got out and walked to Abe's door. Faith went to the door, as Abe was reclining on the sofa in the dining room.

"This here the Starkweather place?" the tall one asked. He had a hoarse voice and a way of speaking that Faith had not previously heard.

"Yes, it is," Faith said. "But if you're salesmen, we don't want any. One blamed salesman after the other stopping by these days."

The tall man laughed; the short one smirked a little.

"Nah, we ain't salesmen. Your old man home? Abe's his name, right?"

"Yes, my husband's home."

"Say, what does 'Abe' stand for anyway?"

"Stands for Abraham," Faith said, her curiosity rising about these two well-dressed men.

"Sounds right out of the Bible," the tall man said.

"You some kind of evangelical church guys wanting to convert us or something?" Faith asked. She stood with her hands on her hips.

Now both the big man and the little man began laughing, loud, too.

"Nah, we ain't much for religion, but we'd like to talk to that husband of yours," the tall man said. So far the little man had not said a word, but kept looking around, staring in all the corners of the kitchen, looking out the window to the outside, even staring at the ceiling. Faith wondered if he had some kind of deficiency.

"Abe," Faith called.

A weak "Yeah" came from the dining room.

"Couple men here wanna talk to you."

"Whadda they want?" came from the dining room.

"What is it you gentlemen wanted?" Faith asked.

"It's personal," the tall man said.

"They don't say," Faith said toward the closed door of the dining room.

After a few minutes of uneasy silence, Abe shuffled into the kitchen. He wore pants but no shirt and was in his stocking feet. He had not shaved in several days, and his hair stood on end in several places.

Abe looked the two men up and down for a few moments and said, "Yeah?"

"We was wondering if we could talk to you in private," the tall man said.

Abe motioned toward Faith, and she disappeared through the dining room door, shutting it behind her.

"I'm Bernardo, and this here is Little Louie," the tall man said.

"You got last names?"

"Yeah, but you don't need to know 'em," Bernardo said.

"This guy ever say anything?" Abe asked, motioning toward Little Louie.

"Nah, Little Louie don't say much. Don't need to. He's got his voice tucked under his arm," Bernardo said.

"Under his arm?"

"I gotta spell it out for you?" Bernardo asked. Little Louie patted something under his coat.

"Well, what was it you wanted to tell me that my wife couldn't hear?"

"Heard you know how to make potato beer?" Bernardo asked.

"How'd you hear about that?"

"Word gets around. You got any of it left?"

Abe laughed. "Hardly. Stuff all blew up. Busted every bottle. Paid good money for them bottles, too. Stuff stunk like hell."

"Heard you got some good equipment," Bernardo said.

"Ain't that good. Stuff I made woulda worked better as bombs than something you'd wanna drink."

"You interested in a better recipe, something that'd turn out good?"

"Might be," Abe said, scratching himself on his bare chest. "But how do I know you guys ain't workin' for the government and just wanna set me up so you can send me to the slammer?"

Now both men commenced laughing.

"We work for Al in Chicago," Bernardo said. "Yeah, big Al. You know about him?"

"Yeah, sure, I know about Al," Abe lied.

"Well, Al wants to set up some cooperative arrangements, especially up here in Wisconsin," Bernardo said.

"Cooperative arrangements?"

"Yeah, we get you started in business, provide you with the know-how, and help you through the first couple months, and then Al will buy your product. Pay you a good price, too."

"Well, I don't know," Abe said, scratching his weeklong growth of whiskers. "Don't want no repeat of my potato beer."

"No more potato beer. We'll show you how to make the good stuff. No more bottles blowing up."

"I'll have to give this some thought," Abe said.

Bernardo looked to Little Louie. "Louie, you got a bottle of the stuff in your coat."

Little Louie dug out a small bottle of clear liquid and handed it to Bernardo, who in turn handed it to Abe.

"What do you call this stuff?"

"Got a bunch of names. We mostly call it purified corn water."

"What?" Abe said, as he had not heard the term before.

"Yeah, that's what we call it. Purified corn water. Since Prohibition came along, people in Chicago took to drinking regular water. Made 'em sick. So we started selling them purified corn water. It's safe to drink, better than water by a long shot. Take a swig, see what you think."

Abe unscrewed the cap from the little bottle, lifted it to his lips, and took a big swallow of the clear liquid. A big smile spread across his face.

"Best water I ever tasted," Abe said in a near whisper as the clear liquid had about taken his breath away.

"We'll be back in a week," Bernardo said, "with the recipe and a little extra equipment."

Little Louie gave one more look around, then Bernardo opened the kitchen door and the two men left. The big black Packard roared off into the dark night.

"What'd those big shots want?" Faith asked when she heard the men leave and returned to the kitchen.

"Want me to make some purified corn water for 'em. Said the drinking water was bad in Chicago and there was a market for this special water."

"Never heard of purified corn water before," Faith said. "This another one of those dead-end projects, like when you wasted a bunch of good potatoes?"

Purified Corn Water

Summer 1920

*J*ust as they had promised, Bernardo and Little Louie drove into the Starkweather farmyard a week later, an hour or so after dark. This time Abe was waiting for them. During the week, he had cleaned up the mess the exploding potato beer had left in his secret room in the back of the potato cellar, swept up the broken glass, and brushed down the cobwebs that had accumulated in the corners. He'd even shaved, combed his hair, and put on a clean shirt.

Bernardo walked up to the kitchen porch where Abe stood. Bernardo was smoking a big black cigar.

"You like a cigar, Abe?" Bernardo said by way of greeting.

"Sure," Abe said. He had never smoked a cigar before. He mostly smoked an old corncob pipe with strong tobacco he bought at the mercantile in Link Lake.

He stuck the big cigar in his mouth; it felt like a small tree limb.

"Here, I'll light it for you," Bernardo said as he struck a match and held the yellow flame to the long black cigar. Soon a big cloud of gray smoke swirled around Abe's head.

"Pretty good, huh?" Bernardo said, taking another big drag on

the one he was smoking. Little Louie was walking around the farmyard, peering behind the buildings, opening doors here and there.

"What's he doin'?" Abe asked.

"Oh, just lookin' around. Can't be too safe, you know. Never
know what's out there hidin' in the corners and movin' in the dark."

"You thought about our proposition?"

"Well, I have given it some thought," Abe said.

"What'd you come up with?"

"Decided I'd like to give your idea a try. Can't hurt none to try
somethin' new. Always said that. Can't hurt to turn in a new direction once in a while," Abe said.

"Pleased to hear it. Al'll be pleased, too. Won't he, Little Louie?"
Little Louie had appeared around the corner of the house. Abe
hadn't heard or seen him coming. Little Louie shook his head up and
down a couple times.

"You got that recipe for this here purified corn water?"

"Got her right here. What say we go over to your office and discuss it," Bernardo said.

"Yeah, my office," Abe said, not sure where he would take them.

"The place where you made the wild potato beer."

"Yeah, sure. First let me light this lantern. Little dark there in the
potato cellar."

Abe lifted the globe on the barn lantern, then struck a match and
touched it to the cloth wick.

"Just follow me over here to the potato cellar. Got a special room
in the back, all boarded off so those not needin' to see what I'm doin'
can't," said Abe.

The threesome walked across the farmyard toward the little
building, now hidden in the shadows. A slice of a new moon hung
in the eastern sky, and a hoot owl called away off in the deep woods
to the north. A whippoorwill called its name again and again from
somewhere on the hillside near the pond.

"Dark as Hades out here," Bernardo said.

"Does turn a little dark when the sun goes down. Like it that way though. Like it when it's dark," Abe said.

"Not me. I like the lights. We got electric lights in Chicago you know. Had 'em for years," Bernardo said.

"Don't think I'd like that," Abe offered. "Some things best left in the dark."

They arrived at the potato cellar, and Abe pushed open the outer door, holding the lantern high so the two men could see their way inside.

"Can't see a blamed thing in here. Even with your lantern, it's still dark."

"You get used to it," Abe said, fishing in his pocket for the key to the padlock on the door to the secret room. Once inside, the two men began inspecting Abe's equipment, looking at each piece of it.

"Pretty good stuff you got here, Abe. Will work just fine for making purified corn water," Bernardo said.

"You got the recipe with you?" Abe asked.

"Little Louie, Abe wants the recipe," Bernardo said. He snapped his fingers.

Little Louie fumbled in one pocket and then another, finally coming up with a folded piece of paper. He handed it to Bernardo.

Bernardo handed it to Abe. "Here it is. Let me hold your lantern so you can read."

Abe began reading:

PURIFIED CORN WATER

40 pounds of corn (dry and ripe field corn)
20 gallons of water (rainwater is best, but any clean water will
   do)
4 cups of yeast

Directions: Put the corn in burlap bags and wet with warm water. Place bags in a warm, dark place and keep moist for about

294

ten days. When the sprouts are about ¼ inch long, the corn is ready for the next step. Wash the corn in a tub of water, rubbing the sprouts and roots off. Throw the sprouts and roots away, and transfer the corn into your primary fermenter. With a wooden pole, mash the corn, making sure all the kernels are cracked. Next, add boiling water. When the mash is cool, add yeast. Seal fermenter with a water-sealed vent. Fermentation takes seven to ten days. When fermentation is done, pour into your still's kettle, filtering the material through a clean bed sheet to remove all the solids. Heat the kettle and catch the liquid at the end of the condensing coils. The liquid that comes off first is best and most powerful. To test for purity, put a little of the liquid in a spoon and touch a match to it. It should burn with a blue flame. If it burns yellow, don't drink it. It may kill you, as something has gone wrong in the process.

"Well, what do you think?" Bernardo said when Abe finished reading.

"I think I can do it. I got lots of corn. Can grow more here on the farm. Got a good water well. When the wind blows and the windmill turns, I got lots of good water. Think I got what's needed."

"Then we got a deal?" Bernardo said. "You make it; we'll buy it."

"Got a deal," Abe said as he and Bernardo shook hands. Little Louie had once more disappeared.

"We'll be back in a few weeks to see how you're doin'," Bernardo said. A big cloud of gray smoke came from his mouth before he spoke.

"Bring you some more cigars, too," said Bernardo.

The two men got into their big Packard, fired up the engine, and turned down the road.

"Well?" Faith said when Abe came into the house.

"Well, what?"

"You gonna do what those guys want?"

"Yup, gonna make a pile of money, too."

"Let's hope so. Price of milk doesn't amount to much these days. Sure could use a little more money around here."

Purified Corn Water—Summer 1920

"Be a bunch more money once I get the hang of makin' this purified corn water," said Abe. He took another big drag on his half-gone cigar. The gray smoke settled under the ceiling of the kitchen. Faith waved her arm to move the foul-smelling smoke away from her.

51

Living High on the Hog

Summer 1922

*T*wo years passed. Money from Abe's "purified corn water" project poured in, making him and Faith even more money than they made selling gravel. Bernardo had made it clear to Abe, though, that he shouldn't tell anybody what he was doing. Bernardo said some people wouldn't understand the importance of purified corn water, especially certain people in authority, and more especially federal officers who prowled the countryside looking for operations like Abe's.

Even with no marketing whatever, Abe had a rather steady supply of customers who came to the farm, always at night. Abe would plead ignorance to anyone stopping by in the daytime. He'd tell them they must be mistaken and should look elsewhere for what they wanted.

Abe's neighbors suspected what he was doing, but they weren't about to tell anyone. Abe had turned most of his cultivated acres over to corn growing. He added a few hogs to his livestock collection. If someone passing by asked about the acres of corn he grew, he told them he fed it to his pigs. He did. But most of it found its way to the little room in the back of the potato cellar where smoke came from the stovepipe nearly all hours of the day and night.

Anyone who didn't suspect Abe and Faith had an outside source of money thought this young couple had become exemplary farmers. Everything was neat and tidy around the place. The house was painted, the grass kept clipped. They also had a full-time hired man who milked and cared for the cows and did the field work, the plowing and planting, and the corn harvesting. No other farmer in this rather poor community could afford a hired man. Even with the extra help, Abe insisted on building and repairing fences by himself, something that made no sense to anyone, especially to the hired man, who was happy to do the work. Abe also walked the fields after plowing and soil preparation, with his head down and his hands behind his back. This made even less sense, but it was a reminder of what his father had done until the very end of his life.

Besides the hired man, Faith also employed a full-time maid who took care of the housework, cooked meals for Abe and Faith, did the washing and ironing, and generally kept the house in order. She had a room upstairs in the house.

Unlike any of the other neighbors, the Starkweathers hooked up to electricity. The village of Link Lake got electricity in the early 1900s, when the miller installed a water-powered generator. Abe personally paid for setting electric light posts and stringing wire from the village to his farm. Faith ironed with an electric iron. She washed clothes with a washing machine powered by an electric motor. Electric light bulbs illuminated every room in the house and in the barn and all the other outbuildings, including the potato cellar. A light fixture high up on a post lighted the farmstead and was kept on all night. Abe had become quite concerned about those who might try to steal some purified corn water. Word of the high quality of his product had gotten around, and everyone, it seemed, wanted some of it, whether they had money to buy it or not.

Faith dressed in the finest clothing she could buy. Each fall she took the train to Chicago to buy new clothes. She stayed overnight at the Palmer House and spent a couple of days shopping at Marshall Field's for the most stylish and up-to-date clothing available.

Where once folks around Link Lake had seen Faith Starkweather as a young, energetic farm woman, they now thought she'd begun putting on the dog a good deal more than she ought.

One day when she and Abe were eating breakfast, Faith said, "We need a new barn. This old barn we have just won't do anymore. We need something new, something more modern, something up-to-date."

"Well, I guess we can afford it," Abe said, smiling. He had just returned from one of his weekly trips to Chicago, where he had delivered a load of purified corn water to one of Al's several warehouses. Abe never knew where to deliver the product until the day before he left. He would get a short phone message: "Number Two." That was the extent of it. The warehouses had coded numbers that only a select few people knew.

"What kind of a barn should we build?" Abe asked.

"I've been paging through the new Sears Roebuck catalog. Those Sears barns look mighty appealing."

She had her eye on what Sears called its "Blue-Ribbon Modern Dairy Barn." She selected the largest one of this type. It was 36 feet wide and 140 feet long. The haymow would store 210 tons of hay.

"I think this is the one we should buy," Faith said. "As you say, we can afford it."

Two weeks later Abe got a call from the depot agent in Link Lake. "Your new barn is here," he said. "Came in a couple train cars. Come fetch it anytime you want."

Abe got in touch with the dray company in Link Lake that now used trucks rather than horses and wagons. It took several truckloads before the precut pieces of the barn sat in a big pile near the site for the new building. Local carpenters put the pre-cut pieces together. Before two weeks passed, a big, new, impressive barn stood in front of the old one, where people could see it easily from the road. The barn featured vertical cedar siding, a row of windows stretching along both sides, double doors on the ends, two metal cupolas on the roof, big double doors at each roof peak through which hay could be unloaded. It was clearly the most modern, to say nothing about the most beautiful, barn in all of Ames County.

About the same time the carpenters finished with the barn, Bernardo and Little Louie arrived at the farm one dark night. Abe hadn't seen them for more than a year.

"Got bad news," Bernardo said. He was chewing on a big cigar.

"What is it?" Abe said.

"The feds are tightening down."

"What does that mean?"

"It means they are on the lookout for operations like yours. They come in, bust up everything, and dump the product on the ground."

Little Louie, as was his style, took to looking around the farm, inspecting the new barn, walking around the house.

"Who around here knows about your operation?" Bernardo asked.

"A few regular customers," Abe answered.

"They know how to keep their mouths shut?"

"I . . . I think so," Abe said. He had begun to perspire.

"Well, if they don't, you can expect visitors some night, and they won't be customers. They carry guns, and they ain't afraid to use 'em."

Abe began perspiring even more.

"One more thing. Them feds are setting up roadblocks and stopping any vehicle that looks like it might be carrying product. Let's see, you drive to Chicago about once a week with a load, right."

"Never been stopped," Abe said.

"Well, you will be; count on it," Bernardo said.

"When they find the stuff, they arrest the driver, take his vehicle, and dump the product in the ditch."

Abe began fishing for his handkerchief to wipe the sweat that had begun dripping into his eyes.

"Just wanted you to know," Bernardo said as he and Little Louie climbed back into their new black Packard and tore off down the road, a cloud of dust visible in the moonlight drifting behind them.

Abe didn't tell Faith what he'd just heard. A real possibility existed that their easy money might come to an end and that he might end up in jail. He didn't sleep that night, tossing and turning and running through his mind how he could keep his operation a relative secret, at least to the nosy feds.

Around four that morning, in the gray dawn of the new day, Abe came up with a solution for hauling his purified corn water to Chicago without being arrested.

All day Abe worked at modifying the trailer that held the big tank in which he hauled the corn water. That evening he stood back and looked at his effort and said, "I think this will do it."

That night he slept without waking up once, even though the next day he was scheduled to make his weekly run to Chicago. In the morning, he filled the tank and then covered it with straw. He had constructed a penlike structure on the trailer, with the top of the flat tank serving as a floor for the pen. He walked his big boar, a rather dirty-white crossbred pig, up into the trailer and headed off to Chicago. No federal officer would think to stop a farmer hauling a hog to a Chicago packing plant, which is what he would say if for any reason some officer stopped him.

For the next two years, that very same pig made a round trip to Chicago once a week. The animal had come to look forward to the journey as much as Abe did. Abe swore that the boar was even smiling as they chugged down the road, carrying the precious cargo.

52

Sorrow~Joy~Sorrow

1925

Sophia celebrated her seventy-fifth birthday in early 1925, but her health had been going downhill steadily for the past several years. Abe or Faith looked in on her every day, and Faith's maid spent part of each day at Sophia's cabin, preparing her meals and helping keep the place tidy. Sophia refused to move to the "big house," as she called it. "This log cabin is my home," she said. "It was here that Silas and I started our lives together."

Sophia was pleased with her son's good fortune and the fine farmstead they had built. But she knew, as mothers have a way of knowing, that most of Abe and Faith's income did not come from their herd of dairy cows. True, they had one of the finest herds of Holstein cattle in all of Ames County. They had a fine barn and several silos and milked their cows with milking machines. It was clearly a showplace farm; people drove by on Sundays just to see the place.

Sophia didn't say anything about Faith's fancy clothes, her expensive jewelry, her regular trips to Chicago—where she not only shopped but attended the theater and hobnobbed with some of the city's wealthiest people. She knew that the little room in back of the potato cellar and the clear liquid that flowed freely into the trailer tank that now made the trip to Chicago two times a week was the source of their money. Deep inside, she knew this was wrong, morally wrong, and also illegal. She also knew that she would never tell the sheriff, because, after all, Abe was her son, her only living child. She worried that one day officers would come by and arrest him, and he would spend many years in prison. She would be disgraced. She wanted to tell him about how wrong it was to do what he was doing, but she didn't have the strength, didn't know how to do it.

Sophia continued spending several hours a day in her gardens. Flowers grew in front of the cabin, as they had for years. And vegetables of every description grew in her vegetable garden a few yards from the house. Just beyond this was the big patch of lupines—Sophia made sure to keep the self-seeding trees and shrubs away from these beautiful blue flowers that each year attracted bees and butterflies, especially the little Karner blue butterflies no larger than her thumbnail. Sophia spent hours just sitting by the lupine patch in late May when the flowers came into bloom, looking out over the expanse of blue and watching the little butterflies flit about. When Sophia sat absolutely still, the little butterflies would sometimes sit beside her on her bench and occasionally would even rest on her open hand, where she could watch them up close.

One early afternoon in late May, when the lupines were in full bloom, Abe stopped by the cabin. The maid had earlier made Sophia lunch and then returned to the big house, which was her regular schedule.

"Ma," Abe called when he opened the cabin door and stepped inside. It was always much cooler inside the cabin, as the thick logs provided a natural insulation.

"Ma," Abe called again. He guessed that she must be taking a nap. He looked into the bedroom, a lean-to that had been attached to the cabin many years ago, when he was but a little boy.

The bed was made and no one was in it.

Abe walked back outside toward the vegetable garden and the big patch of wild lupines. There he saw his mother sitting on her favorite bench, her back to him.

"Ma," Abe called softly. Usually, when he found his mother sitting on the bench she would turn and greet him, a big smile spreading across her face. For all his shortcomings, Sophia never stopped loving her son.

This time she didn't turn. Abe called a little more loudly, "Ma." But no response.

When he faced his mother, he saw her eyes were closed and she had a big smile on her face. He immediately thought she was napping, something she often did on warm days with the spring sun high in the sky.

Gently he touched her shoulder, but she didn't move.

Three days later, another tombstone appeared on the hill above the cabin. Sophia Starkweather joined her husband Silas, and her first-born, Elsa. Sophia's tombstone read:

Sophia Reinert Starkweather
Born: April 21, 1850, in Germany
Died: May 30, 1925

To the surprise of his neighbors and his hired man, Abe dug the grave, which took him most of an afternoon. "It's the least I could do for my mother," Abe said. But, of course, he had other reasons for wanting to dig it.

With his mother laid to rest, Abe pulled shut the door on the cabin, the little building so much a part of his family's history. He decided to leave it just as it was, as he remembered it from his growing-up years.

Faith had become ashamed of the little cabin and with Sophia's death said to Abe, "Now we can tear down that eyesore."

"The cabin will remain standing," Abe said firmly. Seldom did he take a stand against the wishes of his rather headstrong wife, but the little cabin with its garden and lupine patch had become quite special to him, although he wouldn't admit it to anyone.

A few weeks later, at the breakfast table, a very surprised Abe heard some unexpected news.

"I think I'm pregnant," Faith said.

"You're what?" a disbelieving Abe asked.

"I'm going to have a baby."

"But you're too old to have children. We've never had children."

"I'm only forty-one."

The following May, when the lupines were in full bloom, a baby girl became a part of the Starkweather family. They named her Emma.

Emma grew rapidly; in many ways she took after her grandmother Sophia. She loved the outdoors and followed her father everywhere; except, of course, she was kept away from the secret room in the back of the potato cellar, with its special smells and the wood smoke coming from the metal smokestack that stuck out in back of the building.

Emma helped her mother in the garden, followed the hired man doing the barn chores, watched him milk cows, and, as she got older, insisted that she help with the cattle.

Faith dressed her daughter in the finest clothing, but Emma preferred denim overalls so she could crawl around in the dirt, inspecting worms, looking at wildflowers up close, and watching the activities of an anthill for hours.

Abe continued making his twice-weekly trips to Chicago with his load of precious liquid cargo. Al had continually encouraged Abe to produce more product, as the demand for it had continued to increase through the later years of the 1920s. But Abe refused to cut any corners. He could have produced a lower-quality product—some of his competitors were and were getting away with it. But he had high standards when it came to his special "Link Lake Purified Corn Water," as Al and his people had begun calling it some years earlier.

Abe knew he was pushing his little equipment to its ultimate capacity. By the early 1930s he had planted almost every acre of his farm to corn, and nearly every kernel found its way to the back of the potato cellar. Some passersby commented that, for all that corn, the Starkweather hogs seemed skinnier than most hogs. Of course it was true. There was little money in feeding corn to hogs. By now, though, Abe had selected a new boar to make the trips to Chicago. This pig got special treatment. He had his own pen and his own water supply and, of course, received ample amounts of corn in his diet.

By 1932, the country had fallen into a deep economic depression. The price received for milk from the Starkweather cows had fallen to its lowest level in anyone's memory. The price of pork was at rock bottom. Abe had even seen a decline in the demand for Link Lake Purified Corn Water. Now he made but one trip to Chicago a week.

On May 30, 1932, a few friends—those rather well-to-do—gathered at the Starkweathers' to celebrate Emma's sixth birthday. She had just completed first grade at Link Lake School, so it was a double celebration. Her mother baked a big cake, and Emma received many presents, including a special one from her father, whom she adored. She had been begging him for a pony for more than a year, and now she had one. The pony was named Ben, and he came complete with a shiny bridle and saddle.

"Can I ride him? Can I ride him?" Emma said when her father led the little surprise gift from the barn.

"Of course, he's your pony," her father said.

Abe helped his little girl into the saddle and led the pony around the yard as the partygoers clapped. This was clearly the happiest day in Emma's young life.

Emma fell asleep that night thinking what a lucky girl she was to have such a fine father and wonderful mother and to live at such a wonderful place as Blue Shadows Farm. And besides that, she now had her very own pony.

Sometime in the middle of the night, the time when Abe usually made his special corn water, it happened. A huge explosion lit up the sky and shook the house, awakening little Emma and her mother.

"Oh my God," Faith screamed when she looked out the window and saw that the potato cellar had blown to bits. She immediately got on the phone to alert the telephone operator that there was a huge fire at the Starkweather farm. Soon, their farmyard was filled with cars, everyone working as a bucket brigade to put out the fire and keep it from spreading to the house, barn, and other buildings.

"Hottest fire I've ever seen in a potato cellar," one of the volunteer fire fighters from Link Lake said. Most people fighting the fire didn't say anything, because they knew why it burned so fiercely.

Once the fire was out, the men began searching through the rubble, as no one had seen Abe. They found his body, badly burned, in a corner of the potato cellar. Another gravestone joined those on top of the hill. It read:

Abraham Lincoln Starkweather
Born: February 12, 1876
Died: May 30, 1932

Faith and six-year-old Emma stood with heads bowed over Abe's grave. Now four headstones stood on the lonely hill above the old cabin. Faith and her young daughter had a difficult decision to make. Would they, could they, continue to stay at Blue Shadows Farm now that Abe had died and their main source of income had disappeared? Perhaps it was time to move away, to Chicago where Faith had some friends. She knew staying in the Link Lake community would be difficult—she had almost no neighbors who would even talk to her. But without a source of income, what would she do in Chicago?

Depression, Then War

Summer 1932

*T*he Depression's strangling impact moved from the great cities to the countryside. No one escaped. Unemployed men rode the rails, traveling from town to town looking for work and settling for a meal. Scarcely a day went by but that two or three men, people called them tramps, jumped off the Chicago and Northwestern freight train when it approached Link Lake, hoping this little farm town would offer more than the place they'd just left.

"Mommy, mommy!" Emma called. "A strange man is at our door."

Faith, still mourning the tragic loss of her husband in the explosion and fire, came to the door. She saw a man so thin that his dirty, threadbare shirt hung loose, like a garment on a metal hanger.

"Spare a hungry man a slice of bread?" the man asked in a quiet voice.

Faith had heard about men like this, but this was the first one she had ever met in person.

"I'll split a pile of wood for a sandwich," the man said. His long, black, tangled hair stuck out from under his dirty hat in several directions. He smelled of coal smoke and perspiration.

"Fine little girl you got here," the man continued. "Back home I have a little girl like this."

Faith stood for a moment, speechless. "We . . . we don't have anything extra," she finally stammered.

"Then I'll be on my way," the man said. "Thank you anyway. And the Lord be with you and your little girl."

The man slowly made his way down the driveway and onto the dusty country road. Emma watched him as he slowly walked away, his head bowed, like he was looking for something on the road, or perhaps not wanting to consider what he might see ahead of him.

"Mommy, we've got extra bread," Emma said. "Why didn't we give him some? He looked hungry."

Faith bristled at the question. "He's a no-good tramp looking for a handout. He should find himself a regular job."

"But he looked hungry, Mommy. He was skinnier than any animal we've got here on the farm."

"Go play with your dolls," Faith said, turning away from her daughter and holding her head in her hands.

For a long time Faith sat at the kitchen table, staring off into space and thinking about Emma and herself now that Abe was gone. It didn't occur to her that the skinny man asking for a handout bore considerable resemblance to her own future self. At the time she didn't realize that she had lost not only her husband and their main source of income but something more precious—the support and concern of her farm neighbors. Too often in recent years, Faith had flaunted her wealth, had snubbed her considerably less-well-off neighbors, and had become the neighborhood show-off. Nobody in the Link Lake community had the kind of money the Starkweathers had at that time. Faith wasn't above letting people know it, either. For instance, she wore her fine dresses, expensive jewelry, and hats to town when she grocery-shopped at the mercantile. Ordinary folks in Link Lake didn't like to have their noses rubbed in the fact that they couldn't afford such finery. Faith seemed to enjoy showing off, which soon proved an enormous problem for her and for her daughter.

Folks in the Link Lake community had a long history of helping each other with threshing, silo filling, corn husking, pig butchering, and, of course, with pitching in when someone was ill or had gotten hurt. Now the Starkweathers, in the eyes of their neighbors, were no longer a part of the neighborhood where they lived. When Faith and Emma needed help, there wasn't any. Faith was also too stubborn to ask. So that fall, when people drove by their farm, they saw Faith driving the team on the corn binder and little Emma walking along behind, pulling the corn bundles out of the way.

As one neighbor had said a week or so after Abe died, "That Faith Starkweather has been shot right in her fancy petticoat. If anyone deserved a comedown, she certainly did." Country folk don't forget easily, especially when they believe a neighbor has gone to extremes to act like they are several notches better than everyone else. In the country, a little humility goes a long way.

Faith soon discovered that the income from their dairy herd would not cover their expenses, so she had to make some hard decisions. For the first time in several years she did not travel to Chicago that fall. She would miss the new shows in the theaters and would have to pass by the opportunity to buy new clothes for Emma and herself.

She soon learned that she would have to cut back even more. In early winter 1932, she decided to hold an auction to sell most of their prize Holstein cattle. She would keep a dozen of the best ones and move them to the old barn, the one that had stood vacant since the new Sears barn arrived.

The auction went reasonably well, but the income from the cattle was only about half of what these prize animals were worth.

A few days after the auction, Faith fired both her maid and her hired man. "I'm sorry," she told them. "But I just can't afford you anymore."

Emma and the maid, Florence Taylor, had become close friends. Florence played with Emma more than her mother did. She read books to Emma, books about birds and insects, about wildflowers and butterflies. Books about castles and dragons and knights on white horses. Florence also told Emma stories that she had made up. Florence would ask, "Give me the names of two characters," and Emma, thinking a bit, said, "How about Emil and Frank, who are green frogs living in a small pond covered with pond lilies?"

Florence would spin a tale about the adventures of these two frogs that spent their evenings going "Harrumph, harrumph." Whenever Florence "harrumphed," Emma giggled.

Florence hugged Emma as she stood on the porch, her meager belongings in one well-worn leather suitcase.

"Where will you go?" Emma asked, tears streaming down her face.

"Back home to Waupaca," Florence said.

The hired man, Henry Lackelt, had left earlier that morning. He had simply gotten up, packed his bag, and left. No goodbyes for him. By the time Faith and Emma had gotten up, he was on his way, joining that huge parade of out-of-work men who rode the rails and walked the dusty country roads, searching, begging, looking, hoping, but being generally disappointed.

Dry weather settled over central Wisconsin in 1932, diminishing the corn crop by nearly half, cutting short the hay crop, and drying up the cow pastures.

With some of the money from the sale of the dairy cows, Faith purchased more hogs. Even with the drought, she knew she would have more corn than the few pigs Abe raised could consume.

Faith worked harder than she had in years. By now, she had made up her mind to stay on the farm—she had few choices with the Depression creating so much havoc in the country. She became adamant that she would not lose Blue Shadows Farm because she couldn't pay the taxes. She knew it had been in the family since her father-in-law had homesteaded the place in 1866. Faith had heard about farmers around Link Lake who had lost their farms, because of the low prices during the Depression, and joined the growing throng of the displaced and unemployed. She was far too headstrong to let that happen to her. Besides, she had grown up on a farm. Her parents had both died several years ago, but she remembered well the lessons she had learned from her folks.

As the 1930s passed, Faith and Emma survived with hard work, careful attention to their farm, and good health that allowed them to keep working. As Emma got older, she took over much of the vegetable garden, which provided them with the majority of their food, from peas and potatoes to sweet corn and green beans. Every summer, the two of them spent many hours in their hot kitchen, canning vegetables so they would have plenty of food during the long, cold, Wisconsin winters.

Coincidentally, by December 5, 1933, the Twenty-first Amendment to the Constitution had been ratified by thirty-six states, and Prohibition was officially over. The Starkweathers' source of outside income from their "purified corn water" would have ended even if Abe had lived.

Another bit of baffling behavior continued on Blue Shadows Farm. Faith knew that Abe, for all his faults, wanted to keep the fences on their farm in good order. So, as busy as she was with other farm matters, she worked at keeping the fences repaired, setting new posts when necessary and stringing new barbed wire when stretches of the fence had been destroyed. Of necessity, she had to keep the fences around the cow pastures in good repair. No one wanted a phone call in the middle of the night from a neighbor informing you that your cows were in his corn.

It seemed to Faith that the 1930s, with Depression and drought, would never end, yet she had become confident that she and Emma would survive, no matter what.

On December 7, 1941, everything changed once more. With the Japanese attack on Pearl Harbor, the United States was again at war, this time with Japan, Germany, and Italy. In 1941, Emma was fifteen and her mother was fifty-seven.

Farm prices shot up during the war; milk rose from $1.20 to $2.50 per hundred pounds. Pork prices climbed from $6.00 to $10.00 per hundred. Now the Starkweathers had a little more money to spend on a new coat of paint for the house and barn, some new furniture in the house, and even some new clothes for Emma, who was now attending Link Lake High School.

The work didn't get easier, and it had clearly been taking its toll on Faith, who suffered from hands riddled with arthritis, knees that were essentially worn out from milking cows, and shortness of breath from a bad heart. The doctor in Link Lake told her not to work so hard, that it was time to take it a little easy. But she would hear none of it.

"Farm is finally making some money; this is no time to slow down," Faith said. Of course, Emma worked as hard as her mother during these war years when nearly everything was rationed—sugar, tires, gasoline, clothing, canned goods, coffee, shoes, and more.

Emma graduated from high school in 1943. She had been going steady with Johnny Jensen, a classmate, since they were juniors. She and Johnny, who farmed with his father near Pine River, had big plans for the future.

But right after graduation, Johnny was drafted into the army. Before he left for basic training at Fort Leonard Wood, Missouri, he proposed to Emma and slipped a little diamond ring on her finger. They spent the evening together, enjoying each other and making plans for the future.

"I will write to you every day," Emma said. "And I will wait for my Johnny to come marching home."

But Johnny did not come home. He was killed in the Battle of the Bulge. A tearful Emma wrestled with her dashed hopes for the future.

54

School Board Decision

Emma
November 2000

I was baking bread on that cold and rather dreary November day. November days could be like that, not really fall and not winter, either. I always considered November just sort of a "blah" time. The trees had lost their leaves, and a hard frost had killed all the flowers. A good time to do something creative like baking bread—I still do all my cooking and baking on the old woodstove that has nearly as much history as Blue Shadows Farm itself. I remember the story my father told about when he and my mother first moved into the big house, where I live now. Some of the neighbors had asked, "Why bother to move that heavy old cookstove? If you have a new house, you should have a new stove." Pa said to them, "That old stove was good enough for my ma and pa, and it's gonna be good enough for Faith and me." And it was good enough. I love this old stove—it's been repaired several times and had its grates replaced at least twice. Nothing beats it for baking bread and pies and cakes. Something about the kind of heat that comes from burning wood, I've decided. But I suspect this is only my opinion.

I've always liked baking bread, kneading the dough, watching the loaves rise, and then enjoying the smell of them baking. Several smells on the farm stand out in my mind and I suspect are buried in my childhood memories—fresh-baked bread, new-mown hay on a warm evening in early summer when the sun is sinking in the west, apple blossoms from the old tree that stands in the field back of the cabin. I suspect some folks would think it a bit strange to compare fresh-baked bread to new-mown hay and apple blossoms, but these would be folks who hadn't spent any time on a farm and probably have forgotten how to smell anyway.

I was pulling the last loaf of bread from the oven—I always baked three loaves, two for myself and one to give away—when I heard the phone.

"Hello," I answered, perhaps a little more gruffly than I intended because the sound of the phone had startled me and I touched my finger on the hot oven door.

"It's Kate."

"How are you, Kate?"

"You heard the news?"

"What news?"

"About the school board's decision on nature hikes?"

"Nope," I said. "Haven't had the Willow River radio station on this morning. Been busy baking bread. Got an extra loaf for you, if you want it."

"Of course I want it. Nobody makes better bread than Emma Starkweather."

"Well, what'd they decide?"

"Not good, Emma. They voted, four to one, to eliminate all nature field trips. Said it was a money-saving decision. Said the school district couldn't afford to send buses out on field trips. But more than that: The school board's attorney told them that their liability insurance would likely go through the roof."

"How'd the discussion go? As if it matters now."

"Well, Ruth Prescott led the charge. Boy, she's a piece of work, that one. Gotta give her credit, though. She's a take-charge woman. Charging all the way—no matter who she runs over. Anyway, when they got to talking about nature hikes at your farm, she said they just weren't necessary anymore. Kids could get a much better nature education with the Internet and with DVDs and computer simulations. Then she got onto the dangers of kids in the wild. I wrote down what she said: 'We just can't take a chance these days of subjecting our children to the wild, where they can be stung by bees, bitten by wood ticks, exposed to poison ivy, to say nothing about being struck by lightning.' When Prescott mentioned that the school's liability insurance was likely to go up, I knew right then what the vote would be."

"I'm not surprised," I said. "Sounded like the board was headed toward a 'no' vote when we met with them."

"Something else happened, too," Kate said. "The board voted unanimously to give you an award for allowing Link Lake school children to visit Blue Shadows Farm every spring and fall."

"Really," I said, with more than a little cynicism in my voice.

"They voted for you to receive an engraved plaque, to cost no more than $50 and to be presented at the next school board meeting."

"Well, how about that?" I said. "Pat me on the back with one hand, and slap me in the face with the other. What a bunch of hypocrites. What a plug-ugly deal."

"You decide to sell your place yet?" Kate asked, changing the subject.

"Not yet, but I expect what the school board decided may push me along."

"Anytime you want to talk about all this—one friend to another—just let me know."

"I'll bring your bread to town this afternoon, after it's had a chance to cool a little."

"I'll be here."

I pulled on my warm jacket and cap, walked outside, and breathed deeply. Nothing like a crisp November morning for a walk. I had moseyed along for a hundred yards when I heard the sharp crack of a rifle in the distance—I'd forgotten that it was deer season in Wisconsin. As I hiked along with my trusty walking stick, I thought about what it would be like without children tramping on these trails every spring and fall, busloads of children enjoying the outdoors firsthand, learning about the environment. The smell of fall was in the air, fallen leaves, dried grass, and clear, clean air blowing in from Canada, a hint of the winter to come. A ruffed grouse exploded in front of me, giving me a start. No matter how many times I've kicked up a grouse, I always jump. What a beautiful bird it is, with reddish-brown, black-tipped feathers. It flew in a zigzag trajectory through the naked tree limbs.

Should I sell this place? This thought tumbled to the top of my mind no matter what I was doing these days. It's probably time I did. There comes a time for everything—says that in the Bible someplace, at least I think it does. Truth of the matter, maybe it is time that I hang up my fiddle. I've been living on this farm for a coon's age.

This nature group is probably the right organization to buy the place. Merrifield seems like an all right kind of guy—different from their skinny sales rep. The company seems to believe in environmental education, even though I must say I don't understand all the stuff they make. There are so many electronic gadgets on the market these days that I don't know a blamed thing about. And I guess I don't want to learn, either—too much of a bother when you can just sit down with a good book. Besides, you don't have to plug in a book or stuff batteries into it. Works just by turning the pages. Can you imagine that?

I saw something running through the trees. I looked up to see an enormous buck standing not more than a hundred yards in front of me on the trail. Its sides were heaving; obviously it had been running hard. Its white tail was up, and its ears flicked back and forth.

I stood motionless, the buck and I staring at each other. The big deer's ears were listening for every sound. Its head was high, so the animal caught every scent in the woods. We stared at each other for a minute or so before it bounded off, its long, white tail flashing and its tawny body disappearing into the brown of the woods.

Watching deer is something I'll surely miss when I sell this place. Seeing any wild creature is a thrill. No matter how many pictures I look at, nothing can replace seeing such a beautiful animal in the wild.

Part 8

55

Threshing Days

August 1945

The farmwork continued. These last days before the war ended, it was threshing time and it was the Starkweathers' turn to host the threshing crew. Somehow Faith had gotten back into the good graces of the neighbors so they at least would help with threshing. Mort Reinert, her husband's cousin, ran the old Reinert farm with his bachelor sons, Ellsworth and Vernon. In 1945, Mort was seventy, Ellsworth forty-eight, and Vernon forty-six. After buying more land, Mort and his sons farmed nearly 500 acres. Faith and Emma still farmed their original 160.

Mort was as bald as an ostrich egg and plump as a stuffed turkey and about as arrogant as a politician who'd just won an election with 50.1 percent of the vote. Besides that, he was deaf as a stump and talked so loudly you wanted to run in the other direction when you saw him coming. Nobody cared much for the guy, but he owned the threshing machine and the tractor that powered it.

Faith had no time for him. He'd sniffed around a couple times when he heard she hadn't been feeling well, hinting he'd like to buy Blue Shadows Farm.

"The nerve!" Faith said. She figured he already had more land than he could handle.

The day set for threshing dawned hazy and hot, a good day for the grain, a tough one for the crew. Mort, on his new Farmall H tractor—somehow he'd wrangled a way to buy it during the war when no one else could—drove into the yard hauling his J. I. Case threshing machine behind.

"Where you want it set up this year?" he yelled over the sound of the idling tractor. The red Farmall shined. Mort likely had ordered one of his sons to wipe off the dust so he could show off the tractor to the neighbors. None of them had one; they all still farmed with horses.

Faith pointed over behind the barn and directed him to the exact place she wanted things set up. Mort revved up the Farmall and pulled it into place, unhitched, and backed into the drive belt.

"How many acres you got this year, Faith?" he asked, with a kind of smirk on his face. Faith knew he grew close to a hundred acres of oats, and she had but fifteen.

"About the same as last year," Faith answered.

"You got enough help lined up?" Mort asked.

"I think so. Got three teams, a field pitcher, and three men carrying grain to the granary."

"Kind of a slim crew. This here machine needs to keep a-runnin'. Ain't got time for it to be sittin'. Got lots more jobs to do."

Faith didn't answer; she was getting red in the face, and that usually meant she had something to say. She chose not to speak.

The first wagonload of oat bundles slowly made its way up the driveway; one of the Meadows boys was driving his family's big pair of Percherons on the bundle wagon.

He eased up to the threshing machine, yelled "whoa," tangled the leather driving lines around the wooden bolster, and grabbed his pitchfork. He signaled Mort to bring the machine up to speed. Soon the pulleys and belts began moving; the machine began shaking, and a cloud of dust rose over the entire operation. The Meadowses' team shied back a little as the machine came up to speed.

Mort signaled to begin tossing bundles, and the day's activity began. Emma, at age nineteen, in addition to helping Faith in the house with the noon meal, had the job of sitting on the threshing machine and pointing the straw-blower pipe in the right direction. All winter, Faith bedded the cows with oat straw. She also used it to add some comfort to the laying hens and provide a birthing nest for the sows. So the Starkweathers needed a properly made strawstack that withstood the weather.

About eleven or so, Emma crawled down from the thresher; she was dirty from head to toe, for running the straw blower is about the worst job in the entire threshing operation. She washed up as best she could and hurried into the house to help her mother with the noon meal.

A threshing meal is really a kind of thanksgiving dinner, as the threshers are celebrating the harvest. Anyway, it's a lot of work to feed a hungry threshing crew. Used to be that the neighbor women would help each other at threshing time, but not so much now. The Starkweathers didn't have as many neighbors as they once did. Several farmers had lost their farms during the long and drought-ridden Depression. And some of the neighbors still remembered the days when Abe made moonshine in the potato cellar and Faith had acted a little too big for her britches. The older farm women continued to remind the younger ones of Faith's transgressions, even though more than a decade had passed. In the Link Lake neighborhood, folks have long memories. Too long. And lots of prejudices. So nobody offered to help Faith with the threshing dinner this year, even though most people knew she'd had some health problems. When Emma hurried into the house, Faith was working over the stove, mashing a big tub of potatoes. A huge hunk of roast beef lay on a platter to the side.

"Cut the meat, if you would, please," Faith said to Emma when she entered the kitchen. "And finish setting the table. How many are out there?"

"Eight, counting Mort."

"Wish we didn't have to deal with that old buzzard," Faith said. "About the only thing he's got on his mind is money. And he made a pile of it during the war. Every time I see that man, I remember hearing that he sold a bunch of black-market pork in Wisconsin Rapids."

Emma said that she'd heard that, too. But nobody much talked about it, at least not so that Mort ever heard.

Promptly at noon the threshing crew gathered by the house. Emma set up washbasins on the kitchen porch where the men could peel off some of the grime, but layers of dust still covered their clothes. Some of the men even had dust on their back ends. When they sat down at the dining room table, a little cloud of dirt surrounded their chairs.

The crew soon finished the beef, scraped the bottom of the mashed-potato bowl, downed all the carrots and peas, ate a big jar of dill pickles, and put away both an apple and a cherry pie, in addition to drinking nearly a full pot of boiled coffee that sat on the back of the cookstove.

The men sat around outside for half an hour or so, smoking, telling stories, and discussing what it would be like now that the war would soon be over. Then they got back to work. By about midafternoon, the Starkweathers' oats were threshed, and the men drove home, ready to start again the next day at a new place.

Mort readied the threshing machine for travel, hitched up the Farmall, which was now covered with dust, pulled up in front of the kitchen porch, and stopped, shutting down the engine. He came up to the kitchen door and knocked. Faith had been sitting down, resting after she washed and dried the dishes. After the noon meal

Emma had gone back to steering the straw blower and building a reasonable strawstack.

"Got her done," Mort said, in his loud voice. "Not the best crop in the world, but you got a few bushels of oats and a fair-to-middling strawstack." He handed Faith a slip of paper with the cost for the work, so much for each bushel of grain threshed. (The machine had a little recorder that registered how many bushels of grain passed through it.)

"Say, Faith, this may not be the time to bring it up. But I know you ain't been feeling top-notch lately. You ever wanna sell this place, I'd be glad to take it off your hands," he said, smiling.

"Oh, I think we'll keep it for a while," Faith said, quietly. Emma could see her face redden again, and she knew her mother wanted to tell off the greedy old bugger but thought better of it.

"Well, just thought I'd mention it. One relative to another," Mort said as he walked out the door, climbed on his tractor, and headed down the driveway, the threshing machine wheels turning up little puffs of dust, and a gray thread of smoke belching from the tractor's exhaust pipe.

56

Postwar

August 1945

After atomic bombs wrecked havoc on major Japanese cities, World War II ended on August 14, 1945. The Village of Link Lake sponsored a big parade celebrating the war's end. World War I veterans marched down Main Street, firing their rifles periodically. People lined the streets, waving American flags and cheering.

Emma Starkweather did not attend the celebration, nor did her mother. Emma still grieved the loss of her Johnny, who had come home in a wooden box. Johnny's grieving mother had given the Purple Heart he received to Emma.

"He would have wanted you to have this," the grief-stricken woman said.

Every day before Emma went to sleep, she took the medal from its little box and held it close to her. And the tears flowed.

Some semblance of normalcy returned to Link Lake and the farming communities that surrounded the village. People once more bought sugar, tires, canned goods, and shoes without rationing stamps. But even greater changes, far-reaching changes, appeared on the horizon. Tractors became readily available, and most farmers bought one. Being a conservative lot, they also kept their horses, not willing to trust the dependability of these shiny new horse replacements. For those farmers who did not have electricity, the REA (Rural Electric Administration) Electric Cooperative rushed to set poles, string wires, and connect them to the rural community.

With tractors to till the land and electrically powered machines to do everything from pumping water to milking cows, some farmers began expanding their operations. They mostly did this by purchasing land from their neighbors. Tired from years of Depression and war, older farmers were ready to sell. They sought quiet retirement in the Village of Link Lake, fishing, gardening, and watching the seasons change.

Emma worried about her mother. She wouldn't slow down even though the doctor warned her that her heart wasn't up to all she asked it to do. She bought additional dairy cows, purchased a new John Deere B tractor with a two-row cultivator, and even looked at an Allis Chalmers grain combine, though she didn't buy it.

"These combines will destroy the threshing rings. Every community needs something to pull it together," she said. "And a threshing ring does that."

Every day Faith worked from first light until she fell exhausted into bed by nine each evening. So did Emma. Emma discovered that the harder she worked, the easier it was for her to sleep. She had fewer nightmares, fewer dreams about what her life would have been like had Johnny not died in the war.

In 1946, the same August day that the war had ended the year before, Emma and her mother were milking cows. They now had a herd of twenty and had once more begun using the big Sears barn that had stood vacant since the death of Emma's father in 1932.

Faith's health seemed to have improved a little over the summer.

With their new tractor, and the assistance of a hired man for a few weeks, the barn's haymows were filled with bales of hay. Faith hired a man with a custom hay baler to do the work.

They had two milking machine units; Emma took care of one and her mother handled the other. Emma, working on the far end of the barn, heard a commotion on the other end, where her mother worked. One cow bellowed, and several others rattled their stanchions, devices fitted over their necks to confine them to their stalls while they were milked.

Emma found her mother slumped over a milking machine unit, the teat cups of the machine on the floor making a loud sucking sound.

"Oh, no," Emma said. "Oh, God, no."

One more headstone joined the others on the hill behind the log cabin, looking down on the patch of lupines.

Faith Hanson Starkweather
Born: May 1, 1884
Died: August 14, 1946

Over the past year, Emma had had many interesting talks with her mother—almost as if her mother knew that her time was short. The message in nearly all of these conversations concerned the farm and its future. "Take care of Blue Shadows Farm when I'm gone, Emma. No matter what, take care of the land. It's the land that matters. We all depend on the land."

Emma remembered the days back during Prohibition when her mother regularly traipsed off to Chicago and spent money on everything from fancy clothes to expensive parties. And then the money abruptly stopped coming in—and her mother changed. Likely not because she wanted to but because she had to. Necessity also changed Emma's ideas about money.

Emma thought about all of this as she now took full responsibility for the farm, even though she was not yet twenty-one years old. Scarcely a month after her mother's death, a knock came on Emma's door one evening, after she finished the barn chores. It was Mort Reinert.

Emma heard that the Reinerts had bought out their neighbor to the south. She guessed what Old Mort wanted.

Ever since Emma's father, Abe, had made purified corn water during Prohibition and took in a pile of money doing it, the Reinerts had had little to do with the Starkweathers. Emma thought they were probably jealous that Abe was hauling in money by the sackful at the time. Or maybe they were down on Emma's mother because she had been showing off a little with new cars, fancy clothes, and trips to Chicago.

Or still another reason for their aloofness might be their negative judgment of Emma's father, who clearly had been no prince, even though he knew how to make money. Now Old Mort stood at her kitchen door.

"May I come in?" Mort said politely.

"Of course, come in," Emma said. "Can I offer you a cup of coffee and maybe a cookie? Baked sugar cookies this afternoon."

"That would be nice," Mort said. He tossed his straw hat in a corner. "Terrible thing what happened to your mother," Mort said. "Just terrible."

"She hadn't been well," Emma said quietly.

"But to be killed by a kicking cow, well that's awful," Mort said.

"Didn't happen that way," Emma said.

"That's the talk in town. One of your big unruly Holsteins kicked her in the head when she was putting the milking machine on it."

"The doctor said she had a heart attack," Emma said. "The cow didn't kick her."

331

"Well, that's what I heard in town. That's the story."

Emma got up, walked to the stove, and retrieved the coffeepot and refilled Mort's cup. He was already biting into his second sugar cookie.

"Sure good cookies, you wouldn't happen to have another one?"

Emma walked over to the cookie jar and brought it to the table, setting it in front of Mort.

"I thought I'd stop by to see how you were doing. Big job for a young girl to take care of a farm like this, milk all these cows, take care of the crops, all this without having a man around."

Like her mother, Emma never liked Mort Reinert, and now she knew why. He was a pompous cuss.

"I'm twenty years old," Emma said proudly, "and I've been work- ing this farm with my mother my whole life."

"It just doesn't seem right for you to be here all alone, trying to make a go of it by yourself. You got a boyfriend, ain't you?"

Emma bristled with the question as Mort knew full well that Emma's fiancé had been killed in the war but two years ago.

"No, I do not have a boyfriend," Emma said, trying to remain civil to her cousin.

"Oh," Mort said. "'Spect you'll have one soon."

"I doubt that," Emma said, looking down at the cup of coffee in front of her and thinking once more of Johnny.

"Was wondering about your plans," Mort said. He had his hand in the cookie jar again.

"Don't have any plans, outside of keeping this place going."

"Well, in case you ever wanna sell, maybe move off to Milwaukee or Green Bay, someplace like that, you have a standing offer from me."

"Thank you," Emma said. She was glad Mort couldn't see what she was thinking. Not enough time had passed for her mother's grave to grow grass, and Old Mort was already sniffing around try- ing to buy Blue Shadows Farm.

Mort shoved back his chair, retrieved his straw hat, and stood up. He took Emma's hand. "Just remember, anytime you wanna move off this place, just give me a holler. I'll be happy to take it off your hands. That's what relatives are for . . . to help each other out in time of need."

Emma hadn't thought much of selling the farm, although it probably would have made sense to do so. But after the conversation with Mort, her stubborn streak kicked in. "I'll show that old geezer," she thought. "I'll run this place by myself."

57

Jim Lockwell

August 1946

*E*mma soon discovered that operating the farm by herself was more than she could handle, even at age twenty. She fell into bed each night exhausted, only to rise again at five the next morning to do it all over again.

With a milking machine, milking cows was certainly easier than doing it by hand, but milking twenty cows was still exhausting work. And that wasn't the half of it. She had to fetch them from the pasture each morning at five-thirty, sometimes walking more than half a mile one way through the mists and dewy grasses to do it, and she had to tend to the calves, take care of the chickens, and keep the pasture fences in good order. When she had some extra time, which was almost never, she weeded the garden and tried to keep the flowers around the house looking presentable. The last thing she wanted was to have the neighbors talking about how Blue Shadows Farm had gone downhill since Faith died and Emma took over its operation.

September was but a few weeks away, and Emma would have to figure out how she would cut corn and fill the silo. She knew the cows needed the feed during the long winter when they would remain in the barn. Thankfully, they had completed threshing grain before her mother's death.

One cloudy morning in early September, when she was a little sleepier than usual and had just gotten the morning milk into the cooling tank, Lloyd Gunderson, the milk hauler, arrived.

"Lookin' a little frazzled this morning," Lloyd said.

"Overslept," Emma confessed.

"Lot of work for a young lady," Lloyd said. He was a big man and wore a canvas apron to keep his clothes dry from the dripping-wet ten-gallon milk cans he pulled from the cooling tank, carried to his truck, and hoisted inside.

"I gotta do it," Emma said. "I gotta keep going." She brushed back a piece of damp hair that had fallen over her face. "Promised my ma I'd take good care of Blue Shadows Farm, no matter what."

"Ever think of hirin' somebody to help you?"

"Tell you the truth, I've been too tired to think since Ma died," Emma replied.

"I know a guy in Link Lake who could use a job. Nice guy, but kind of bunged up from the war. Lost an eye and was shot in the leg. Limps a little because of it. Name is Jim Lockwell."

"I don't think I can afford a hired man," Emma said. She remembered the days when her folks had both a hired man and a maid.

"He'll work cheap. Want me to talk to him? I know him pretty well."

"Suppose it wouldn't hurt to talk to the guy," Emma said. Every muscle in her young body ached.

A couple days later, about midmorning, an old black Model A Ford car pulled into the Starkweather yard and stopped by the house. A slightly built man with a definite limp stepped from the car and started slowly toward the kitchen door.

"I'm out here in the garden," Emma said, waving her arm.

The man, who wore bib overalls and a gray felt hat, heard her and ambled on toward the garden. Emma stood up, brushed the dirt from her hands, and wiped them on her apron.

"I'm Jim . . . Lockwell," the man said. "Heard . . . you . . . were lookin' . . . for a hired man." He spoke slowly and deliberately, as if he had to think of each word before speaking it.

"I might be," Emma said. "Let's go sit on the porch in the shade." Emma led the way to the two chairs on the kitchen porch.

"Would you like a cup of coffee?"

"That . . . would be . . . nice," Lockwell said. He had removed his sweat-stained hat, revealing short brown hair.

Emma disappeared into the kitchen and soon returned with two cups of steaming coffee. Like her mother, she always had a pot of coffee simmering on the back of the stove.

"Heard you were hurt in the war?" Emma inquired quietly.

"Yeah . . . them Nazis . . . got me . . . good. Lost . . . an eye. Got me . . . in the . . . leg, too." Jim stopped to touch his injured left leg. "Besides . . . now . . . I don't talk . . . real good . . . either," Jim said.

"Got lots of work around here, cows to milk, a silo to fill, maybe make a late crop of hay before cutting the ripe corn. Think you could help do it?" Emma asked. She looked him straight in the face. His remaining eye was a deep blue. A vacant scar took up the space where the other eye had been.

"I . . . I know how . . . to work," Jim said slowly but firmly. "If . . . somebody . . . would give me . . . a chance."

They talked for a little bit about wages, and the milk hauler had been correct. Jim Lockwell would work for little more than a roof over his head and three meals a day.

"I'll let you know," Emma said when they had finished their discussion. Jim limped to his car and chugged off down the road.

That afternoon Emma thought about this injured war veteran. Earlier she had learned that he was only thirty years old, and someone had said he was shell-shocked, which was why he talked so slowly. He looked ten, maybe fifteen years older. She wondered if he could do the work—farmwork was hard. Having but one eye probably didn't matter, but having an injured leg did. Farmwork included lots of walking and lifting where two good legs certainly made work easier.

Other matters concerned Emma more than Jim Lockwell's disabilities. What would the neighbors say if she hired a one-eyed, bum-legged, slow-talking man? People would think she didn't have enough money to hire a decent, full-bodied hired man and, even worse, she didn't have enough sense to select an appropriate one, a man that was healthy and all together. She could hear them talking now: "That Emma, when she was little she had lots of money and little common sense. Sure showing up now, her hiring a cripple to do farmwork."

That night Emma woke up around three and said aloud, "I don't care if the neighbors get all fired up, I'm gonna give Jim Lockwell a try."

The next day she was on the phone to the Link Lake Hotel, where Jim had a room. She told him he had the job and he could start the following day and that, if it was all right with him, he could stay in the old log cabin on the property and take his meals with her in the big house. For a long time she heard nothing in reply, but then she heard a quiet, "Thank you. I'll be there . . . bright and . . . early tomorrow." His voice sounded as if he was crying.

Five-thirty the next day the little Model A pulled into the Starkweather farmyard, and Jim Lockwell got out and limped directly to the barn.

"Good . . . morning," he said, a big smile spreading across his face.

"Good morning to you, Jim," Emma said. She was putting a milking machine on the first cow.

"Do you know how to run a milking machine?" Emma asked.

"I . . . do," Jim said. When she had talked with him earlier, she had forgotten to ask such important questions as what he knew about farming and farmwork. Later she learned that he had grown up on a dairy farm in Clark County, where his father had one of the first milking machines in the area.

Jim Lockwell was filled with surprises. He knew how to drive a tractor and appreciated that Emma's John Deere B had a hand clutch, which meant his bad leg didn't make a whole lot of difference when he drove it. Mostly, he knew how to work, and he didn't have to be told what to do. When he saw a job to be done, he did it. When he spotted a broken fence wire, he fixed it. When it was time to cut corn for the silo, he informed Emma of the fact and hitched the tractor to the corn binder and began cutting.

He also played the harmonica. Each evening, when the chores were done, he sat in a rocking chair on the log cabin's porch and played tune after tune. Mostly mournful tunes, the kind that brought tears to your eyes. Tunes like "Old Shep," "The Lamplighter," and "That Silver-Haired Daddy of Mine." Music that hung in the air on humid late summer evenings and floated toward the big house where Emma sat reading. She heard the music and appreciated it. But mostly she appreciated Jim.

Of course, as the years went along, people did talk, and stories floated around Link Lake, mostly coming from the Link Lake Tap, where the regular customers excelled in starting rumors.

"Hear that young Emma Starkweather out south of town is sleepin' with that one-eyed Jim Lockwell?"

"You don't say. Not suprisin'. She's quite a looker, in spite of how hard she works."

"He lives right there on the premises, in that old log cabin they shoulda torn down a long time ago."

"I know that. Also know one-eyed Jim ain't as old as he looks. Probably has more lead in his pencil than most of us."

58

Fishing

August 1947

A year after Emma hired Jim Lockwell, she still didn't know much about him. It was obvious he was a hard worker and he seemed to enjoy everything that he did. She remembered hearing him whistling one day when he was cleaning out the chicken house. Shoveling chicken manure is one mean job no matter how you look at it. It's dusty and dirty, and, besides, the smell is so strong it burns your eyes. But there was Jim. He'd worked up a considerable sweat shoveling chicken droppings through the chicken house window into the manure spreader and was whistling a tune while doing it.

Emma worried a little bit about him climbing into the upper reaches of the haymow during haying season with his bad leg and all. She was even more concerned when he crawled up into the silo on the narrow metal ladder. But heights didn't seem to bother him, even with his gimpy leg.

He surprised her in other ways, too. Emma always prepared an especially good Sunday dinner with pork chops, fried chicken, or roast beef, plus mashed potatoes, carrots, and peas from the garden (in season, or from what she'd canned), and a big apple pie. Jim liked apple pie. He'd take a big piece—she always cut her pies into five slices. He'd finish off his slice, and she'd ask him if he'd like another. He'd always say, "I expect . . . one piece would do me." But then he'd smile and slide another hunk onto his plate.

Jim wasn't much for talking. He may have been a little ashamed that he couldn't spit out the words as fast as he wanted. But that was no matter to Emma, especially when she got used to hearing him. When he did open his mouth, he usually had something to say. This made him about 90 percent different from most of the folks she ran into those days.

Sometimes they'd eat an entire meal and about all she'd get out of him was, "Thank you. That . . . was sure . . . a fine meal." Otherwise he just sat and ate.

One Sunday noon, after he'd polished off his second piece of apple pie and pushed back from the table, Emma asked him what he'd planned for the afternoon. Of course, it was none of her business. Sunday afternoon was his to do with what he wanted.

"I was . . . thinking . . . of going fishing," he said.

"I didn't know you liked to fish."

"Yup, . . . grew up fishing . . . with my pa. Just the two of us . . . we'd go off to the lake . . . and spend an afternoon. Caught a . . . bunch of fish, too. Pa's . . . no longer with us . . . but I remember those days."

"Would you mind if I came along?" Emma asked. She remembered an old cane pole tucked under the eaves of the corncrib, one Silas probably used years ago. She didn't recall that her dad, Abe, had ever gone fishing. He never had taken Emma along, if he did.

"I don't know much about how to do it," Emma said. "It's been a long time." She didn't want to share that she'd never fished a day in her life and didn't know one end of a fishing pole from the other. Jim found the old cane pole and said it was in good order but the line had rotted off. He said he had some extra line and would fasten some onto it, knot on a hook and bobber, and it'd be all set.

340

He tied the pole, which was fourteen feet long, across the top of his old Model A Ford, and they drove off toward Link Lake. Someone at the Link Lake Mill had told Jim that the fish were biting; Emma guessed that's the reason he'd mentioned it.

They stopped at Paul's Bait Shop, located right on Link Lake and just south of the village, where they rented an ancient wooden boat. Jim had a casting rod and reel, something his dad had given him for his birthday many years ago. And he also had some fishing lures, wooden things with hooks coming out from all sides. Some were red and white. Some green and white. One was all green and sort of shaped like a frog. They bought a couple dozen fishing worms from Paul, climbed in the boat, and pushed off.

Emma remembered several things about that day, beyond the fact that the boat leaked and seemed about ready to sink after they'd been on the lake for an hour or so. Jim showed Emma how to bait her hook and how to adjust the bobber. "You want . . . the worm a couple . . . feet off the bottom. And then, when your . . . bobber commences . . . bouncing," he said quietly, "wait for it . . . to go all the way under . . . before you do anything."

Jim rowed over to a little bay, around the shoreline so they couldn't see the village, a quiet little place where pond lilies grew and willow trees hung over the water.

"Should . . . catch . . . a few here," he said, smiling. He cast out his line, and Emma, after a little struggle, had her hook and line in the water with a big red-and-white bobber sitting a few yards out from the boat.

"Sometimes it . . . takes . . . a while . . . to get a bite," he said. He was cranking on his reel and watching his line, while at the same time glancing over to see if Emma's bobber had any action.

For a time they both sat quietly, the only sound from some birds in the willow trees, a red-winged blackbird perched on a cattail, and the gentle lapping of water on the side of the boat. After a while Emma's feet began feeling wet.

"I think the boat is leaking," she said, trying not to suggest any alarm in her voice.

"Oh, . . . these old wooden boats . . . all leak," Jim said, not taking his eye off his fishing line. "Just keep . . . looking at . . . your bobber," he said, without even glancing down to see the several inches of water that had already accumulated in the boat's bottom.

Then out of the blue, Jim asks, "You . . . like farming?"

"Well . . . ," Emma hesitated. "Guess I do, or I wouldn't be doing it. But we've sure got lots of work to do." She had turned twenty-one back in May, and since her mother died, she had done little but work.

"Yeah . . . we've been busy . . . for sure we've been busy."

"I guess I've got farming in my blood," Emma said. "Never thought much about doing anything else. Don't know what I'd do besides farming. I promised Ma when she got sick that I'd try to keep things going."

"You ever . . . thought of marrying?"

Emma smiled at the question and hesitated before answering.

"I did," she said. "All set to do it, too."

"Don't mean . . . to be prying," Jim said as he tossed out his line. The lure landed among a cluster of pond lilies. A good place for largemouth bass.

Emma hadn't thought much about Johnny for some time; having lots to do and many things to worry about had taken her mind off things that can be hard to forget. And, of course, her mother's passing was still on her mind as well.

"It's okay," Emma said, trying to hold back tears that hadn't flowed for many months.

"Sorry . . . Emma . . . I shouldn't have asked. Shouldn't . . . have asked," Jim said as he touched her arm.

"His name was Johnny," she blurted out. "He was killed in the war."

"Oh . . . Oh," Jim said. A most sorrowful look came over his scarred face.

Emma sobbed quietly, trying to watch her bobber through her tears. Then she realized that both her feet were wet, and when she glanced down, the water had come up above her shoes.

"Jim, this boat is sinking!" Emma said.

"Not for . . . another fifteen minutes," he said, glancing at his watch and smiling.

"Jim, you picked this boat on purpose, didn't you? You knew it leaked," Emma said. "Trying to play a little trick on me?" She lay down her pole and put her hands on her hips.

He chuckled but did not reply. In a few minutes, he helped Emma wrap up her fishing pole, reeled in his line, and began rowing back to Paul's dock, the cool lake water sloshing around their ankles.

59

New Year's Eve

December 31, 1949

*E*very New Year's Eve as far back as Emma could remember folks around Link Lake brought in the New Year at the Lakeside Pavilion, a dance hall located on the shores of the lake and just a half-mile north of town. The wooden building was built during the flapper era of the 1920s and now was beginning to show its age. It needed a coat of paint, having faded from a rather bright white to a nondescript gray. Yet, the place had a wonderful hardwood dance floor that the owners kept in top-notch condition.

The pavilion hung partly over the lake—providing a beautiful view of the water, especially nice on moonlit nights. Of course, the place had a reputation. The religious fuddy-duddies in town, mostly overly nosy, pious women, claimed the place was the devil's playground. There might be some truth to the comment, depending on one's point of view. Common knowledge suggested a fair number of babies had been conceived in the pavilion's parking lot or along the sandy beach that led in both directions from the dance hall.

When Johnny and Emma were courting, they regularly danced at Lakeside, as the place was fondly called. Lakeside held dances every Saturday night throughout the year and, of course, on New Year's

Eve, no matter what day of the week the celebration fell. Admission was fifty cents. When young people reached eighteen, they could crowd up to the bar, which was located on one end of the dance hall. They could drink beer but no hard liquor until they were twenty-one. On the other end of the dance floor was a small restaurant, which filled up about midnight with those who had a little too much drink and needed some food to clear their heads and steady their hands so they could drive home without plowing into the ditch or, worse, into another driver in a similar condition.

Emma hadn't been to Lakeside for a long time, not since Johnny went off to war. But now, another New Year's Eve was coming and she thought it might be fun just to go there and listen to the music. As an afterthought, she wondered if Jim might like to go along. She was long past worrying about what other people would think if she and her hired man went dancing on New Year's Eve.

At their noon meal that day, Emma asked Jim if he'd like to go with her to the dance. "I don't . . . think I can dance . . . like I once could," he said, "but sure . . . I'll come along."

Emma suggested they leave about nine. Promptly at that hour, Jim stood waiting near her car. He wore nicely pressed gray slacks, a neat blue dress shirt, and black shoes that he'd obviously polished. He had freshly shaved—Emma could smell his shaving lotion—and he had combed back his brown hair. The night was warm for this time of the year, maybe twenty degrees or so; they'd had snow cover since back in November.

"Aren't you the handsome one," Emma said when he got into the car. She could see that he was blushing.

"You . . . look nice . . . too," Jim said.

They arrived at Lakeside a few minutes later, and already the place was jam-packed with dancers. Augie Meyers's Five Notes band sat on the little stage on one side of the dance hall. The Five Notes had long been one of the most popular polka bands in this part of Wisconsin and beyond. Each musician sat in front of a little cardboard music stand with his name printed in front, along with five notes. Augie played the concertina, Sonny the trumpet, Joe the banjo and guitar, Fritz played a saxophone and clarinet, and Shorty blew on a tuba that hung over his shoulder.

A few heads turned when Jim and Emma walked around the edge of the dance floor, where they found a couple empty chairs pushed up against a little round table. Emma wore one of her nicest dresses. It was blue and a little low cut, probably considered a lot low cut by some of the matrons in the community. She hadn't worn it for several years and was pleased how well it still fit. She thought when she pulled on the dress, "A little hard work does keep one fit and trim." Most of the folks who knew Emma had never seen her in a dress. So she let them gawk as she walked with her head high, Jim Lockwell, with a big smile on his face, limping along beside her.

"Would you like a beer?" Emma asked Jim after he held the chair for her and she sat down. "My treat."

"Sure," he said. Emma got up, walked into the bar, and brought back two bottles of Schlitz and set them on the table in front of them.

"Figured you didn't need a glass."

"Nope," Jim said as he held up his bottle, then said, "Cheers."

The band began playing an old-time tune, "The Blue Skirt Waltz," and soon dancers filled the floor. What a collection of people, a cross-section of those who lived in the Link Lake community. A few of the young men wore their insulated deer-hunting boots, Emma suspected just to prove they could dance in them. She pitied their girlfriends, who had to put up with bruised feet from these foot-smashers. Young and old attended the dance. Little kids jumped up and down, trying to keep time with the music and avoid being run over by the dancers. Men and women in their sixties and even seventies were there, smiling and dancing the slow dances.

"Like another beer?" Emma asked Jim when she noticed he'd downed the first one in no time at all.

"Let me . . . buy this round," he said as he got to his feet and limped off to the bar.

Emma noticed Mort Reinert's sons, Ellsworth and Vernon, sitting across from them. They wore their dark-blue church suits, and each sported an identical red necktie. Emma wondered why these guys were there. By now they must be in their fifties. They were lifetime bachelors. Their old man had kept them working every day of their lives, but here they were, sitting as stiff as dried-oak boards, with not so much as the hint of a smile on either of their faces. She suspected Old Man Mort had told them to take the night off and go find themselves a wife. It wouldn't be beneath him to do something like that, the old rascal.

"You having a . . . good time?" Jim asked.

"I am," Emma answered. "Thanks for coming along."

"Thank . . . you," he said quietly. "Thank you . . . for tonight. And . . . for giving me a job."

"Couldn't make the farm work without you," Emma said, touching him on the sleeve.

"You have a . . . wonderful farm," Jim said.

"It's a lot of work," Emma said. She hadn't finished her second bottle of Schlitz before Jim already had his third in front of him.

"Do you . . . know what I like best about your place?" Jim asked.

"I surely don't."

"The . . . nights."

"The nights?"

"All the stars . . . in the sky. I never noticed them much until I lost my eye," he said, touching the long scar on his face. His words seemed to come more easily, with little hesitation. Was it the beer, she wondered?

"And on dark nights when the moon comes up and the countryside is . . . filled with moon shadows. Blue shadows this time of the year . . . as the moonlight filters through the bare branches of the trees . . . and bounces off the snow-covered fields."

"Jim, that's beautiful," Emma said. "I didn't know you paid attention to such things."

"Lots that folks . . . don't know about me."

"You like to dance?" she asked. The Five Notes had begun playing a slow tune, "Stardust," it was.

"I don't . . . know if I can," Jim replied, somewhat flustered by the question. "What will . . . people think?"

"I don't care what people think, let's give it a try."

They moved onto the dance floor and slowly danced to the strains of that great old tune. "What a wonderful night this has been," Emma thought as they slowly moved around the floor, Jim doing his best with his bad leg.

As midnight approached, Augie of the Five Notes began the countdown to the New Year, starting at fifteen seconds. People began kissing their partners and wishing them the best for the coming year. Jim and Emma sat at their little table. Emma leaned over, kissed Jim on the cheek, and said, "Happy New Year, Jim." He blushed a little and said, "Happy New Year . . . Emma."

"I'll buy you . . . a cup of coffee," Jim said.

"How about I make some at home?"

They drove home slowly, and Emma parked the car near the big house. She started the fire in the cookstove and soon had a pot of coffee brewing. Earlier, she'd baked an apple pie. She cut two pieces, a big one for Jim, a smaller one for her.

They sat quietly, eating pie and drinking coffee. The big clock in the dining room struck two.

"Jim," Emma said quietly, looking him in the face. "Would you like to spend the rest of the night with me?"

For a time he said nothing, but stared at his empty pie plate. Emma began to feel embarrassed for asking the question.

Finally he said, "I'd love to, Emma. . . . But I can't." She noticed a tear running down his face.

Part 9

60

Green Growing Farms

Summer 1960

The years passed, and the Starkweather farm prospered with Emma and Jim working as a team. But people continued to talk. One Saturday evening, Emma and Jim had been buying groceries at the Link Lake Mercantile and were walking to their car. They had to pass by the Link Lake Tap, and just as they did, a young fellow who had obviously drunk a little too much staggered up to Jim and Emma.

"Well, if it ain't old one-eyed Jim and his squeeze, Emma."

You'd think the fellow had hit a stick against a hornet's nest for what happened next. Emma handed the sack of groceries to Jim, grabbed the fellow's shirt collar with both hands, and about lifted him off the ground.

"You creep," she said, looking the fellow right in the eye. She had gotten his attention.

"You say one more word about Jim Lockwell, and one of *your* eyes will come up missing. You hear me?"

"I . . . I hear you," the young man said. His face was red, his eyes were bulging, and a wet place appeared in his crotch.

Emma let go of him; he staggered and fell down. Loud laughter came from the open door of the saloon, as several tavern patrons had been watching the confrontation.

"And that goes for the rest of you curs, too," Emma said toward the open door. She took the sack of groceries from Jim, and they continued toward their car.

That little incident got everyone in Link Lake talking. The result was that nobody ever mentioned "one-eyed Jim" again, at least not when Emma was in earshot.

A few days after the episode in town, just after lunch, a knock came at the door. Emma thought maybe it had something to do with what had happened in front of the Link Lake Tap, and she was prepared to defend what she did. Jim had already left the house for the barn to do the noon chores. She opened the door to meet a man with an outstretched hand. "I'm with Green Growing Farms," the man said enthusiastically. He had a rather limp handshake.

"What can I do for you?" Emma asked. She suspected he was some kind of salesman—he looked the type—in his forties, a belly that hung over his belt, and a thick red nose that suggested he'd tipped one too many at some bar.

"You've surely heard of Green Growing Farms," he said.

"Well, as a matter of fact, I haven't. What are you selling?" By this time in Emma's life, she had little patience for salesmen. A parade of them came by the farm every year. If it wasn't the Watkins man or the Raleigh guy—she sort of enjoyed these characters—it was somebody trying to sell her some mineral for the cows, a new kind of fly spray for the barn, or seed corn guaranteed to yield at least 150 bushels per acre.

"I'm not selling," the fellow said, removing his cap, embroidered with a farm scene and the letters "GGF." "I'm buying."

"Well, that's a switch, if I say so myself. What is it you'd like to buy? Let's see, I might have a little extra hay for sale. Got a couple of veal calves ready for market. Got a half-dozen hogs we're gonna ship off to the stockyards in a couple days. Even got a couple cows I could let go." Emma was only half kidding as she rattled off the list of things she was ready to part with.

The fellow laughed. "What I'd like to do is buy your farm."

"What?" Emma said, too loudly, wondering if she'd heard right.

"We'd like to make you an offer for your land." This time the guy wasn't laughing.

All Emma could think to say was, "Why?"

"Because you've got the kind of land we're looking for."

"What'd you say your outfit was called?"

"Green Growing Farms."

"Now I remember. Heard about your company in town just the other day. Fellow couldn't remember the name but said somebody was traveling through the neighborhood trying to buy land."

"That's us. You've got just the kind of land we're looking for. Rather sandy and good for growing potatoes and cucumbers and sweet corn, those kinds of crops."

"Really," Emma said.

"But I've got a question for you. One of the problems with your farm is all those blamed fences. Why've you got barbed wire fences going this way and that, back and forth?"

"Something my grandfather did," Emma answered. "He said we should take care of the fences and never let them fall."

"Why'd he say that?"

"Because smaller fields were easier to farm, and the wind didn't blow the soil away."

"Of course, the first thing we'd have to do with the place is tear out all the fences."

"I hate to interrupt, but aren't you forgetting an important question?"

"And what would that be?" the fellow asked.

"Don't you wanna know if the farm is for sale?"

"Oh, it's for sale all right," he said, rather arrogantly.

"You didn't hear that from me."

"I will," he said, "when you hear how much per acre we'll offer."

Emma had just about enough of this arrogant windbag. As the years passed, she had quit trying to be nice to these kinds of people. "Outspoken" is how some people described her. So be it. When she had something to say, she said it.

"What if I said you could take your offer and stick it where the sun doesn't shine?" Emma said, looking the man square in the face.

"What?" the fellow asked in surprise, seeming not to have heard what she just said.

"You heard me. You take your land offer and get outta here. And don't forget your goofy cap," Emma said, tossing it toward him.

"Well, . . . well, if that's how you feel, madam."

"That's exactly how I feel. And by the way, if you're looking for a madam, this isn't the place." She slammed the door behind the fellow as he stumbled toward his car, somewhat shaken by what she'd said.

Good God, she thought after he'd left. The nerve of the guy. What in the world is happening these days—the money people trying to take over everything, even farms?

That night, when she told Jim about her visitor, he laughed. "Good for you, Emma. Good . . . for you."

61

Holding On

Emma
June 1980

*E*mma loved the late weeks in May and the early weeks of June. Each year around her birthday (May 15) she looked forward to the lupines; she now had an entire hillside of them leading up to the cemetery on top of the hill above the old cabin. Almost every evening during these first weeks of spring, when the chores were done, she and Jim walked up to the little cemetery among the lush blue flowers. Jim had come to love the lupines as much as she. Neither of them was so young anymore—Emma had turned fifty-four on her birthday, and Jim had turned sixty-four back in February. So they took advantage of the evening hours to relax after the hard days of preparing the soil and planting crops—potatoes, oats, corn.

Jim never ceased to amaze Emma. One evening she remembered so well, he had along with him his copy of Emerson's *Nature*. What surprised her—she didn't know why it should—was how much Jim read and, perhaps even more surprising, what he read.

"Do you mind . . . if I read a few lines?" he asked. "What Mr.

Emerson said . . . seems to fit this place." Jim turned a few pages in the book he held and began, "The health of the eye . . . seems to demand . . . a horizon." He paused before continuing. Emma had been looking to the far reaches of the farm, to where a row of oaks lined the wire fence that Grandpa Starkweather had built. The trees formed the horizon, with a cloudless sky meeting the green treetops.

Jim continued, "We are never tired . . . as long as we can see far enough."

"Oh, Jim," Emma said. "That so fits this day, when the sky is so blue and the air is so clear."

They both sat, neither saying anything, as the first hatch of Karner blue butterflies flitted about, one landing on Jim's finger for both of them to watch. So tiny, yet so beautiful, this little creature with its blue wings and orange spots.

When the sun began slipping below the line of trees to the west and streaks of red and pink stretched overhead, they slowly walked down the hill, Jim going to the log cabin that he had come to love so well, and Emma to the old house, empty and silent. She'd purchased a television set some years ago, but she watched nothing except the news and the weather. She'd offered to buy one for Jim, as a present, but he said, "No, I wouldn't know . . . what to do with it." Jim did have a radio to keep him up with what was happening in the world. He had lined the walls of the cabin with books. "These are . . . my friends," Jim said one day when Emma stopped by to bring him a special apple pie.

"What's the pie . . . for?" he asked.

"I just wanted to do it," Emma said. She hadn't stepped into the old cabin for some time and was not surprised at how neat and clean it was—or how many books he had.

The same week that Jim had read from Emerson, the *Link Lake Gazette* carried this front-page article:

Holding On—June 1980

University Agricultural Economist Claims the Small Family Farm Irrelevant

Chicago, Illinois
June 12, 1980

At a national meeting of farm experts in Chicago today, Professor Sidney Wilson Golightly IV declared the end to the mythic family farm, as he described the institution.

"All that remains is the burial," this noted agricultural economist, who teaches at Wisconsin State University, said in his keynote address to 500 agricultural leaders from across the United States.

"We've held onto this icon of American agriculture far too long," he said. "The small family farm, as a viable producer of food and fiber, died a couple of decades ago, and we just didn't notice." Golightly wrote the bestselling book *Family Farms: It's Time to Forget Them.*

"The industrial model that has been extremely successful in every other part of our economy fits agriculture like a glove," he said. "The sooner we in agriculture adopt the industrial model, the better off we all will be." Golightly went on to compare the manufacture of an automobile to the operation of a factory farm. "In both instances, we have inputs and we have outputs," he said. "The key words are 'efficiency' and 'scale.' The two words go together. The larger the factory, the more efficient it can be. The larger the factory farm, the more profits, because a factory farm can become as efficient and productive as any other kind of factory.

Professor Golightly, in a bold attempt to quell his critics who argue smaller farms allow the operator a closer relationship to

nature and the land, scoffed, "We've learned how to control nature years ago. What is nature anyway? Some kind of religion?
The factory farmer can ignore nature completely. We have the
modern tools to do so—chemicals, genetics, irrigation systems—
nothing is left to old undependable Mother Nature."

Emma finished reading the article and thought, I surely don't
agree with this Golightly's ideas about factory farming, but his com-
parison of nature with religion—that's interesting. Caring for nature, taking care of the land—a kind of religion? That old out-of-
tune professor just may have struck on something.

Emma also thought about what Jim had read the other night
from Emerson. Sidney Wilson Golightly IV sees little beyond the
next quarter, the next three months. Caring about nature requires a
longer view, a much longer view—a need to see "far enough."

62

Longtime Relationship

1986

*E*mma tried to ignore the Professor Golightlys of the world, the bankers and loan agencies that encouraged borrowing to buy more land and equipment, the university extension specialists who proclaimed the need for farmers to get big or get out, and the factory farmers who were held up as models for the future. But it was difficult. In her own neighborhood, where once within a few miles she could count a dozen small farms, today there were but three, her own included. She missed the threshing, silo filling, and corn shredding crews that came by each summer and fall—neighbors helping each other with the harvest. Neighbors who knew each other, enjoyed each other's company (with exception, of course), and depended on each other to help harvest their crops. The neighbors were gone, and the neighborhood as she remembered it had disappeared. True, some of the old-timers had never forgiven her father and mother for what they had done and, in turn, had been reluctant to help her. But most of these people had died or moved away, and those who had remained had been good neighbors to Jim and her.

Now she hired a custom operator to combine the twenty acres of oats that Jim and she planted each year. She hired a man with a corn picker to harvest their twenty-acre corn crop. She bought a second-hand forage harvester, which Jim used to cut corn for silo filling.

Emma increased the size of their dairy herd to forty milk cows, which was the capacity of her dairy barn, and she purchased a bulk cooling tank to replace the ten-gallon milk cans they had used for years. The Link Lake Cheese Factory manager had encouraged her to build an addition to the barn and buy more cows, but she refused. "Forty cows are about all that Jim and I can handle," she told him. "If I added more cows, I'd have to hire more help, and I don't want to do that."

She noticed the changes not only in rural Link Lake and Ames County—with abandoned farms, absentee owners, and a few large farms remaining—but in town as well. The gristmill had closed in the 1970s—it had become a gift shop that attracted many visitors because of its picturesque location on the banks of the millpond near the old dam. The mercantile had been transformed into an antique store. The once prosperous hardware store housed a craft shop; Link Lake Seed and Feed had been abandoned, the building slowly falling down. And what had been Gorman's Harness Shop was now headquarters for the Link Lake Historical Society.

In the early 1980s, land prices fell, and Emma was pleased that she had not bought more land like her Reinert cousins had. Farmers had gone bankrupt all over Ames County, with the banks taking over the land and holding auctions. Just like during the Depression. The Reinerts lost most of their land—they had but 160 acres left when the bank got through with them. Emma's farm had been 160 acres from the time her grandfather Silas Starkweather had homesteaded the place, and she meant to keep it that size.

People in the Link Lake community had developed a new respect for Emma and her hired man, Jim. They had survived the early 1980s with few problems, mostly because their land had been paid for and they had few debts.

By 1986, when Emma was sixty and Jim seventy, the farm was making enough money so they could live comfortably and not worry about financial problems. Jim had slowed down considerably in the last couple years, and Emma, too, appreciated taking a little more time to enjoy her garden, walk in the lupines each spring, and watch the sunsets.

Emma and Jim had developed a great respect for each other. They clearly loved each other, but not in an intimate, physical sense, although Emma would have enjoyed sharing her bed with Jim. They never talked about it, but when Emma first hired Jim, they desperately needed each other. That need, at several levels, continued over the years—indeed continued to 1986.

As the years passed they had become a great team. They kept Blue Shadows Farm going through thick and thin, and they had a good time doing it, a wonderful time doing it. Emma had always loved nature, but Jim taught her a new appreciation for everything in the outdoors. He was always quoting something from Henry David Thoreau or Ralph Waldo Emerson, Aldo Leopold or John Muir. With her two good eyes, she learned to see some of what Jim saw with his one. He constantly discovered new things on the farm, a new wildflower, a new bird, an unusual growth on a tree.

One July morning in 1986, Emma arrived at the barn to milk their cows, and Jim was not there. He had always preceded her to the barn; she could count on him to start the milking. But this morning, the cows stood in the barnyard, waiting.

"Jim," Emma called quietly, thinking he was somewhere in the barn and had not opened the door for the cows to enter.

"Jim," she called again. But there was no answer. It was not like him to oversleep. Emma couldn't remember that this had ever happened before. She hurried to the little log cabin that had been Jim's home these many years, pushed open the door, and quietly called, "Jim, Jim." The cabin had a faint smell of wood smoke. She walked across the big bearskin rug, from the bear her grandfather had killed so many years ago. She walked by the bookshelf where Jim kept more books than she had at the big house. She saw his harmonica resting on the homemade wooden table.

She rapped on the door of the bedroom. "Jim," she called again. She pushed open the door. In the dim light of the dawn, she found him in bed. He had a peaceful look on his face. He had not overslept.

Yet another tombstone appeared in the Starkweather cemetery behind the cabin, overlooking the patch of lupines.

James Alonzo Lockwell
Born: February 20, 1916
Died: July 17, 1986
We are never tired if we can see far enough.

Within a week following Jim's funeral, Emma sold her dairy herd. She didn't want to farm without Jim. For five years, she rented her fields to her neighbors, who grew corn, oats, and alfalfa hay. But with Social Security and the money she had from selling her cows, Emma decided to do something different with her life for the years she had remaining.

Offer

Emma
November 2000

*I*t was a cool, clear, fall morning. Frost covered everything, the dead grass, the dead wildflowers, the barn roof. I walked to the mailbox to fetch the mail as I did every day around eleven. One thing about mailman Bill Swenson, you can set your clock by him. Unless the roads are slippery or it's Christmastime.

I flipped open the rusty mailbox door and pulled out a wad of junk mail and a bunch of catalogs. And one pale green envelope. It was a letter from Modern Nature Educators, with my name in big print on the outside—"Ms. Emma Starkweather, R.R. 1, Link Lake, Wisconsin 54987." I leaned my walking stick against the mailbox and slit open the envelope with my pocketknife—that's one good thing Pa taught me. Never go anywhere without a knife in your pocket. Never can tell when you'll need it.

I glanced at the signature; it was from Winston Merrifield, Ph.D. And then I began slowly reading. When I finished, I let out my breath and said aloud, "Well, I'll be danged." It was an offer for Blue Shadows Farm at nearly twice the going rate for land in this part of

Ames County. The land around here had shot up in price since a few big farmers began irrigating and discovered they could grow sweet corn and peas, and cucumbers and green beans, and even bumper crops of field corn. So the land wasn't cheap.

I grabbed my walking stick and hurried up the driveway, clutching the letter in one hand. Once in the kitchen, I immediately went to the phone and rang up Kate.

The phone rang two or three times.

"This is Kate."

"Kate, this is Emma. I've got news."

"Got news for you, too, Emma. But you go first," Kate said.

"Got an offer from Modern Nature Educators," I blurted out. I couldn't hide my glee. I read the letter slowly and stopped just before I got to the money part. "They've ponied up real good."

"Well, how much did they offer you?" an ever-impatient Kate asked.

I told her, and all I heard was a big "Wow."

"Unbelievable," Kate said. "Absolutely unbelievable. They must really want your farm."

"Sounds that way, doesn't it," I said.

"But I have some bad news for you."

"Bad news?"

"Remember I wanted to find out more about Modern Nature Educators before I wrote a story for the paper?"

"Yes, remember you saying that."

"Well, I got glowing reports from all over the place. The company is doing interesting things, and they're pushing into new areas with computers and virtual learning. But they've got a dark side, as well."

"A dark side?" I asked, wondering what Kate had learned.

"Well, I called the newspapers in both St. Paul and Omaha and heard back from both this morning. In both cities, MNE has been cited for violating pollution rules."

"Pollution rules?" I said, not fully understanding the meaning of what she was saying.

"Yeah, pollution rules. They run sizable printing plants, and in both cities they got caught dumping toxic wastewater from their factory—into a nearby lake in one instance and a stream in the other."

"Really" is all I could think to say.

"Worse than that, their high-powered lawyers got them off with a few bucks' fine. A company official was quoted in the St. Paul paper saying, 'Paying a fine is the cost of doing business these days—with the government wanting to regulate everything we do.'"

"Well, blast it all," I said. "The factories are still going, aren't they?"

"Yeah, they are. But they are on some kind of watch list because of their past behavior."

"Well, blast it all," I said again. "Do you suppose they see my pond as a place to dump some waste out of the regulators' sight?"

"Don't know, Emma, but it makes you wonder, doesn't it."

"Dang it," I said. "Why does life have to be so complicated? Can't even sell my farm without a problem developing."

"Just thought you should know," Kate said. "My story on Modern Educators comes out tomorrow. You'll wanna read it."

"You bet I will," I said as we finished our conversation.

I hung up the phone. Just when something looks good, it goes sour. I threw the letter on the kitchen table and poured another cup of coffee. I wondered if I was being snookered.

I got my copy of the *Link Lake Gazette* the next day. Headlines on the front page shouted: "The Dark Side of Modern Nature Educators, Inc."

The story covered much of the front page. Kate wrote about the potential employment opportunities and the increased tax base. She told how the company, with its huge investment, would put little

Link Lake on the map. She also wrote about their pollution violations in St. Paul and Omaha, and she quoted Joe Crawford at length. She ended the piece with one of Joe's statements: "No computer simulation, no CD or DVD can ever replace the joy and wonder that comes when children hike a trail in the woods and pay attention to what is around them."

After reading the piece, my mind was jumbled. I have a chance to sell to a supposedly reputable company that may or may not be honest. I was hoping they'd learned their lesson about polluting—how could they not? They claimed to support the environment in every way. They offered me good money for my place, and I'd about decided it was time I left this farm to someone else. And now these new questions.

I decided to drive to town and have a talk with Kate. When I got to the newspaper office, I found her working at her computer with a deep frown on her face.

"Hi, Emma," she said. "Thought I might see you."

"Get any reaction to your story?" I asked.

"Sure did," Kate said, pushing back in her chair. "Wasn't fifteen minutes after the paper hit the street when our good Mayor Jessup tore in, mad as could be."

"Well, what did he think of your story?"

"He threw the paper on the counter; his face was flushed, and the veins in his neck stuck out. He yelled, 'What in blazes do you think you're doing?'"

I knew that the mayor and Kate never got along, so I wasn't especially surprised by his reaction. "That all he said?" I smiled, hoping to ease the tension that hung heavy in the room.

"No . . ." Kate let the "no" drag out for a bit. I could tell from the tone of her voice she was still thinking about the confrontation.

"I tried to tell him I wrote the story from several perspectives, and then he yelled out something about how the *Link Lake Gazette* was no different from those supermarket rags that invented scandals for the sake of newspaper sales."

"And you said?"

"I've got a bit of a temper, as you know. I bit my tongue and said something about how I was doing my job. Well, when I said that, he exploded. He said the only reason I quoted Joe Crawford was because he's my boyfriend, and besides, he said, Joe didn't know what he was talking about."

"You did quote Joe a lot," I said.

"Well, I think Joe happens to be right. Jessup also said that including the information about Modern Nature Educators' pollution problems was not necessary. They'd paid their fines, and the matter was closed."

"Sounds like the mayor knew about the fines already," I said.

"Seems that way, doesn't it? Anyway, he wagged his finger at me and said, 'Mark my word, Kate Dugan, if this deal falls through, you're gonna pay. You won't have a single advertiser left. Not a stinkin' one. I'll see to it myself.' He stormed out of the office and slammed the door behind him."

"Kate, should I sell my farm to these people?"

"Can't tell you what to do," Kate said. She put her hand on my arm. "Sounds like a good offer, in spite of everything. Suspect every company has its secrets, its dark side. That's the way it is these days."

Secrets

Emma
November 2000

After hearing Kate's new take on Modern Nature Educators, I couldn't sleep all night. I didn't know what to do. I had a chance to sell Blue Shadows Farm at a price way beyond anything I could have hoped for. Didn't even have to dicker over the amount. If I sold, I would be able to spend the rest of my days living right up there on top of the heap. I could buy a place in Link Lake and still have enough money left to cover my living expenses. Besides, if I accepted the offer, I'd be helping the community. With the company's investment, the tax base for the community would increase, a bunch of new jobs would come to town, and I suspect Link Lake would gain a little status. Most folks around here believe Link Lake has been getting the short end of the stick for way too long. Modern Nature Educators coming to town could change that.

Yet, I couldn't get Joe Crawford's words out of my craw. I have a lot of respect for him. He's a good teacher, and I think he's right when he says kids can't learn about nature in front of a computer or

TV screen. Of course, the school board's vote not to allow any more field trips meant the kids couldn't hike my trails anyway, even if I turned down the offer to sell.

I kept wondering why Modern Nature Educators broke pollution laws? It made no sense to me. Why would a company that seemed concerned about nature and the environment not practice what it preached? In both cases that Kate turned up, the company paid a small fine and that was the end of it. Perhaps it was just a mistake on their part. A small blemish in their history. Maybe I'm barking up the wrong tree with my concern.

I was up early the next morning, still fretting about what I should do. I decided to continue sorting things in the loft of the old log cabin. I went back to the green metal box and what it contained. I'd read most of my grandfather's journals, and now, digging deeper, I found two faded envelopes. I opened the first envelope and unfolded the yellowing sheet of paper.

TOP SECRET
BILL OF LADING
UNION ARMY

Date: February 12, 1865
From: Link Lake, Wisconsin
To: Camp New Orleans, New Orleans, Louisiana
Contents: Two Uncut Diamonds
Value: Extremely Valuable

Why did my grandfather have this old Civil War bill of lading? And where did uncut diamonds fit into the picture? Maybe I'd learn more by looking in the second envelope, which contained a letter addressed to Silas Starkweather, Camp New Orleans, Louisiana. I carefully read:

April 14, 1865

Dear Private Starkweather:

In response to your recent letter inquiring about the possibility of diamonds being found in central Wisconsin, I can offer you the following information. First, there is a chance you might find diamonds there. The glacial till the last glacier deposited in the terminal moraine (where the glacier stopped) could contain alluvial deposits of gems, including diamonds and ore deposits such as copper. Of course, most of the till contains rocks of many sizes and shapes, and any diamonds would be few and far between. Yet, there is a possibility they might be found and be extremely valuable. There has been knowledge of diamonds in Wisconsin since the 1670s, when the Jesuit fathers told of finding diamonds near Green Bay.

I hope this information is of some help to you.

Sincerely,

J. A. Lapham, Engineer

"This is it!" I said aloud. I now had the answer to the mystery that's been in my family for three generations—why my grandpa Silas came here in the first place and dug more postholes than needed digging, walking tilled fields hour upon hour, and why my father inspected load upon load of gravel shoveled from the farm's gravel pit. Grandpa wasn't crazy as a loon, like some people thought.

I dug deeper, to the bottom of Grandpa's haversack, and found a small leather pouch, bulging and tied at the top. I untied the leather throng and peered inside. "Holy Blue Shadows Farm!" I said as I identified the contents. The pouch contained a big uncut diamond and a slip of paper with the word "Elsa" and the date April 17, 1872, the day after Grandpa and Grandma's first child died, and when Grandpa Silas dug her grave and apparently found the diamond.

I stared at the big, green, rough stone that I held in my hand, a ray of sunlight from the little loft window reflecting from it. I guessed it had been worth a lot of money when Grandpa found it. Of course, it was worth a lot more now. I put it back in its little leather pouch and returned it to the metal box.

It's strange. Grandpa Silas found the treasure he came looking for, but he hid it away, telling no one he had found it. Now, as I pondered whether to sell Blue Shadows Farm, I thought about Grandpa Silas. He'd come to Link Lake in search of diamonds and wealth, but as the years passed, he must have changed. He discovered the love of a good woman, the joy (and challenges) of children, the comfort of good neighbors and what it meant to be part of a community. Above all, he'd developed a love for this old farm. Why else would he have pressed lupine flowers in an old copy of *Walden* and preserved a tiny Karner blue butterfly in its own little box? An uncut diamond, a pressed wildflower, and a little butterfly, all carefully saved and stashed away. "Land sakes," I said.

I packed everything back in the metal box and shoved it into the corner where I'd found it. I decided to tell no one about the possibility of finding diamonds, not even Kate Dugan. I thought if word got out about the gem, a horde of diamond seekers would descend on Link Lake. I'll bet Grandpa Silas reasoned the same way. Probably why he never let the cat out of the bag.

The nagging feeling that had nearly overwhelmed me for weeks came into focus. Tomorrow I would tell the Modern Nature Educators people my decision. A huge weight lifted from my shoulders.

Epilogue

Present Day

Back in 2000 when Emma Starkweather discovered the metal box with her grandfather's things, she not only learned why he had been digging holes, but she discovered that he had found something else. As his journals revealed, at first he hated farming and had no ambition to continue beyond obtaining clear title to his land. Yet, over the years he found that he loved the place.

A final entry in Silas's journal, written in June 1905, only a short time before he died, added another dimension to the story.

June 15, 1905

I'm not feeling well these days. Old age is creeping up on me, and I fear my days are numbered. The grim reaper is waiting in the shadows. I have had a good life, much better than I thought it would be. Sophia has been a wonderful wife. Unfortunately, almost every day I think about my little Elsa who died so many years ago. My son, Abe, has been a great disappointment. He is lazy, drinks too much, and hates farming. I had planned to tell him earlier that my main reason for coming to Link Lake was to search for diamonds. Now I must tell him soon, or it will be too late. Abe is not to be trusted. I have told no one that I found a diamond, not even Sophia. Though I will tell Abe about my quest for these valuable gems, I will not tell him that I found one. Let him look for himself, if he wishes. If I told him about the diamond I found, he'd sell it and leave Blue Shadows Farm in an instant. I want Blue Shadows to stay in the family. Not telling Abe about the diamond will ensure that this happens, at least for as long as he lives.

Of course, with the information about the diamonds, Abe continued digging postholes and inspecting loads of road gravel; he even insisted on digging the graves of his parents. He was distracted from his search when he discovered the great demand for purified corn water during Prohibition.

Modern Nature Educators couldn't believe that Emma Starkweather would turn down their lucrative offer. She never told them the real reason. When Mayor Jessup heard she wasn't selling, he blamed the newspaper article for changing her mind. He started a campaign to discredit the *Link Lake Gazette* and dry up its advertising revenue. His vindictive effort backfired, and he lost the next election. Jessup and his wife moved back to Milwaukee. No one seems to know what he's doing these days.

Modern Nature Educators bought land near Omro, on the Fox River. They built a much smaller version of the project they had planned for Blue Shadows Farm.

Joe Crawford and Kate Dugan married in 2003. They currently live in the big house at Blue Shadows Farm, which is now known as the Blue Shadows Nature Center. Kate continues to run the newspaper, which has its challenges but is surviving.

Joe quit teaching and started the Blue Shadows Farm Foundation in 2002. The foundation receives money from environmentally conscious businesses from across the country. Within two years, it raised enough money to buy Blue Shadows Farm from Emma, with the proviso that she could spend summers living in the old log cabin that her grandfather built. During the winter months, Emma lived in a little house on Link Lake, overlooking the water.

Joe Crawford remodeled the big Sears dairy barn into a nature and training center. Teachers from throughout the Midwest spend up to two weeks at Blue Shadows Farm all seasons of the year, hiking the trails, studying the pond, and learning about the plants and wildlife there.

In early spring and fall, schoolchildren visit the property by the busload. Emma, through her attorney, quietly sold her big diamond and gave most of the money anonymously to the Blue Shadows Farm Foundation, to be used for grants to schools to pay the transportation costs for bringing children to the nature center and to fund the cost of liability insurance for nature hikes. The Link Lake School District overturned its decision preventing children from going on nature hikes when it heard of the fund to pay for liability insurance. The diamond money also provides scholarships for teachers who spend an extended time at the center in the summer months. More than twenty families garden at Blue Shadows Farm each summer.

Emma Starkweather told no one (except her attorney) about the secret box or about the diamond she found in her grandfather's things. To make sure no one learned the secret, she buried the box and its contents next to Grandpa Silas's tombstone.

In 2008, Emma quietly passed away; she is buried on the hilltop above the old log cabin, next to Jim Lockwell, her longtime friend and partner. Her tombstone reads simply:

Emma Sophia Starkweather
Born: May 15, 1926
Died: June 1, 2008

Epilogue—Present Day

Joe Crawford made a plaque with Emma's photo, which he placed on the wall in the training center: "Emma Starkweather, 1926–2008. She loved this land."

Now on cold winter nights, when the snow is piled high and the moon is bright, Kate and Joe walk the quiet country road that trails by their place and they marvel at the blue shadows they see displayed on the white expanse of snow. In the spring, during the month of May, they regularly hike to the lupine patch and watch the Karner blue butterflies flit about. And as they look at the tombstones in the little cemetery on top of the hill, they recall the stories of Silas and Sophia, of Faith and Abe, and of Emma and Jim. So many stories connected to this piece of land. So much history. So many changes.

Suggested Reading

For Further Information

Go to www.blueshadowsfarm.com to learn more about Blue Shadows Farm—lupines, Karner blue butterflies, diamonds, community gardening, and nature education for children. Information about the Ames County series is also included here.

Other books in the Ames County series include

The Travels of Increase Joseph. Middleton, Wis.: Badger Books, 2003. How an eccentric preacher from New York State founded Link Lake, Wisconsin, in 1852. He preached the importance of saving the land.

In a Pickle: A Family Farm Story. Madison: University of Wisconsin Press, 2007. Link Lake in 1955, when many of the small family farms began disappearing and the village and entire community suffered as a result.

Also learn about other books Jerry Apps has written about farm life, rural history, and rural community activities. Find out about the possibility of locating minerals and rare gems in glacial till.

Reading List

Children and Nature

Louv, Richard. *Last Child in the Woods.* Chapel Hill, N.C.: Algonquin, 2006.

Suggested Reading

Louv makes the point that for healthy development, children must have the opportunity to experience nature directly, to hike a trail, walk in the woods, and get their hands dirty.

Classic Books about Nature and the Environment

Carson, Rachel. *Silent Spring*. Boston: Houghton Mifflin, 1962.

Rachel Carson (1907–1964) makes the case for the detrimental affects of insecticides on the environment.

Christofferson, Bill. *The Man from Clear Lake: Earth Day Founder Gaylord Nelson*. Madison: University of Wisconsin Press, 2004.

Gaylord Nelson (1916–2005), a Wisconsin native son, was a state governor and U.S. senator and did much to influence legislation protecting the environment. He organized the first Earth Day, April 22, 1970.

Emerson, Ralph Waldo. *The Selected Writings of Ralph Waldo Emerson*. New York: Modern Library, 1992.

Writing in the mid-1800s, Emerson (1803–1882) saw nature through the eyes of a philosopher and poet. He was a close friend of Henry David Thoreau. This book includes the essay *Nature*, which was first published in 1836.

Lapham, I. A. *The Antiquities of Wisconsin*. 1855. University of Wisconsin Press, 2001.

Increase Lapham (1811–1875) was born in New York State and moved to Wisconsin in 1836. His interests included botany, geology, meteorology, archaeology, cartography, and history. He was Wisconsin's chief geologist, 1873–75. He wrote several books, *Antiquities* being one of his most popular.

Leopold, Aldo. *A Sand County Almanac*. New York: Oxford University Press, 1949.

Leopold (1887–1948) was a University of Wisconsin–Madison professor of wildlife ecology who developed the term "land ethic." He continues to be seen as one who brought environmental and land-use questions into focus for the nation. He was a gifted writer, combining philosophy with careful research.

Muir, John. *The Story of My Boyhood and Youth*. Madison: University of Wisconsin Press, 1965.

Born in Scotland, John Muir (1838–1914) grew up in southern Wisconsin, where he developed his love for the land and his concern for

378

preserving natural places. In 1892, he and his supporters founded the Sierra Club.

Olson, Sigurd F. *Listening Point.* Minneapolis: University of Minnesota Press, 1997.

Olson (1899–1982) is remembered as a wilderness ecologist as well as a gifted writer. He is best known, along with others, for establishing and protecting northern Minnesota's Boundary Waters Canoe Area. *Listening Point* is one of several books he wrote about canoeing in the wilderness.

Thoreau, Henry David. *Walden.* 1854. Boston: Houghton Mifflin, 2004.

Thoreau (1817–1862) was a naturalist, a philosopher, an author, and one who followed his own drummer. To this day, *Walden* remains one of the most complex, revealing works about a person's relationship to nature.

Wisconsin Geography and Biology

Curtis, John T. *The Vegetation of Wisconsin.* 1959. Madison: University of Wisconsin Press, 1971.

Curtis describes the biological tension zone and Wisconsin's varied plant communities.

Ladd, Doug. *Tallgrass Prairie Wild Flowers: A Field Guide to the Wildflowers, Grasses, and Woody Vines of the Tallgrass Prairie.* 2nd ed. Guilford, Conn.: Globe Pequot, 2005.

Ladd's book contains descriptions and photos of hundreds of plants found in the Midwest's tallgrass prairies.

Martin, Lawrence. *The Physical Geography of Wisconsin.* Madison: University of Wisconsin Press, 1965.

Martin's book includes information about Wisconsin's glaciers, land formation, interesting materials found in glacial till, and much more.

Tekiela, Stan. *Wildflowers of Wisconsin.* Cambridge, Minn.: Adventure Publications, 2000.

A pocket-size field guide to hundreds of Wisconsin's wildflowers with full-page photos.

Wisconsin Agricultural History

Apps, Jerry. *Old Farm: A History.* Madison: Wisconsin Historical Society Press, 2008.

Suggested Reading

This history of the author's farm includes essays on land use, solitude, prairie restoration, vegetable gardening, and more. It includes a history of the place from the days of the glacier to the present.

Current, Richard. *The History of Wisconsin.* Volume 2, *The Civil War Era, 1848–1873.* Madison: State Historical Society of Wisconsin, 1976.

This well-crafted and carefully researched book provides context to Wisconsin's history from the mid- to late 1800s.

Schafer, Joseph. *A History of Agriculture in Wisconsin.* Madison: State Historical Society of Wisconsin, 1922.

This excellent reference for the early history of farming in Wisconsin includes extensive coverage of the wheat-growing years.